BRAIDED LEARNING

Susan D. Dion

Braided Learning

ILLUMINATING
INDIGENOUS PRESENCE THROUGH
ART AND STORY

PURICH
BOOKS

Copyright © 2022 Susan D. Dion

All rights reserved. No part of this publication may be reproduced, stored in a retrieval system, or transmitted, in any form or by any means, without prior written permission of the publisher, or, in Canada, in the case of photocopying or other reprographic copying, a licence from Access Copyright, www.accesscopyright.ca.

Purich Books, an imprint of UBC Press
2029 West Mall
Vancouver, BC, V6T 1Z2
www.purichbooks.ca

Printed in Canada on FSC-certified ancient-forest-free paper (100% post-consumer recycled) that is processed chlorine- and acid-free.

Library and Archives Canada Cataloguing in Publication

Title: Braided learning : illuminating Indigenous presence through art and story / Susan D. Dion.

Names: Dion, Susan D., author.

Description: Includes bibliographical references and index.

Identifiers: Canadiana (print) 20220149887 | Canadiana (ebook) 2022015466X | ISBN 9780774880787 (hardcover) | ISBN 9780774880794 (softcover) | ISBN 9780774880800 (PDF) | ISBN 9780774880817 (EPUB)

Subjects: LCSH: Indigenous peoples – Study and teaching – Canada. | LCSH: Canada – History – Study and teaching. | LCSH: Canada – Race relations – History – Study and teaching. | LCSH: Canada – Ethnic relations – History – Study and teaching. | LCSH: Indigenous peoples – Canada – History. | LCSH: Indigenous peoples – Canada – Ethnic identity. | LCSH: Multicultural education – Canada. | LCSH: Storytelling – Canada. | LCSH: Indigenous arts – Canada. | CSH: Indigenous artists – Canada.

Classification: LCC E76.6 .D56 2022 | DDC 971.004/970071—dc23

Canadä

UBC Press gratefully acknowledges the financial support for our publishing program of the Government of Canada (through the Canada Book Fund), the Canada Council for the Arts, and the British Columbia Arts Council.

This book has been published with the help of a grant from the Canadian Federation for the Humanities and Social Sciences, through the Awards to Scholarly Publications Program, using funds provided by the Social Sciences and Humanities Research Council of Canada.

*This book is dedicated to my siblings –
Paul, Ann, Jim, Michael, and Kenny.*

*Every day,
you teach me that our connection is our survival,
our inheritance is love, care, and protection.*

Anushiik wak Katawaliil

One's voice is individual, but as it communicates shared cultural experience, it is also ancestral and capable of transcending time. In words, there is eternity.

– N. Scott Momaday, in *Ancestral Voice*

CONTENTS

Acknowledgments / ix

Introduction: Indigenous Presence / 3

1 Requisites for Reconciliation / 18

2 Seeing Yourself in Relationship with Settler Colonialism / 31

3 The Historical Timeline: Refusing Absence, Knowing Presence, and Being Indigenous / 74

4 Learning from Contemporary Indigenous Artists / 100

5 The Braiding Histories Stories / 128
   Co-written with Michael R. Dion

Conclusion: Wuleelham – Make Good Tracks / 203

Glossary and Additional Resources: Making Connections, Extending Learning / 209

Notes / 237

Bibliography / 247

Contributors / 254

Image Credits / 257

Index / 259

ACKNOWLEDGMENTS

When he was just learning to talk, my young grandson Samuel would say to me, "Auntie Claire catches babies, Auntie Vanessa makes art, and you make knowledge." I loved the way he understood my work as a researcher, learner, teacher. The making of knowledge is not accomplished in isolation; creating new/old ways of understanding is accomplished through collaboration. This book derives from myriad conversations, short exchanges, and extended discussions.

While I had been contemplating writing a second book for a few years, it was a conversation with Judi Kokis at the Ontario Ministry of Education that convinced me. Her words, "It's how you tell the story, your attention to who is listening," were my guide as I wrote these stories down. Thank you to Judi and to the team of educators who worked on the First Nations, Métis and Inuit Collaborative Inquiry Initiative, including Denise Baxter, Troy Maracle, Nick Bertrand, Gail Brant-Terry, Debra Cormier, Libby Stephenson, Sue Hearn, and Pam Tylee. I am grateful to the students and classroom teachers who participated in the project; the audience members who attended talks, listened, and asked questions, teaching me about the work of learning; and, most importantly, the Elders, including Felicia Waboose, and Indigenous community members, whose commitment to improving schooling experiences for Indigenous students informed our work. Anushiik to my research community.

Although we do not always agree with each other, there is a shared commitment to transforming education among my friends and colleagues in the Faculty of Education at York University. As much as institutions of formal schooling are fraught spaces for Indigenous people, the faculty and the broader university community create space for me to be the academic I want to be. Anushiik to my colleagues.

To my grandchildren, Sam, Lilly, and Owen, thank you for your questions, and your joy. Matthew, Claire, and Vanessa, you are out in the world researching, teaching, learning, bringing your stories home, and sharing them with me; I am grateful for your presence in my life. Ann, your steadfast commitment to care and protection is formidable. I have benefited from it my whole life; I know it in my blood, in my bones. To Michael, for your interest in hearing and telling people's stories – my love of teaching and learning is strengthened by your interest in and consideration for other people's stories. This book would not have been possible without you. Vanessa, your contribution to my understanding of and appreciation for the work of visual artists contributes to the strength of the book. Thank you for introducing me to the artists and their work, and for always responding to my calls for assistance. Anushiik to my family.

To Sara Roque, who assisted me in identifying artists and organizing Chapter 4, thank you for sharing your knowledge and understanding. To my friends and colleagues, including Kathy Absolon, Jan Hare, Karleen Pendleton Jiménez, Ingrid Mündel, Hannah Fowlie, Jen Gilbert, Tanya Senk, Myra Lefkowitz, Verna St. Denis, and Carl James, and to Roger Simon, whose engagement with my work taught me to be a researcher. To the team of graduate students who assisted; Ixchel Bennett, Marianne Groat, Georgie Groat, and Tasha Smith, your work as Indigenous Education Warriors gives me hope. To the students in the Wabaan Indigenous Teacher Education program, the Urban Indigenous Education cohort, and the PhD cohort. To the Elders Council at the Toronto District School Board Urban Indigenous Education Centre, including Duke Redbird, Joanne Dallaire, Pauline Shirt, and Clay Shirt; I am grateful for the many conversations and the learning opportunities you provide. Anushiik to my teachers and students.

To research assistant Elena Cremonese. To the team of editors at UBC Press, including Nadine Pedersen and Katrina Petrik. To an excellent editor, Merrie-Ellen Wilcox. And to the anonymous reviewers whose feedback strengthened the manuscript. Anushiik.

And to my partner in love and life, Carla Rice, Canada Research Chair at the University of Guelph; our day-to-day conversations nurture my spirit.

Nii eloongomatii Anushiik waak katawaliil

BRAIDED LEARNING

INTRODUCTION
Indigenous Presence

"We can do a project about Indigenous people," the teacher said. "What would you like to do?"

"I want to make a book about my community for the teachers and kids in this school because they don't know a thing about us," nine-year-old Tamara responded. "They think we live in tipis down that road."[1]

I tell and retell this story with purpose. It reminds me that Indigenous children and youth are aware of what people know and don't know about our histories, cultures, and worldviews. They are bothered by this lack of knowledge and want to do something about it. Ultimately, this book is for them. However, the change that Tamara and others like her are hoping to accomplish requires engagement. More specifically, then, this book is for those who want to engage, hear, and learn from Indigenous voices telling Indigenous stories. It is about the relationship between Indigenous Peoples and settler Canadians and the ways in which colonialism informs our relationship. Illustrating Indigenous humanity, ongoing presence, and worldviews through art and story, each chapter addresses Indigenous Peoples' survival, ongoing presence, and future visions.

Although Tamara could not articulate it, she was responding to a reality that was purposefully created. Until the early twenty-first century, in countries around the world, stories about Indigenous Peoples positioned us as Romantic, Mythical, primitive people of the past.[2] Sami, Maori, Cree, Inuit, Mapuche, Maasai – many people share this experience. Stories and images of us are used to produce and reproduce ways of knowing that keep us locked in the past. Dominant representations of Indigenous Peoples justify the theft of our lands and resources to generate the wealth of nation-states established on our lands, erasing our existence. In settler states, including Canada, the United States, Australia, and New Zealand, the attempted eradication of Indigenous Peoples included policies aimed at genocide. In other places, including South America, Scandinavia, and Southeast Asia, to achieve eradication, Indigenous Peoples were almost completely absorbed into the colonizing population, or wholly isolated. Yet while these policies and practices had and continue to have devastating impacts, Indigenous Peoples survive and flourish. We continue to resist and are working to re-establish our ways of living, taking care of each other and the land. Our work includes teaching others that we did not disappear. Our ways of knowing and being are legitimate, and we continue to thrive. We have always known, and the United Nations Declaration on the Rights of Indigenous Peoples affirms and protects, our collective and individual rights, including our right to cultural practices, control of our economies, and leadership in social and political institutions.

In the current context, particularly in Canada, there is a growing interest in understanding and learning from Indigenous Peoples. This turning toward recognition of our ongoing presence has not occurred in isolation: it comes from the efforts of Indigenous leaders, activists, artists, and educators who have vigorously and unstintingly worked for needed change. Seeking to recover from the violence of colonialism, to gain access to ancestral teachings, and to recuperate Indigenous languages and worldviews, students, families, and communities advocate for the inclusion of Indigenous education in schools and sites of public education, including art galleries, historic sites, and museums, and through film and media. The Truth and Reconciliation Commission of Canada's Calls to Action both crystallize and amplify Indigenous Peoples' demands for recognition of our ongoing presence, concrete improvements in our access to and control of land and resources, and the right to self-determination.[3]

In part, this book is written in response to the Listening Stone Project: Learning from the Indigenous Education–Focused Collaborative Inquiry Initiative. As the principal researcher on this four-year project, I worked alongside Indigenous and non-Indigenous educators and community members from across Ontario. Presenting on the research brought me into conversations with local, national, and international audiences. The research focused on improving Indigenous student well-being and achievement. Findings emphasized the ongoing need for knowledge and understanding of settler colonialism and its impacts. When asked about their biggest challenge, consistently 90 to 94 percent of educators over the course of the project identified their lack of knowledge and understanding of Indigenous people's history and culture and their fear of making a mistake when teaching.[4] Whether I was talking with high school students in northern Ontario, teacher candidates in Vancouver, school board trustees in Toronto, or teacher educators at conferences in Chicago or Washington, DC, I heard the same message: *We do not know the history. Even if we want to support Indigenous people, we do not know where to start. We are afraid of doing it wrong.* As part of the research, I interviewed and surveyed close to four hundred educators, and their concerns were consistent with the broader field of research addressing Indigenous education in institutions of public schooling. Among educators, lack of knowledge is well documented.[5] Godlewska, Moore, and Bednasek refer to it as "cultivated ignorance or an ignorance that has been taught, learned, and embedded in the curriculum."[6] In this book, I am responding to what is, for me, an alarming lack of knowledge and understanding of Indigenous Peoples, our experiences, and our perspectives.

Settler Colonialism and Education

Anti-colonialism and anti-Indigenous racism call for settlers to understand the complexities of whiteness and settlement. Settler colonialism occurs when colonizers come to stay and form their own governing systems, eliminating the already existing nations.[7] Indigenous Peoples are pushed aside to build settler states on expropriated land. Veracini aptly identifies this as the "colonizers' demand that Indigenous populations 'go away' whether through literal/physical death or through figurative/social forms of death through assimilation or absorption into the settler polity."[8] White supremacy plays a vital role in settler colonialism, as it relies on the assumption that whiteness and white ways of being are superior to Indigenous Peoples' ways of being and are therefore to be desired. It requires the Indigenous population to want to and be forced to assimilate into the settler population.

Colonialism is a structure and a process that operates at all levels in our education systems, including the hierarchical organization of schools, the competitive approach to schooling, the content of the curriculum, how curriculum is taught, and who is doing the teaching. The shortage of self-identified Indigenous teachers in schools across Canada is well known to those working in the field. For example, in Alberta, where the Indigenous student population is 7 percent, Indigenous teachers make up less than 1 percent of the teaching population.[9] The under-representation of Indigenous people in the teaching profession impacts all students. Not surprisingly, it is Indigenous students who identify it as significant.[10]

The most significant manifestation of colonialism in our schools is the near complete erasure of Indigenous Peoples, our experiences, and our perspectives. This erasure is both material (physical presence) and ideological (knowledge). Canada is a settler colonial nation-state – Indigenous land and people were colonized by the French and British, and colonization continues through government policies and practices. Settler teachers have limited knowledge of the history of Indigenous–non-Indigenous relations and treaty and traditional rights, or the current issues impacting our communities, including the loss of land, resource extraction, and imposed governing systems. This entrenched ignorance in mainstream or settler-stream education is a critical issue for all Canadians.[11] Schools are colonial institutions, and teachers – like all Canadians – are impacted by what they did and did not learn in schools.

My commitment to the project of decolonizing schools is both personal and professional. I am an Indigenous educator (Potawatomi/Lenape/Irish/French) and strongly agree with Senator Murray Sinclair, who said about the Indian residential school system, "Education got us into this mess, and education will get us out of this mess – the use of education at least in terms of residential schools – but education is the key to reconciliation."[12] After thirty years of work in the field of Indigenous education, I know that this is complicated. In many ways, what Indigenous people want and need Canadians to learn is what many Canadians do not want to know. Like other Indigenous educators, I am somewhat weary of the need to educate non-Indigenous people. However, as Tamara's experience, described in the first paragraphs of this introduction, demonstrates, Indigenous people live in a relationship with non-Indigenous people. If we want new, better, more equitable and just relationships, all Canadians need a better understanding of the history that informs our relationship.

Afro-Indigenous Solidarity

I argue strongly that if you live on Indigenous land, you are in a relationship with Indigenous people. Just as strongly, I believe that how you came to live on this land matters a great deal. Not everyone or everyone's ancestors arrived by the same routes, nor did they experience the same privileges when they arrived. As important as it is to recognize diversity within the Indigenous population, it is equally important to recognize diversity within the settler population.

Settler colonialism and the attempted genocide of Indigenous Peoples did not happen in isolation. The theft of Indigenous lands occurred alongside the enslavement and forced movement of Africans. The violence and oppression experienced by Black and Indigenous people connects us with each other. Our experiences are different and the same. From the time the first Africans were forcibly brought to our land, we have had experiences of solidarity and conflict. There are stories of care and protection, as well as stories of violence and discrimination perpetrated against each other. Increased knowledge and understanding of how white supremacy and settler colonialism have been used against us, and used to position us against each other, is contributing to increased commitments to Afro-Indigenous solidarity.

Black and Indigenous people are becoming increasingly committed to working together, developing deep alliances, and supporting each other's work to dismantle white supremacy. A move toward establishing deep alliances is evident in the stories of Elders watching over young people during the Black Lives Matter protests, doing their work as protectors, and stories of Black activists bringing food to protesters and travelling to protest alongside their Indigenous brothers and sisters during the Idle No More, Wet'suwet'en, and LANDBACK protests.

Deep alliance requires deep commitment to supporting each other, refusing to compete with each other over who is more oppressed, refusing to keep our interactions at a surface level through public expressions of support or appreciation. It involves working together and learning from each other's knowledges and experiences.

These alliances are making it increasingly possible to recognize and hear the voices of Afro-Indigenous people. Identified primarily on the basis of visible markers of their Blackness, their identities as Indigenous people have historically been silenced or erased. In learning about the experiences of Indigenous people, it is absolutely critical to hear a diversity of voices. My intention in this book is to encourage the recognition and significance of difference, prioritizing respectful relationships. Rather than judging each other's worthiness, it is possible to learn from and with difference.

Our Perspectives

I have been working in the field of Indigenous education for over three decades, and I have spent considerable time thinking about questions of representation. I am particularly interested in what non-Indigenous people hear and learn from the stories Indigenous people tell. I am writing this book in collaboration with my brother Michael Dion. We grew up with our four siblings, basking in the warmth of our parents' love for each other. The shadow of colonialism eclipsed that warmth. While our father shared stories of his childhood, stories of an Irish-Catholic family leaving home and arriving in Quebec City, our mother was almost silent about her childhood experiences growing up on Moraviantown Reserve Number 47. My strongest memory from when I finally found a way to talk with our mother about her life was her sense of insult. Her words stay with me: "They judged us incapable, as if we did not know how to take care of ourselves and our children." The disdain she expressed toward those who judged reflected a deep sense of pride in her own and her family's capacities to take care of themselves and each other.

Michael and I began writing together in the early 1990s. At the time, I was an elementary school teacher and Michael was working in downtown Toronto restaurants. We had many conversations about being Indigenous and what it was like growing up in a small southern Ontario city, living with anti-Indigenous racism that was not, at that time, even identified as racism. I shared with Michael my experiences as a teacher, including the time I was assisting one of my English as a Second Language students in her history class and heard the teacher say, in reference to the building of the railroad across the western plains, "It was no problem – there was nothing out there but some buffalo and a few hundred Indians." When I told Michael about my children – his nieces and nephew – coming home with images of Indians dressed in buckskin and feathers, we started to discuss the idea of writing about Indigenous people. We wanted to share our stories, to provide readers with opportunities to learn, from our perspective, what it means to be an Indigenous person in Canada. The words of that history teacher still sting, and I know he was not the only one. His words are emblematic of teachers' lack of knowledge and, consequently, students' lack of learning opportunities.

Why Art and Story?

In his book *Why Indigenous Literatures Matter*, Daniel Heath Justice writes, "Story makes meaning of the relationships that define who we are and what our place is in the world; it reminds us of our duties, our rights and responsibilities and the consequences and transformative possibilities of our actions."[13] In my teaching and research encounters, I have come to know that many Canadians are unfamiliar with Indigenous literature. At the start of each academic year, I ask students in my university classes if they have ever read a book by an Indigenous author. Students report that while they have all read Shakespeare, many have read Hemingway, and some have read Margaret Atwood, very few have read a book written by an Indigenous author. More than once I have heard, "I didn't even know that Indigenous people write books." Heath Justice echoes Indigenous storytellers – King, Momaday, Archibald, Vizenor – who, informed by centuries-old storytelling tradition, recognize the centrality of story for making meaning of our lives.[14] Heeding their words, my brother and I are sharing our stories with intention. We agree that the stories we hear and do not hear – the stories we tell and do not tell, about ourselves and each other – matter a great deal.

My faith in the power of story comes from my experience and my understanding of the use of stories as teaching and learning tools within Indigenous cultures. Sitting around the supper table after the plates were cleared, around the campfire, or waiting for the clothes to dry at the laundromat, my parents told stories. Some of the stories were about fond memories, difficult times, or loved ones. Mom's stories were usually about the exciting and amusing events of the day. I appreciated listening to the stories as much as my parents enjoyed telling them. The stories were a form of entertainment, but they were also much more. The stories provided me with a sense of belonging and purpose, an understanding of my connections. They taught me about who I am and about the importance of respect for and responsibility to my ancestors, myself, my family, and all living things.

They inspired feelings of confidence and belonging that nurtured my spirit and my capacity for action.

In our writing, Michael and I draw on Indigenous storytelling practice. As we write, we are conscious of our responsibilities as tellers, and we recognize the significance of establishing a relationship with our readers. Within an oral practice, "storytelling implicates the listener [reader] into becoming an active participant in the experience of the story."[15] Jo-ann Archibald of the Stó:lō Nation describes the synergistic interaction between storyteller, listener, and story as a critical storywork principle.[16] The relationships between the teller, the listener, the text, and the meanings they co-construct within the storytelling context is for us part of the potential power of storytelling. Although this book provides access to our stories through reading, we are, in some respects, asking our readers to become "hearers" with the responsibilities of listenership. Within Indigenous storytelling traditions, careful attending is the responsibility of the audience. Archibald (2008) writes that it is vital to listen and then to go away and think deeply about the meanings of the story. She reminds us that listening is an active role that must be deliberately accepted. An interest in or a concern with the story is not sufficient; members of a listening audience must be willing to do the work of listening.

These elements matter to the story being told and the story being heard. Michael and I write stories that invite readers to lean in, hear, and make their meanings. We document the diversities and complexities of Indigenous people's lives. We include our meaning-making experiences of and responses to the suffering and profound losses brought about by settler colonialism. Just as importantly, the stories document how Indigenous people draw on ancestral teachings to survive and thrive. Writing ourselves into the story and sharing our meaning-making creates space for readers to see themselves in the story and to make their meaning as part of the process. We take our demands on readers seriously and recognize "the need to speak clearly and truthfully, the need to understand that when you speak, you are calling upon others to commit time and attention."[17] This understanding of the responsibilities that go along with being storytellers informs our writing. Michael and I are co-writers of the Braiding Histories stories that appear in Chapter 5. He provided writing and editing support to the settler Canadians whose stories appear in Chapter 2. He is also a writing mentor and editor for me.

Chapter 4, "Learning from Contemporary Indigenous Artists," was completed with assistance from Sara Roque. In her position as Aboriginal Arts Officer at the Ontario Arts Council, Roque played a critical role in supporting emerging Indigenous artists. Her knowledge of contemporary Indigenous art contributed to the organization and selection of artists featured in Chapter 4. It is further informed by my daughter Vanessa Dion Fletcher. Vanessa is a mid-career artist, and my learning about artistic creation comes in large part from my conversations with her about what it means to make art. While I had been including visual art in my teaching for some time, Vanessa helped me understand the way art works as a teaching and learning strategy. "My art is a response to questions that I am thinking about – I don't necessarily know what those questions are until I am finished the work."[18] This conversation made me realize that, in part, art is an invitation to observe and experience the artist's process. Thus, I understand engaging with art as an observational and experiential teaching and learning exchange. The images in Chapter 4 are meant to be looked at and talked about before, during, and after reading the stories that accompany the images.

Indigenous Pedagogy

Stories have always been valued within Indigenous cultures as a means of teaching and learning. Stories are not just entertainment but power. They reflect the deepest, most intimate perceptions, relationships, and attitudes of a people and can be used to bring harmony and balance to all beings that inhabit their nation's universe.[19] Within Indigenous conceptions of story and history, the concern is not with a chronological telling of events; history is neither linear nor steeped in notions of social progress and evolution.[20] As Vine Deloria Jr. of the Sioux Nation has written, "The nation's stories reflect what is important to a group of people as a group. Historical events were either of the distant past and regarded as such or vivid memories of the tribe that occupied a prominent important place in the people's perspective and understanding of their situation."[21] Michael and I are sharing stories that are "vivid memories" of events that occupy a prominent place in our perspective and understanding of our situation. These texts inform and reflect who we are and our experience of being Indigenous in Canada. We are sharing with good intentions and hoping to engage readers in learning from the stories we tell. We aim to expand and deepen readers' understanding of Indigenous people, of themselves, and of themselves in relationship with Indigenous people.

This book is framed by my understanding of Indigenous pedagogies. My interest in pedagogy is rooted in my desire to understand how and what people learn, what gets in the way of learning, and how to accomplish teaching and learning that contributes to well-being. In my work within Indigenous education, I have come to know and value Indigenous approaches, including story, observation, and experiential learning. The stories in this book are meant to be experienced, reflected on, questioned, talked about, and talked back to. Visual art is included to recognize the work of contemporary Indigenous artists and their contribution to disrupting the dominant narrative. Importantly, I know that images portraying Indigenous people as Romantic, Mythical people of the past continue to circulate in the public domain, significantly contributing to what and how people "know" about Indigeneity. The work of the artists disrupts those narratives and gives access to alternative ways of knowing ourselves and each other.

About Positionality

In a traditional storytelling setting, there is a connection between the storyteller and the story listeners. Speakers and listeners have a shared understanding of their responsibilities. Furthermore, they are speaking and listening from a collective body of shared knowledge.[22] In her discussion of cross-cultural/cross-racial oral events, Jocelyn Donlon suggests that when crossing cultural and racial boundaries, tellers risk finding listeners who do not share their "critical beliefs" – that is, beliefs that contribute to accomplishing understanding between themselves and their listeners inside a "mutual belief space."[23] Kimberly Blaeser explains the challenges Indigenous writers confront:

> In their work, they often find themselves negotiating against the authority of the very written tradition in which they are engaged: challenging the rules of writing, challenging the truth of historical accounts, challenging the privileging of text. Their work often rewrites, writes over, writes through, writes differently, writes itself against the Western literary tradition. Native writers often tell a different story, tell it from a different perspective, from a different worldview. They challenge the reigning literary conventions and the enshrined styles of writing both in principle and in practice.[24]

Michael and I write from this position, with the realization that our readers may not be familiar with our approach. What is more, it may feel alienating. We encourage readers to hear the story being told, to not interrupt the storyteller in order to absorb and respond to the whole of the story, to make their meaning within the context of their lives. We also realize that readers may need additional information and may want to check facts and get names, dates, and definitions; a glossary therefore provides details, background information, and links to additional resources to extend learning.

More about the Chapters

All of the chapters in this book draw on Indigenous theories of teaching and learning. Relying on art and story, my intention is to cultivate relationships between readers and storytellers, between readers and artists. While Chapters 1 through 3 work best read sequentially, in

Chapters 4 and 5 readers are invited to move back and forth between art and story. The glossary and additional resources at the end are intended to be used throughout the reading of the book.

Chapter 1 sets the context for the book, with a discussion of the growing awareness on the part of many Canadians that Indigenous Peoples, our experiences, and our perspectives are relevant to all people living in Canada. Utilizing the "Perfect Stranger" concept introduced in *Braiding Histories*,[25] I describe a shift in people from being comfortably unaware to uncomfortably aware of how much they don't know and their emerging realization that they want and need to know more. I introduce "Requisites for Reconciliation," including Implication, Investment, Shared Interest, and Impact, explaining how prior learning cultivates a particular stance necessary for reconciliation to happen in respectful ways. The chapter prepares readers for engaging with the content of the book.

In Chapter 2, three settlers share their stories of coming to see themselves in relationship with Indigenous people. Libby Stephenson, Sheyfali Saujani, and Joe Wild each share their experiences and struggles with understanding what was missing from their knowledge of being Canadian. In the telling of their stories, they address issues and concerns, including appropriation, stereotypes, fear, anger, and guilt. This chapter reflects the work required to recognize implication and responsibility.

In Chapter 3, I tell the history of Indigenous–non-Indigenous relationship as a cohesive narrative that can be read from beginning to end. I frame the chapter with my questions about what happened in the relationship between Indigenous people and newcomers, from first contact to today. Reflecting on what I learned in school and the confusion I felt about being Indigenous, the chapter focuses on the dominant narrative of Canadian history and what was missing from that narrative. I address how Indigenous Peoples, initially friends and allies of the newcomers, became the "Indian problem," and how the reserve system, the Indian Act, and residential schools were a response to the problem. The final section addresses recuperation and resurgence, including a response to the 1969 White Paper, the birth of the National Indian Brotherhood, and the ongoing resistance movement. This is a story told in broad strokes. It is my story of coming to understand what happened and why Indigenous Peoples, who once had sovereignty over our lives and territories, now live under the rule of an imposed state authority. However, our political difference has not been erased and continues to live on.

Inspired by the oft-quoted words of Métis leader Louis Riel, "My people will sleep for 100 years, but when they awake, it will be the artists who will give them their spirit back,"[26] Chapter 4 uses the work of contemporary Indigenous artists to expand on crucial issues and concerns introduced in Chapter 2. Through their artistic practice, many contemporary Indigenous artists are drawing on ancestral teachings to make sense of and contribute to knowledge and understanding of history. Chapter 4 includes images that inspire engagement, provoke questions, and initiate learning. Drawing on both the artists' statements and discussions with educators and art critics, each image is followed by three to four paragraphs of text that provide readers with opportunities to engage deeply with ideas introduced in the artwork. Topics include residential schools, child welfare, land, community, and Indigenous language, worldviews, and family relationships.

Chapter 5 is a collection of stories that provides opportunities for readers to engage with the specific impacts of colonialism on Indigenous people's lives. As a collection, titled "The Braiding Histories Stories," these stories focus on individual people, showing how policies and practices impacted individuals, their families, their communities, and their nations. For example, while many Canadians know about the building of the railroad, they do not understand how the need for control of land on the Prairies is implicated in the starvation of the Cree and their forced removal to reserve land. This chapter includes previously published stories about Shawnadithit, Mistahimaskwa, and Audrey Dion, addressing both early contact and the impacts of disease, overhunting, and the Indian Act.[27] It includes stories about a post-secondary Mi'kmaq youth, a mother of mixed

Indigenous/non-Indigenous ancestry, a Black-Indigenous educator/activist, and an adult artist/educator.

The conclusion provides a summary and review of the critical issues addressed in the book, and a discussion on next steps. Returning to the requisites for reconciliation introduced in Chapter 1, it highlights some significant changes achieved since the final report of the Truth and Reconciliation Commission was published and challenges readers to consider their roles and responsibilities in accomplishing new and better relationships with Indigenous people and all of creation.

Informed by my understanding of Indigenous pedagogy, this book relies on theories of learning that put relationship, responsibility, and respect at the centre. I appreciate that readers may need specifics about some of the key events, concepts, policies, and practices referred to. The expanded glossary and additional resources at the end of the book provide these details. Each entry begins with a quote from the book, putting the term or concept in context, followed by a definition and detailed description, as well as background information and additional resources to extend learning.

1

REQUISITES FOR RECONCILIATION

A group of high school students are on a twelve-day canoe trip in Algonquin Park. The students attend a private school, and most are from upper-middle-class families. They are almost exclusively white. It is early in the term, but the students have been together long enough to have learned a little bit about each other. In particular, they know that one of their classmates is Indigenous. It is Day 5 of the trip and the fifth straight day of rain. The sixteen students and their two teachers have stopped for lunch. They have paddled to shore and are sitting in their canoes, trying to stay warm. Brenda turns to Niki and asks, "Niki, don't you know how to do a rain dance or something to make it stop raining?" When Niki turns toward her teachers, they turn away. Niki responds with a deep sigh of exasperation and the moment passes. However, for Niki and for her teachers, the question, the asking, and the turning away never pass.

Brenda's question, premised on stereotypical ways of knowing, exposes her lack of knowledge, creates discomfort, and, though likely unintentionally, causes harm. It imposes an expectation and a responsibility on Niki, as if – by virtue of her status as an Indigenous person – she is in some way responsible for providing a solution to the group's less than pleasant experience in the natural environment. When Niki turns to her teachers for assistance, the teachers, who know enough to know that the question is problematic, turn away, pretending that they didn't hear. In turning away, they abandon their responsibilities to both Niki and Brenda. Brenda's question draws attention to Niki's difference with no consideration for her difference. For me, the significance of this exchange is not whether we can tolerate the asking of such questions but whether we can recognize the teaching and learning potential of such questions, work through our discomfort, and reflect on what they reveal. Might an understanding of what is at stake when we turn away motivate a turning toward?

Recognizing and Working Through Discomfort

During the past thirty years, my teaching and research have focused on identifying and understanding how to engage Canadians in teaching and learning from Indigenous people's experiences and perspectives. When I started this work, I wrote about resistance, identifying what I called the Perfect Stranger position.[1] In my experience, educators, like many Canadians, positioned themselves as perfect strangers, telling me, "I can't teach this content, I know nothing about Indigenous people, I have no Indigenous friends, I didn't grow up near a reserve, I didn't learn anything when I was in school. I am a perfect stranger to Indigenous people."[2] I wrote about the allure and enticing nature of this position, explaining how it is ultimately an avoidance tactic. If you are a perfect stranger to Indigenous people, you have no responsibility for doing the work required to accomplish justice and equity in the relationships between Indigenous and non-Indigenous people. In this book I am responding to a hopeful shift – what I am calling the Not-So-Perfect Stranger. This shift reflects a significant move – rather than turning away, many Canadians are turning toward, wanting to know, wanting to understand, and asking, "If this has something to do with me, how do I make sense of it, what do I need to know, what am I to do?"

This turning has potential and thus interests me a great deal. As much as I want to celebrate it, I want, more importantly, to understand, learn from, and respond to the questions and concerns people have as they engage with the challenge of working through[3] the history

Requisites for Reconciliation

and ongoing implications of settler colonialism. Drawing on my teaching, research, and public lectures, in the following section I share my responses to frequently asked questions and comments that I hear from Canadians as they struggle to make sense of the relationship between Indigenous and settler Canadians. The national dialogue on reconciliation has generated interest, yet many people continue to experience resistance when hearing Indigenous people's voices. As much as they want to understand and contribute to new and more just relationships, they continue to encounter challenges. Identifying and reflecting on common points of resistance is a kind of pre-emptive strategy to prepare for learning from the art and stories shared in subsequent chapters. Before taking up those questions, I want to address Brenda, Niki, and their teachers' turning away.

Returning to Brenda's Question

I recognize the desire to avoid questions about Indigenous people and the discomfort those questions cause, but I believe that we cannot afford to lose the potential learning they offer. Investigating why people ask such questions can open them up to how their experiences, beliefs, and desires are projected onto Indigenous people and impede their ability to see and hear Indigenous perspectives. Sometimes people's words and actions in the present are informed by their pasts, and their words and actions make sense "within a frame of perception that is so familiar, so safe, that it is difficult to risk changing it even when they know their perceptions are distorted, limited, constricted by that old view."[4] If, for example, rather than turning away from Brenda's question or simply reprimanding her for an expression of stereotypical ways of knowing about Indigenous people, the teachers turned toward the students, investigating their own and their students' understanding of and reactions to the question, what might they have had the opportunity to learn?

Asking what students know and don't know about the history of Indigenous Peoples in Canada, what stories have they heard and what stories do they tell? In particular, on a canoe trip, in the northern Ontario landscape, with her Indigenous classmate alongside her, what story does Brenda hear and in what ways is it different from the story that Niki is experiencing? And – this is key – Brenda's question draws attention to a significant difference, and ignoring it does harm. Reflecting on and questioning the question opens possibilities for learning. For example, Brenda may have known full well that Niki did not know a rain dance, and her question might have been an attempt to add humour to a miserable situation. While Brenda can afford to find humour in asking Niki to do a dance, for Niki there is nothing funny about the loss of access to her ancestral knowledge.

What might Niki have been able to learn about herself from this question had her teachers supported further inquiry? What might she have wanted to say and teach others?

- I want you to know how much I wish that I *did* know about the dances, songs, and ceremonies of my ancestors.
- I want you to appreciate my sense of loss, how deeply I mourn for the loss of Indigenous knowledge.
- I want *you* to know the stories of *our* ancestors, which brought us to this place where I, an Anishinaabe student, sat with you and the rest of our class and listened to our white teachers teach me how to paddle a canoe.

Attending to disruptive questions illustrates how something that appears innocent may be complicated for Indigenous students. If, rather than turning away to avoid discomfort, the teachers turned toward the students and worked with them and with the discomfort, what might they have accomplished?

Engaging with Art and Story: Attending to Disruptive Questions

We bring to any story an existing narrative frame that helps us order an understanding of how things are connected and why certain actors act as they do. That is, we make sense of the stories we hear based on our existing knowledge frames and beliefs. When listening to a story that originates from outside of that frame (or one that ruptures our frame), our commitments to a given knowledge base and belief system may obstruct our ability to understand the story. In response, we may find ourselves "bothered" by questions that demand our attention, questions that Simon and Armitage call "shadow questions."[5] The answers to these questions are typically not found within the text but are questions that signify an "asking after," something we need to know in order to make sense of the text. While attending to these questions may seem to take us away from hearing the story, I argue that paying attention to the questions addresses our positionality, helping us recognize our differences and the implications of those differences in how we understand and make sense of the stories we hear.

Reading and listening audiences are not the same; the responsibilities of listenership are understood differently.[6] I recognize that, at different times and in different ways, Canadians are listening to Indigenous people's stories from outside of a shared critical belief space. I have come to appreciate that the responsibility of careful attending includes attending to the questions our stories provoke. It is equally important to think about how and to whom listeners pose their questions. As an Indigenous educator, I have accepted a pedagogical responsibility and am sharing stories purposefully, with the intention of provoking questions, and I write conscious of the questions I anticipate from readers. It may be that readers are unable to make sense of my stories without first addressing the shadow questions that limit their understanding. Dialogue and self-reflection before, during, and after reading is critical to learning from the stories.

Rather than setting questions aside, being afraid to ask, we ought to interrogate ourselves about why our questions are important and necessary and what assumptions and judgments they imply. If, rather than allowing our questions to divert us from the story, we use them to begin working through the story by investigating the terms that not only motivate but also define the questions, then we can begin to "hear" the story differently. Asking and responding to our own questions provides a way to scrutinize what constitutes our understanding in order to be conscious of what we bring to the story, opening up the possibility for us to understand differently. We must be able to hold up our responses for scrutiny, allowing us to enter into critical dialogue about our relationship to that which initiated the question.

In the following section, I discuss questions that I hear from people who are engaging with the history of Indigenous–non-Indigenous relationships. These questions help me understand the challenges people confront as they think about reconciliation and what it entails.

Turning toward Questions, Concerns, and Commitments

Learning from Indigenous people's experiences and perspectives initiates a range of questions and concerns. For me it is helpful to reflect on the issues and challenges people confront as they begin to think about themselves in relationship with Indigenous people.[7] Reflecting on what I hear people say, I identify four requisites for reconciliation. I am not concerned here with what reconciliation is or must include; that is a complex and ongoing discussion, beyond the scope of this book. I am suggesting that these requisites are significant as people move from a place of disinterest to actively searching for ways to join the conversation about new and better relationships between Indigenous people and other Canadians.

Requisites for Reconciliation

1. *Implication* – recognizing that all Canadians are in relationship with Indigenous people
2. *Investment* – making a commitment of time and energy to learn from Indigenous people's experiences and perspectives
3. *Shared interest* – appreciating that Indigenous people's well-being is in the best interests of all Canadians

4 *Impact* – wanting my actions to have a positive impact in creating new and better relationships between Indigenous and non-Indigenous people

As more and more Canadians begin to hear Indigenous perspectives, the potential for creating real change in the relationship grows. As much as I would like to focus exclusively on creating the change, I recognize that learning from the history of colonialism poses challenges, and I want to continue understanding, learning from, and responding to those challenges. Understanding why it is difficult, and having some sense of how and why, in spite of the challenges, people are still interested in and willing to do the work of learning, is a useful step toward creating change.

Wrestling with Implication
I was speaking with a group of teachers in eastern Ontario about treaty rights and why it is necessary for all Canadians to learn how our government failed to follow through on treaty promises, when I was interrupted by a familiar question. As I was explaining how broken treaties contribute to the barriers Indigenous people confront in establishing economic security, an audience member asked, "But isn't that what we all want? We all want economic security. Why should Indigenous people get special status?"

This question brings to the surface two critical considerations that many Canadians struggle to understand: Indigenous people occupy a distinctive place on this land, and Indigenous people have not been treated the same as every other Canadian. Canada was established on Indigenous land, and much of that land was acquired through treaty negotiations. Boundaries were determined and access to resources, rights, and responsibilities were recorded in treaty agreements. Understanding the story of Canada requires knowledge of treaty history, including the ways in which broken treaties benefited some and devastated others.

I recognize the desire to forget, to argue that the past does not matter in the present, to collapse difference and say we are all the same. While some may find this comforting, it is becoming increasingly difficult to ignore the perspectives of Indigenous people, presenting evidence that connects broken treaties to the current economic disadvantages people encounter in their day-to-day lives. Hearing these voices challenges the dominant narrative of Canada the good, defender of equity and justice. In many ways, treaty education challenges Canadians' expectations of ongoing entitlement to land and resources. It calls into question the discourse of meritocracy that allows Canadians to believe that individual wealth and well-being is earned and not the result of unfair advantages given to some at the expense of others. To understand current conditions, it is important to learn about who had access to land and who was denied access to land and resources. Indigenous Peoples were removed from their traditional territories to "land reserved for Indians."[8] Our land was transferred to the state and became "Crown lands." Settlers were sold land or in some instances granted land in exchange for their service to governments. In some instances, land was granted to settlers in exchange for their labour, clearing and farming the land. Indigenous Peoples were denied access to our land at the same time as settlers were being granted land. These policies and practices from the past have a bearing on the present.

The phrase *wrestling with implication* is helpful because for many people it is a challenge to recognize that as Canadians they are in relationship with Indigenous people, and treaty history is their history too. Implication and investment are intertwined: as people recognize *implication*, they are often more willing to *invest* in hearing Indigenous perspectives. Sometimes, hearing our perspective triggers a sense of implication and deeper investment.

Investing in Hearing Our Voices
I was doing research in northern Ontario when a secondary school student explained, "We don't even know what we want because we

never had it. Why do our teachers think we know our histories, our languages, our teachings? And why do they judge us and ask us, 'Do you speak your language, how Indigenous are you, what's your clan?'"

Many Indigenous people are participating in resurgence. While we are bothered by Canadians' lack of knowledge and understanding of our histories and contemporary lived experiences, we are most concerned with recuperating and improving access to our languages, traditional knowledge, and cultural practices for ourselves and our children. While Canadians are starting to learn about the impacts of cultural genocide perpetrated through residential schools, most don't know that in Canada laws were passed that made it a crime to speak our languages, practise our culture, and pass on stories and ceremonies to our children and grandchildren. Indigenous students are made to feel ashamed of their own lack of knowledge or are judged by outsiders as less authentically Indigenous because of what they don't know, or both. Most people do not understand that *not knowing* was the goal of Canadian policies of forced assimilation.

Isolating Indigenous people on reserves, and creating policies that outlawed language and cultural practices, contributed to the chasm that exists today between Indigenous and non-Indigenous people. It also meant that many Indigenous people had limited access to language and cultural practices. While this is changing, it continues to be a challenge resulting from colonialism. Creating change means that non-Indigenous people need to learn from and with us, and while Indigenous people have survived colonialism, many of us, especially our youth, also need opportunities to learn. While we all live the legacies of colonialism, not enough of us understand its intricacies. In many ways, we need to reconcile our own histories, our familial and community histories. Both Indigenous and non-Indigenous people need opportunities to learn how their ancestors were implicated in colonialism. We all need a better understanding of what was done in order to recuperate from it.

Hearing and learning from Indigenous voices requires an investment of time, attention, and thought. Many Canadians are recognizing the need to invest time and energy in learning from Indigenous perspectives. Increasing numbers of Indigenous-focused courses are being offered in secondary and post-secondary programs; Indigenous people are much more frequently featured in the media; and Indigenous art, film, and writing is increasingly being produced and shared. Learning from and with Indigenous people and supporting the creation of space for Indigenous people to engage with and participate in cultural practices is an investment in shared well-being. Remember not to judge people for what they don't know; rather, invest in their learning.

Recognizing Shared Best Interests
After I had given a talk for teacher candidates at the University of British Columbia, a small group gathered to speak with me. I was not immediately surprised by the student who explained how, as a settler, she particularly appreciated the space I offered her for learning from Indigenous voices. She asked, "Can non-Indigenous people participate in reconciliation if we are relegated to a place of guilty, greedy, violent oppressor?"

Understanding that the relationship between Indigenous people and settlers was and, in many ways, continues to be premised on greed, power, and control over our bodies and land does not mean that people today want the current relationship to continue. The path to creating new and better relationships requires knowledge and understanding of existing relationships as well as knowledge of how we came to occupy these places in relationship with each other. If non-Indigenous people are locked into positions of the guilty perpetrator of violent oppression and Indigenous people are perpetually required to be victims, new and better relationships are impossible. Historically our relationships have been defined by judgments about the inferiority and incapacities of Indigenous people, and the refusal to recognize and respect difference. The relationship premised on judgments of "less than" that justified the theft of land and resources needs to be identified, investigated, and reconciled. In spite of the attempts at eradicating Indigenous people, we have survived – and must be reckoned with in respectful ways that are premised on the legitimacy of our position as original people.

For me this question surfaces a serious challenge – how to teach about colonialism without reproducing dominant narratives centring violence and oppression that require Indigenous people to be perpetual victims of violence and require non-Indigenous people to be guilty oppressors. We cannot erase the violence of colonialism, but we cannot focus exclusively on violence. We can invest in learning and commit to actions that remediate harm and contribute to renewed relationships.

Contributing to Change and Having an Impact

My teaching and research bring me into contact with many non-Indigenous people who are willing and wanting to engage with learning the history of settler colonialism. My question to them is *why*: "Why are you doing this work? What motivates you to engage with this difficult history?" In response, I am told, "I do it because I want to make a difference, I want to have an impact."

The desire to have an impact is a positive motivating force that inspires people to take action and do the work of learning so as to contribute to creating equity and justice. As much as this desire to make things better is good, it can derive from a problematic place. When the desire to have an impact comes from an uninterrogated place of privilege, it can reproduce the saviour-victim relationship. When an audience member tells me that they want to help and asks what they can do to help, my response is a gentle reminder to take responsibility and investigate the ways in which Canadians have benefited from colonialism.

I ask people to learn about the land they live on: Whose traditional territory is it? When were Indigenous people removed from the land? How was the land used before and after contact? And who became wealthy from the land? In my years of working in the field of Indigenous studies I have found that the vast majority of Canadians want to have a positive impact on the world. Learning to work with consciousness of their own place in the relationship shifts the "how can I help you" approach to "how can I take responsibility for the actions of my ancestors and work to establish/re-establish respectful relationships with you?" My faith in the power of education comes in part from working with people who are committed to acting in support of positive change. These questions and comments inform my understanding of the complexities of speaking and listening across difference. My work is grounded in a profound faith in learning: as Canadians take up the work of learning both *from* and *with* Indigenous people, there is hope.

Settler Colonialism, Anti-Indigenous Racism, and the Not-So-Perfect-Stranger Framework

Disrupting settler consciousness calls for settlers to understand the complexities of whiteness and settlement. Settler colonialism occurs when colonizers come to stay and establish political orders for themselves. It operates through a logic of elimination that aims to accomplish the disappearance of the native in order to build settler polities on expropriated land.[9] White supremacy plays a vital role in settler colonialism in that it relies on the assumption that whiteness and white ways of being are superior to Indigenous ways of being and are therefore desired. It requires the Indigenous population to want to or be forced to assimilate into the settler population, or both.

The Not-So-Perfect-Stranger framework for engaging with and learning from Indigenous art and story is informed by the growing awareness of anti-Indigenous racism, with an emphasis on unstructuring settler consciousness. This requires readers to be vigilant about their tendency to avoid implication, their desire to see themselves as innocent participants in settler colonialism. It asks that readers resist the need to justify or explain away their privilege, to be aware of the ease with which they adopt a condescending attitude that requires Indigenous people to occupy the position of pitiful victims, or damaged people in need of healing. This learning requires recognition of the power of Indigenous people to represent ourselves, accepting the invitation to learn from us in the service of establishing responsible relationships. The goal is not simply to learn, feel bad, and carry on. The goal is to renegotiate the terms of living on Indigenous lands. It is most certainly about the return of stolen land and stolen wealth.

2

Seeing Yourself in Relationship with Settler Colonialism

> Now the rule of law of nations is that what belongs to nobody is granted to the first occupant ... And so, as the object in question was not without an owner, it does not fall under the title which we are discussing ... in and by itself it gives no support to a seizure of the aborigines any more than if [it] had been they who discovered us.
>
> – Francisco de Vitoria, 1532[1]

Learning from Settler Stories

For many people, thinking about Indigenous-settler Canadian relationships is new; others have been participating in these discussions for a long time. Although the labels *ally* and *settler in solidarity* are fairly recent, Indigenous people have been resisting settler colonialism since the time of initial contact, and, as reflected in the epigraph, non-Indigenous people allied with Indigenous people contesting the claiming of our lands as early as 1532. In spite of these actions in support of the recognition of Indigenous rights, the relationship between Indigenous and non-Indigenous people was and continues to be shaped by settler colonialism. Changing the relationship is going to require the participation of all Canadians, and learning from the history of the relationship between Indigenous and non-Indigenous people can be a difficult journey. This chapter includes narratives by three settler Canadians who share their stories of coming to see themselves in relationship with Indigenous people.

The first settler story is written by Libby Stephenson. I first met Libby after my talk at an anti-racism conference in Toronto. We came to know each other well through our work with the Ministry of Education's Indigenous Education–Focused Collaborative Inquiry Initiative. During those years, Libby shared many stories of her learning about colonialism and how her learning was changing her actions. When I asked Libby to write her story, she immediately agreed – and then proceeded to procrastinate. As much as she wanted to tell her story, it was still challenging to write about her learning. Libby is an exceedingly friendly, outgoing, helpful person. While the desire to be a helpful friend is evident in her story, Libby does not get stuck in being a good white settler.[2] She pushes past this impulse, challenging herself to learn, to recognize her privilege and accept her responsibilities, and to share her learning with others.

Sheyfali Saujani and I met when she asked if she could interview me about the relationship between recent immigrants and Indigenous people. Newcomers arrive in Canada at different times and by different routes. If you live on this land, you are in a relationship with Indigenous people – but there are differences in how people have come to live on this land and thus differences in the relationship. Sheyfali describes arriving in Canada and the not uncommon tendency to collapse differences between her experiences as a brown-skinned immigrant woman and the experiences of Indigenous people. Through her friendship with a Kanien'kehá:ka colleague, Sheyfali learns to recognize and appreciate the significance of difference.

In the third settler narrative, Joe Wild describes his process of learning from Indigenous people. In his work as senior assistant deputy minister for Crown-Indigenous relations, Joe has had the opportunity to meet with and learn from and with Indigenous people in communities across Canada. He reflects on the depth of his own not knowing, and the surprise and astonishment that came with learning that his experience of being Canadian is not what Indigenous people experience.

Each narrative addresses the challenges of coming to see oneself in relationship with settler colonialism, thus providing strategies and guidance for others interested in learning.

WHAT AM I GOING TO DO NOW?
Libby Stephenson

There is a row of totem poles in Stanley Park. It's an iconic image, readily reproduced in postcards, tourist brochures, and even high school history books. In 2019 I was visiting Vancouver for the first time, and I was looking forward to seeing them. I approached with expectation, but I was caught off guard. The words on the plaque explaining the poles made me stop, surprised by my own surprise – I caught myself in the act of questioning the narrative.[3]

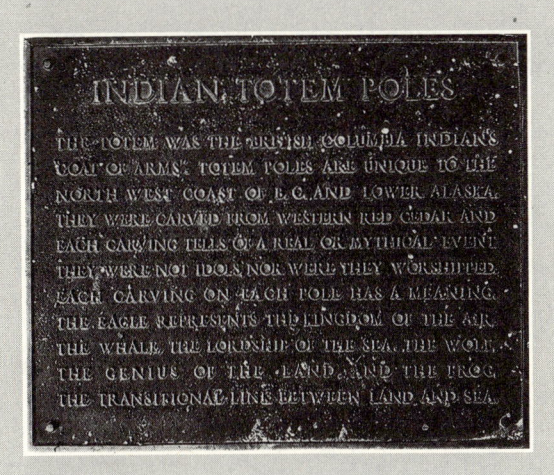

Stanley Park totem poles plaque.

I am starting with this image, this story, because I'm still surprised by it. This questioning was new to me; it was not anything I ever expected. I grew up in a southern Ontario city, went to high school, then university, and became a teacher. I thought I knew the story of Canada. I *taught* the story of Canada, and as a school principal I led a school community in the celebration of Canada. Yet there I was, standing in front of that plaque, questioning.

As I write this story it has no ending.
What is an ally?
Am I an ally?
I know who Christopher Columbus was.
Who is Mistahimaskwa?
I'm shocked, dumbfounded, and embarrassed.
What am I going to do now?

It was a gorgeous, sunny July day in Vancouver. The sky was blue, the heat palpable. My husband and I were in Vancouver for a day before travelling up the coast to Savary Island. We had only a short time and I wanted to see the totem poles. I was looking forward to the experience. Already in my short stay, I felt that Indigenous history and culture were more present and were represented in ways I hadn't seen at home in Ontario. We rented bikes, as many others do. The park was full of people – runners passing by, families out walking, and buses full of tourists. Each person with their own expectations of the day. As we approached the famous totems, I wondered what others' thoughts were, how they saw these totems; did they know the history, the significance of the stories within the carvings – the history of the people? I was overwhelmed by the beauty of the carving and the intricacy of the stories, and then I read the plaque. I felt sad and discouraged when I was so hoping for a feeling of pride. The words weren't from an Indigenous perspective; they were grounded in colonial thinking. So disappointing – the legacy of not representing Indigenous history and cultures continues.

When I stop and think about it, I'm surprised by my response. In this narrative, I share with you my story of re-learning Canadian history, and my understanding of how colonialism has impacted Indigenous people. I am sharing with you from a place of vulnerability and honesty. This is my experience of learning.

I am a white, middle-class woman, wife, mother, daughter, sister, and educator who lives a life of privilege. A privilege I didn't understand completely as I had never really had to reflect on privilege and my white identity. The education system that I was part of never explored the real history of Canada or the power of privilege, and I therefore took these privileges for granted: this was my life, my story. Beginning to understand the privilege of being white and how whiteness has inherently provided me with opportunities for success that others might not have access to has moved me to explore my identity and what it means to me: Can my identity evolve as I understand the role more deeply?

There are moments in our lives that are pivotal. Transformational for me was unpacking my understanding of Canadian history as I was learning and understanding the history of Indigenous Peoples and the impact of colonization – a history I was unaware of until 2013, when I heard an Indigenous scholar, Dr. Susan Dion, share Canada's historical timeline from an Indigenous perspective. It was a history I had never heard.

What was perplexing to me was that I had studied history throughout my formal education. Why was this story never shared? I had only heard Canadian history starting from the landing of Christopher Columbus – how the

European settlers came to our country and settled. I hadn't ever heard the pre-contact story. I didn't know about the first people, people who had survived on the land within their own nations, each nation having traditions, values, and cultures that were unique to their place on the land, with a common understanding of and respect for the land and what it offered to each of them, honouring the land as sacred and cherishing its offerings. People who governed themselves through structures that honoured consensus democracy lived on this land prior to the arrival of European settlers. These truths were never shared in my education.

I realized at that moment that there was a Canadian history that I had not been taught. Dr. Dion's historical timeline, with pre-contact and post-contact stories and examples, jolted me into a reality I hadn't understood. Initially I felt guilt. I felt guilt for what had happened, guilt for being a settler, and guilt for my ignorance. Then angered – how did I not know and why hadn't I known? Saddened that I was unaware. Determined to understand more and deepen my understanding of our true history. I knew now what I didn't before and couldn't leave this knowledge with me alone.

More than just shocked, I was also dumbfounded and embarrassed. I remember going up to Dr. Dion afterward to explain that I had never known any of this. Her response was the pivotal moment in my story. She asked me, "So what are you going to do now?" This question made me realize that I had a part to play in making Indigenous perspectives visible and in rectifying misconceptions. Even as I write this – and, to be honest, I have had challenges in sharing my story – I have lots of doubt about my place in writing. Do I understand enough, am I in a space to continue to keep my goals of supporting others in moving from "I didn't know" to understanding the need to know? I work from home and have less and less contact with others in education settings, and I am feeling farther and farther away from any small impact that I might have had. Is this an out for me, a way to stop doing the work? I know that I want to continue to take on this challenge and understand what, how, and why I must continue my story.

In fact, as I write this story to share it, I realize that it has no ending. Facing inherent racism in our culture is a challenge I accept both personally and professionally. My goal is to be stronger than I have been, to engage in conversations that I wouldn't otherwise have had, to seek to understand the perspective that others may have because, like me, they just didn't know.

I know now what I didn't know then. My perspective has shifted. I had to do work, work on me. I needed to understand that while I value the fact that everyone has a story and I believe I have been respectful of that in my connections with many, I needed to think about my identity, my whiteness. My personal life story didn't involve us having to dig deep into our sense of self and acknowledge what our "whiteness" gave us. I am a part of the dominant culture and yet I knew that I was ready to begin to understand my privilege, challenge my thinking, reflect on my actions – to act on my changed perspective. I didn't want to hear about a history I didn't know and just leave it there, a story once heard. I know myself and I knew I wanted to learn and move forward in a better way.

I knew that I would accept Dr. Dion's challenge, and the timing couldn't have been better. At that time, the Truth and Reconciliation Commission findings and final report had been embraced and accepted as part of Ontario's political agenda. Educators were newly valuing student voices and looking for ways to ensure equity for all learners. Personally, I was open to understanding my inherent biases and was interested in seeking to transform myself from observer to ally. Understanding that one cannot just *claim* to be an ally, I needed to be considered by others to be an ally. I hoped that I could be.

Understanding My Place of Privilege

I began to understand that in order to fully engage in the work, I needed to make my own personal commitment to understand my position of white privilege in a dominant culture. To be honest, I had never realized the space of whiteness – how my white privilege and the dominant culture we so easily live within continues to marginalize others. How so many narratives, images, and symbols of Indigenous people that I see and hear today continue to perpetuate the stereotypes of the "Indian." This is what I had grown up with. "They don't pay tax." "Our cottage is on Indian Land and they could take it back from us anytime." "Most Indians I know are homeless because they are drunks." "Don't give bands any money; they'll just mismanage the funds." And, of course, the images associated with sports teams that we all know. The movies we had watched and continue to watch – think *Pocahontas*, and cowboy and Indian films. The texts I was presented with in school, whether children's books or history books. I know now whose voices were never heard, whose true stories were never shared. I had never questioned those sources of my understanding. Unpacking the overwhelming narrative of the Indian and beginning to know the historical legacy of racist decisions with understanding of the layers of my white privilege wasn't easy for me, yet I knew it was essential. I had to do the work – to understand myself, my bias, my racism, and my perspective. It had to start with me. I concur with John Ralston Saul, who states in *The Comeback* that non-Indigenous people's collective guilt about our colonial past and neo-colonial present is interfering with Canadians' ability to act for the future. Our guilt can be used as an excuse. I did feel guilt and continue to feel it. Yet I cannot and will not let that be an excuse. Even as I struggle with the lack of knowledge, my learning can't stop. As Robin DiAngelo, author of *White Fragility*, states, the antidote to guilt is action.[4] My action.

I made a commitment to action and invested in my own learning, starting with reading books by Indigenous authors. I am an avid reader but had never read any books by Indigenous authors. I couldn't have named an Indigenous author. I have read many now and have some favourites that I share readily with others.

Not the first book I read, but one I couldn't put down, was *Seven Fallen Feathers* by Tanya Talaga. Every Canadian should read about the shocking and disturbing truth behind the story of seven youth found dead in Thunder Bay, Ontario, after leaving their northern reserves to continue their education – their only option if they wanted to finish high school. The truth of our Canadian history, and the tragic impact of deeply held racist beliefs built on political decisions, past and present, are documented here. The legacy of residential schools and reserves, the inadequacy of funding for education, and lack of access to education is what failed these young people – both before and after their fateful move to Thunder Bay. I couldn't help but think that while there are no longer policies that forcibly remove children from their homes, isn't this still the case? Indigenous youth have to leave their homes to attend a secondary school institution because on-reserve education ends at Grade 8. In addition, education for Indigenous students is funded federally – and underfunded in comparison to education funded provincially. How is this inequity still justified?

I had met with Nishnawbe Aski youth in Thunder Bay. My work in education had given me the opportunity to travel and meet with students across the province to understand how our education system needs to respond differently in order to provide better outcomes for Indigenous students. I met with the students from "fly-in communities" attending school in large urban, suburban, and rural communities. These bright and amiable youth showed me on a map of Ontario where their communities were in relation to their schools. I was often dumbfounded as I struggled to grasp the distances many Indigenous students must travel to attend secondary school. This was not my experience of attending school in Canada. Again, my perspective was shaken, my ignorance noted.

As I sat in Circle with secondary school students in different locations across the province, the experience came to be familiar. The Circle opened with a smudge and words of reflection from an Elder or community member. The youth shared how they felt coming into school most days. Often their only safe space was the room where we were meeting, a classroom like many others but with a graduation coach to support the students in the transition to high school. In quiet voices, they openly shared their challenges and successes. Daily they faced racist comments from other students, they didn't feel welcome, they didn't have the money that other students had and often were made to feel less than. Poverty was one of their challenges. Many students who had to travel long distances missed home. They talked of the loneliness of their days. This room for them was the place where there was a caring, supportive adult, helping them to navigate a school system embedded in colonial ways, where they were taught by almost exclusively white teachers. They were truly thankful for the graduation coach. I remember leaving these high school sessions feeling impressed by the students' resilience, their hopes and dreams; awed by their commitment to learning in spite of the many challenges. I couldn't help but think how different this school experience was from my children's experience of school. Would my children have had the strength to face the adversity these youth do? I am not sure. I came home from these trips shaken and deeply moved. How would I, with my limited sphere of influence, keep these youth, whose voices continue to be silenced, in my memory to guide my work in understanding how inequity in education is so present, real, and, for many, still unknown?

I continue to read books by Indigenous authors, a rich world of text I am still discovering. Richard Wagamese is most certainly one of my favourite authors. A prolific writer, his talent with words, creating images through text, is remarkable. Each of his books both teaches me and moves me. I read *Indian Horse* first and was brought to tears. I felt – viscerally – the trauma endured by the main character. I also saw the film with a group of educators at a special screening. The novel was a challenging read; to see it come to life in film was even more so. The event opened with Indigenous songs and drums and closed with words from Elders. I left thankful for the support that filled the room but again saddened that the place we call home has so much to atone for.

As I write this, I often open *Embers: One Ojibway's Meditations*. *Embers* is a collection of Wagamese's thoughts from his daily meditative practice: "They are the embers from every story I have heard. They are the embers from all the relationships that have sustained and defined me. They are the heart songs. They are the spirit songs."[5]

My personal life and professional life came together in a good way at the right time for me. In my work with schools and boards, I was able to be in a space working alongside educators, Indigenous educators, Elders, and community partners. Each time we met, whether in large groups or in small discussions, I felt embraced by so many people. Today I can still hear the words of Elders as they opened and closed our learning sessions. I can feel the vibration of the drums as they played to invite us and the spirits around us into the room. Each session was opened and closed in a good way, guiding us all into the space of openness and honesty. For me, each moment was genuine and pushed me forward to understand the legacy of colonial decisions and the impact on the first people.

Through these experiences, I developed relationships with Indigenous friends, and cherish them still. Each of them has guided me in different ways – treating me with respect and acceptance, opening their hearts and minds.

Today I called Felicia Waboose, an Ojibway Elder who is a member of the Eabametoong First Nation. She attended Pelican Falls Indian Residential School from age nine to fifteen. She now has five children, twelve grandchildren, and five great grandchildren, and lives in Thunder Bay. Since her retirement she has continued to work with educators and students, raising awareness of First Nations culture and issues. I knew I wanted to write about her and the impact of the wise words she shared. I could feel through the phone her smile and optimism. We laughed and remembered our times together. I shared that I was writing this narrative and wanted to talk about her. She said, "Of course – I have no secrets!"

When Felicia and I first began our work together, I was in awe of her patience. When she spoke, with a wonderful twinkle in her eye, her stories were hers and we all listened intently as each story took us to a place of learning and understanding. I understood from her the importance of storytelling, the depth of her spirituality, and the power of culture, customs, and tradition, the significance and value of so much I take for granted. She once said, "We were given two ears, two eyes, and one mouth for a reason." This struck a chord with me. Powerful images filled my head. Still today I think of her and internally often check myself to see if I am being that person – listening wholly to honour other voices, to understand and to question perspective.

Felicia and many others have taken the time to teach me and embrace me in such gracious ways, showing me their strength, resilience, commitment, perseverance, and strong sense of humour, and how to move forward while honouring the past. This has been life changing for me. Throughout the work of the Indigenous Collaborative Inquiries, we listened to educators who shared their fears: fear of making mistakes – fear of doing the wrong thing, fear of culturally appropriating traditions and sacred items. While these concerns are valid (and we *will* make mistakes), it should not be a reason for inaction. Today's schools can be places of change.

I remember the day I walked into a school and inside the front display case were dreamcatchers, tipis, and totem poles made by students in recognition of National Indigenous Peoples Day on June 21. I met with the teacher, wanting to know about the teaching and learning that had taken place. She shared with me how she had used text by

Indigenous authors and worked with her board Indigenous lead and a community partner to deepen both her own and her students' understanding. She had worked in a good way. Non-Indigenous teachers don't have to be experts in all areas of First Nations, Inuit, and Métis histories, cultures, ceremonies, and stories. It isn't expected. There are many First Nations, and each has their own unique traditions and ways of being. More important is for educators to be familiar with the Indigenous territory on which they currently live or on which the school is located. Equally important is to establish relationships with members of the community groups and begin to invite their participation in the inquiries and study within the classroom. Educators then become "co-learners" with their students in the presence of Indigenous lived experience.

In another school, a junior division planned a cross-curricular unit using the expectations in art, social studies, and language. The unit goal was to identify and explore multiple perspectives; interpret the messages in works of dance, drama, music, and visual art; and consider the perspectives found in the works, including understanding issues of fairness, equity, and social justice. To support these outcomes, educators used the art of Norval Morrisseau, an Indigenous artist from Bingwi Neyaashi Anishinaabek, formerly known as Sand Point First Nation, as their resources. This was the change. I know it may seem like an insignificant change, and yet it is a change. In the past, the team would never have considered using the works of Indigenous artists to introduce the big idea of equity. The planning involved working with their Indigenous lead at the district board level, researching, sharing perspectives, and reflecting on their personal bias and lack of knowledge. They moved forward in a good way, not as experts but as learners.

I Am Still Learning

I often reflect on my privilege and think about how fortunate I am. My favourite place to be is on the dock at my cottage on Kawagama Lake in Ontario's Algonquin Highlands. I know that not everyone is as lucky as I am. My life has been and continues to be filled with experiences that many others don't get to enjoy. I now understand and appreciate that I am privileged.

As I sit on my dock and enjoy the gorgeous sunsets and the solitude of the lake, I do understand that the land was well travelled by many before us. My cottage sits on land that was purchased through treaties made with the Anishinaabeg who came before us. I have learned that they were water people who travelled the many lakes and rivers in the area, setting up camps and harvesting maple syrup and birch bark, fishing and trading with others in the spring and summer. They would hunt and trap in the fall and winter. Working in harmony with the land and the climate that was offered by the Creator, they succeeded and thrived. The treaties made with settlers took this away from them.

Cottagers around the lake talk about the beauty of the lake and the cleanliness of the water, a result of much of the surrounding land being Crown land. Through treaties, Indigenous Peoples agreed to share their land. Land now referred to as Crown land by our government was taken at the expense of Indigenous people. I have a better understanding of how that story continues today. On a plaque in our small cottage town, the history of the Anishinaabeg is recognized. It closes with "the legacy of the original inhabitants lives on through the many landmarks, rivers, lakes, and islands that bear Anishinaabemowin (Ojibwe) place names." This plaque was unveiled in 2017. Is it a small step forward?

> **Rooted in the Land**
> **A Brief Indigenous History**
> Information provided by the Mississaugas of the Credit First Nation. http://mncfn.ca/

Plaque on a rock near Dorset, Ontario.

I knew who Christopher Columbus was.
I knew a history that was taught to me.
Today I know differently.
Am I an ally?
Not yet.
I close with this picture.

A brief history it is not. I continue to be challenged by the dominant narrative that is our world, the power of language. I know my perspective has changed and my learning continues. My story never ends.

Afterword

In 2013, I became part of the newly formed Ontario Ministry of Education First Nation, Métis, and Inuit Committee. This working team became the steering committee to support district school boards funded for collaborative inquiry projects. Our committee was made up of both Indigenous and non-Indigenous educators, Elders, scholars, and community members, all committed to Indigenous student well-being and achievement. We were united in believing that all educators, students, and leaders will benefit from student-focused educational inquiries undertaken in schools. Together we mapped out a process to operationalize this work. The result was a four-year project involving school boards from across Ontario in localized collaborative inquiries guided by these three goals:

- To increase Indigenous student well-being and achievement
- To increase the knowledge, understanding, and awareness of Indigenous histories, cultures, and perspectives for all staff and students
- To increase engagement with Indigenous community partners

As a result of this opportunity, I have had experiences that have challenged me, pushed my thinking, engaged me and altered the way I view relationships with Indigenous people, how I listen and to whom, and how I seek out all voices in my own study. This is what I have learned and what I will continue to learn.

A NEED TO KNOW
Sheyfali Saujani

When I think about the things that got me interested in learning more about the history of Canada's relationship with Indigenous people, I find that I have a story in three parts.

Part 1: My Family and Coming to Canada
I was born in Africa. Both my parents were born there: my mother in Durban, South Africa (she went home to have me, her first child), and my father in Uganda, where we lived. My early years there were tumultuous. On the

one hand, my younger brothers and I enjoyed a privileged middle-class childhood of discovery in a beautiful, temperate country whose mountainous elevations made it cooler than many other equatorial nations. On the other, we grew up in a large, tight-knit, and energetically disputatious joint family. Everyone minded everyone else's business because that's how we supported and took care of each other. At the same time, the bickering was endless, sometimes raucous. We lived for and loved a good quarrel. But we loved to laugh, too, and often did at the large, shared meals cooked by our many, many aunties. We still eat and laugh together, and we're all a lot mellower now, but early on I learned to never, ever back down from an argument.

In my case, family arguments often revolved around my stubborn rejection of traditional South Asian gender expectations. No way was anyone going to get me into a sari! (I've worn one exactly twice, both times under protest.)

In August 1972, Uganda's military dictator, Idi Amin, announced the expulsion of the country's sixty to seventy thousand Asians. It was a frightening, confusing experience, whose seriousness I only understood because our familiar squabbling was replaced by a new, mysterious tension, constant fear, and anxiety; the sudden presence of armed soldiers everywhere; whispered conversations among frightened adults; and horrifying rumours running wild among my school friends. We lost our homes, our communities, our property, and our security as citizens. We became stateless because, Amin said, we were not "African" enough, not integrated enough into Ugandan society.

When we left Uganda, in September 1972, it was on an Air Canada flight bound for Montreal via Paris: a twenty-hour ordeal made bearable for me because someone – I don't know who – had brought a book of "Indian" stories, written for children. "North American Indian," not "East Indian."

Back then, we still thought of Indigenous people as "Indian," although as a "real" Indian, with origins in, you know, India, I found the terms confusing. Then I found out that the really confused people were those European explorers who thought they'd found India when they arrived in North America. Those Europeans were also the ones who created the story about how North America's original people were "primitive." I'm not sure if it was the odd Western that we might have seen on our black and white TV set in Uganda, this storybook, or other cues picked up from public culture in Canada, but somewhere along the way I absorbed the notion that North America's Indigenous people were a kind of mythic people from a distant past. The kind of people who showed up in books of fairy tales, fables, or legends like the one we read on that long-ago flight.

I have this vivid memory of lying across my seat in the airplane, while a quiet-voiced adult read us a story about a "native" family during a time of strife. In the story, the parents, who were both ill and dying, made the two older siblings – a brother and sister – promise to take care of their younger brother. As the eldest child in a similar family, I identified deeply with the parental injunction to look out for my younger siblings. In the story, however, the older brother and sister, distracted by their own adventures and interests, soon neglect their baby brother. Abandoned by his selfish siblings, the boy is saved from starvation by wolves, who feed and care for him. And I have this picture in my mind of an illustration at the end of the book. In the line drawing, the elder brother's grief-stricken face is shown as he calls in vain to his younger brother. The neglected boy is shown casting a final reproachful glance over his shoulder as he follows his more caring wolf-family into the forest.

As a child, I thought this was a teaching story, very like Aesop's fables, or tales from the Hindu Ramayana that my father used to tell us at bedtime. It seemed to me a warning tale – about the shame of neglecting and allowing harm to come to our relations. Problematic as that storybook was, it was the last time I encountered what some European editor thought Indigenous moral ideals or ethics might look like. After that, there was the odd chapter or two in a junior high geography textbook about the "disappearing People of the Plains," or how General Brock was assisted by "his loyal Indian allies" in the War of 1812. I didn't learn anything about Indigenous history, politics, or culture, never mind Indigenous intellectual or ethical values, until well into my late post-graduate studies. I certainly never met any people I recognized as Indigenous throughout my elementary, high school, and undergraduate education. They were physically and intellectually absent from my new "Canadian" life.

Part 2: Meeting Lynda
I went to school and university in the 1970s and '80s. Growing up in Waterloo, a small city in southwestern Ontario, we had school trips to see Shakespeare plays at the Stratford Festival, to Fort Henry in Kingston, on the way to see Parliament Hill in Ottawa, and to nearby Mennonite farmers' markets. But, until I began working at CBC Radio, I'm not sure I even knew that the nearby Six Nations territory existed. We were living on Haudenosaunee land, but none of my elementary or high school teachers ever mentioned it. In Ottawa, none of my journalism school professors ever talked about Indigenous issues in the news. The treaties

that authorized the sharing of this land were not part of anything they thought we needed to learn.

In 1989, I landed a job at CBC Radio and eventually found my way to its radio syndication service, then called Infotape. That's where I met Lynda Powless. Lynda is a Kanien'kéha woman of immense character, pride, and intelligence. She's not one to suffer fools gladly and, luckily for me, seemed delighted to engage in verbal jousting with a loud, opinionated South Asian woman not given much to compromise. Lynda and I bonded almost immediately. She's the kind of woman who'd laugh heartily when I smirked about being "a real Indian," you know, the ones Columbus was really looking for. "Yeah," she'd sneer right back, "I wish he'd found you first and left us alone. We wouldn't have missed him." It was good to have a colleague with whom I could commiserate or share a laugh about the irritating assumptions white people made about us brown folks.

We soon became allies pushing for better coverage of "visible minority," or racialized, and Indigenous communities. I would roll my eyes every time the CBC did yet another story about arranged marriages in the South Asian community, and Lynda would mutter with annoyance about yet another radio documentary about Indigenous issues that started with drumming.

She was the person who began to educate me, in her steady, no-nonsense way, about Indigenous politics and issues, most especially those related to Six Nations, which I finally had a chance to visit with her. I met her kids, friends, and colleagues in the community. She knew everything about life on the reserve and took immense pride in all its institutions – the radio station, the local cafés, the newspapers, and the traditional government, not to mention its people, the writers, artists, business leaders, and political

Seeing Yourself in Relationship with Settler Colonialism

figures. She knew her history and was proud of it. From her I learned that in 1924, Canada had sent the RCMP to remove the Confederacy Council (which insisted that Six Nations was a sovereign territory) in an effort to force the community to accept an elected band council, something Six Nations has never fully done. Both governments operate there today. She was determined to keep her Kanien'kéha language skills, but told me quietly that many Elders, those who'd been educated in white-run schools, feared using their mother tongue. She demonstrated how they covered their mouths in fear when they spoke Mohawk. Among the many almost unbelievable things I learned from her was that Indigenous kids couldn't go for dental treatment without the permission of the Department of Indian Affairs (today Indigenous and Northern Affairs Canada). That was just one little example of the routine daily control of Indigenous lives, about which mainstream Canadians like me knew nothing. Everything she said was news to me, but it was often hard to convince our editors to let her tell these stories. And this resistance on the part of mainstream institutions to the truth about Indigenous lives is part of the reason for Canadians' ignorance.

  Over the years, as we covered Indigenous stories in the news, I had to learn more because it was part of my job. Knowing Lynda, I sometimes just consulted her rather than educating myself about all the things she didn't have time to teach me. I also made some foolish assumptions about what I saw as shared experience. For example, I imagined that because my people, too, had experienced loss of property and identity in Uganda, I understood what the loss of land and identity meant for Indigenous people here. I believed that because we both fought against the same racism at work, we came at the problem from the same position.

But we did not. And those differences forced me to think hard about what I thought I knew – and all the things I didn't.

My family and I, South Asian citizens of Uganda, were exiles, deprived of land and legal rights, yes. But when we became refugees and were then accepted into Canada, we became part of the settler community that inhabits this land by virtue of treaty agreements that have never been honoured by the settlers. Loath as we may be to accept it, we are not refugees here. Here, we are settlers, and our experience of life in Canada is very different from the daily realities faced by Indigenous people. Yes, as a brown-skinned woman I have faced racism. But no one ever told my parents they couldn't take me to the dentist when I was a kid. No one took me from my parents, forcibly, to ensure I'd never learn their values or know their love. No one told us we couldn't speak Gujarati at home or in the schoolyard if we wanted to. So I didn't always know where Lynda was coming from on certain things.

For example, the one issue on which Lynda and I disagreed was her oft-repeated insistence that Indigenous reporters should cover Indigenous news. For a middle-class, small-*l* liberal like me, schooled in the bedrock doctrines about freedom of the press, this notion not only seemed restrictive but struck at the heart of my own struggles in the workplace. Visible minority or racialized reporters were only beginning to enter the workforce in Canada. Like many from communities that face discrimination, I badly wanted to have the same freedom to cover any issue a white reporter was allowed to cover. As a person with a disability (I am visually impaired and not able to drive), I worked very hard keeping up with colleagues and competitors in the intense, deadline-driven news environment. I dreaded being pigeon-holed into some news beat deemed appropriate for a South Asian woman or a person with a disability. I wanted the same opportunities that all my white, able-bodied colleagues enjoyed, and I resented the notion that non-Indigenous people ought not to cover Indigenous issues.

What I didn't know, and couldn't fully concede, was Lynda's view that mainstream news coverage overlooked – sometimes astoundingly – so many important issues and nuances of Indigenous society, politics, and experience. Non-Indigenous reporters, for example, assumed there was nothing wrong with elected governments – after all, that's what we had. But Lynda understood that, for Indigenous communities, the RCMP removal of the Confederacy Council was like a foreign overthrow of the government her people had chosen for themselves, on their own terms, in their own traditional ways. After watching non-Indigenous reporters telling stories about First Nations people from European or white mainstream perspectives only, she wanted Indigenous reporters to be allowed to show how *they* saw the news. Because they saw it differently, and we, among the settler community, were not hearing that difference.

Back then, I didn't hear it either. Even though I knew how hard she fought to tell her stories, I thought it was just a matter of persuading editors to change their views, not about ensuring employment opportunities for Indigenous writers and reporters too long denied the right to tell their own truths. I didn't recognize that only more Indigenous voices inside the media – eventually doing all the same kinds of reporting that others could – would begin to correct the biases.

And there was one other hang-up for me. The "community" I come from can be represented in many ways. My parents are Gujarati-speaking members of the South Asian diaspora. There are literally millions of us. The Gujarati language and culture are in no danger of being extinguished by anyone, anytime. It is, moreover, a culture with which I have often been at odds because of those gender norms that got me into so much trouble with my aunties. The ethnic pride, even cultural nationalism, that animates so many racialized immigrant communities makes me uncomfortable. I have first-hand experience, from Uganda – where my South Asian family was not considered "African" enough – of exactly how dangerously violent certain kinds of nationalism can become. This experience sometimes makes me uncomfortable with Indigenous expressions of cultural pride here. I really had not grasped how utterly destructive the legacy of the residential school system was, nor understood how necessary it is to carefully restore cultural practice and Indigenous knowledge in communities that are being brutalized by ongoing colonialism.

In 1994, Lynda launched her own newspaper, *Turtle Island News*. To my surprise, she invited me to contribute as a freelancer based in Toronto. Being an over-stressed, belligerent person steeped in the No-Compromise school of argument, I decided to "win" the argument.

"I can't do that," I said, and waited.

"Why not?" she demanded.

"Because I'm not Indigenous," I said, throwing her call for Indigenous reporters back in her face. I'm embarrassed by the thoughtless one-upmanship of this line now and cringe at how hurtful it must have been.

As a result, I passed up the opportunity to work with one of the leading, multiple-award-winning Indigenous newspapers in North America, run by one of the country's top one hundred businesswomen. And, even worse, I had nearly destroyed a friendship. That moment of intemperate

Seeing Yourself in Relationship with Settler Colonialism

belligerence and the coolness I felt from Lynda for some time after forced me to think hard about how little I really knew about the actual history of Canada's treatment of and relationship with Indigenous people. Because the fact is, even though Lynda wanted more opportunity for Indigenous reporters, she was willing to offer me, a non-Indigenous reporter, the chance to work with her and learn more about First Nations communities. While I was positioned on the thin edge of some abstract "principle," she was taking a far more pragmatic and open approach to what she needed to get her paper off the ground. In fact, over the years, Lynda has hired and trained many non-Indigenous journalists at her paper. It is my great good fortune that she has chosen to forgive me those thoughtless remarks and remains a friend.

Part 3: Taking Responsibility for My Own Learning
After Lynda left the CBC, it dawned on me that I had been wrong, that I had no clue about the factors influencing her attitude and approach. So I began to learn, through university courses, books, and other media. But there was still that meddlesome old family reflex, the one where everyone thought it was right and necessary to poke their noses into each other's business. It's a reflex amplified by colonial attitudes toward Indigenous people, based on prejudices about their ability to govern themselves. In 2002, I had a chance to meet the McMaster University anthropologist Harvey Feit. Harvey, according to his website, has been working with the Eeyou (James Bay Cree) People on "ethnographic and engaged projects" to learn from them about "their ways of living amidst colonialism, dispossession, treaty abrogation, and pervasive ways of shaping conduct." I met Harvey at a time when there were fierce debates

among the Kanehsatà:ke Mohawks about whether Indigenous women who had married non-Indigenous men should be allowed to live on the reserve. News reports (not written by Indigenous reporters) suggested that some women had been threatened with violence. I was troubled by the sense that Canada would hesitate to enforce human rights protections because the "violations" (as they seemed to me) were taking place on a reserve.

"Don't we have an obligation to intervene?" I asked.

Harvey, a gentle bear of a man, looked at me kindly and said no. No. We have to stand back and respect their right to govern themselves, he said, because (and I've never forgotten his words), "they couldn't possibly make it worse than we already have."

They couldn't possibly make it worse than we already have.

That was the moment I realized some important things. First, how shamefully little I actually knew about the capacity of First Nations people to govern themselves; my question was based on lingering colonial stereotypes about "primitive" people not suited to self-government. I knew nothing about the sophistication of Indigenous knowledge or the strength and perseverance of Indigenous leadership. Second, I really had no idea about the exact size and depth of the mess that my country had created – how destructive were the things that Canada had done and continues to do. And it was well past time to learn.

I will tell you that it has been hard to face the truth about the country that gave me and my family refuge. We love Canada and are so grateful for the haven it provided. It is hard to be critical of the nation I now call home, yet, as it is my home, as I am a Canadian, I am also a party to the treaties. As citizens of this country, we have both the duty and the responsibility to participate in the restoration of right relations with the Indigenous people on whose lands we made our home. Gratitude for the welcome we received here should not prevent us from engaging with the fact that it was a colonial state that welcomed us onto lands taken from Indigenous Peoples. And beyond all that is the simple fact of the relationship. I had forgotten, and Lynda reminded me, that families – and friends – can disagree or even quarrel, but we can still sit down and share a meal together. It is the caring for and nurturing of the relationship that matters, and that means listening with respect and humility. We cannot forget our relations, our treaty-relations. And it is for us non-Indigenous people to make sure that when we sit down at the table, we are willing to listen – because we have so much to learn.

THE WORK TO BE DONE
Joe Wild

I sit writing at my kitchen table on lands that are part of the unceded territory of the Algonquin People. I acknowledge and recognize this fact. I extend my respect and thanks to the Algonquin People because my family and I have made our home here on their lands. This land acknowledgment is more than symbolic. It is a foundation on which I, as a settler, acknowledge that I am starting to understand the perspective of Indigenous Peoples in Canada and recognize the need to decolonize our relationship with Indigenous Peoples.

I grew up in the Maritimes and come from a family with roots in Nova Scotia. As in many regions in Canada, the kitchen table symbolizes family; it is at the heart of the home. We gather around the table with family and friends to share meals, play games, tell stories, laugh, and sometimes cry. It is the place where we share in the ups and downs of life and take care of each other. This table is a reminder to me, as a senior public servant with the Government of Canada, to always put people first. I am writing my story at the kitchen table, inviting readers to sit and listen from across the table. We have not done a very good job of hearing the story of colonialism; for many, it is not an easy story to understand. If you sit with me, I will share what I have done, what I have learned, and maybe it will be a good starting place for you.

This is a story about what I have learned from my work over the past six years. Before getting into what the work entails, I want to acknowledge my position as a white, non-Indigenous, English-speaking man. For many, that may make anything I have to say of little value or import. I am humbled by the invitation to tell my story. I am doing so in hopes that it may be of use to others who also need to overcome the fear, guilt, and paralysis that so many seem to experience when it comes time to do the heavy work of dismantling privilege. It is from this perspective, of wanting to assist others in seeing their role in dismantling colonialism, institutional racism, and systems of white privilege, that I am writing. The number one lesson I have learned in my job is the importance of listening to what Indigenous Peoples say about their rights and taking action in support of accomplishing their vision. The voices of Indigenous Peoples on their past and current lived experiences and their visions for the future are the foundations on which reforms must be built. This work must be done in full partnership with Indigenous Peoples and means that those of us who are settlers must do our share of the heavy lifting, including the difficult transition from governing over to respecting Indigenous Peoples' right to govern themselves. It means thinking about what we need to learn so that we can hear Indigenous people's perspectives.

As I tell my story, parts of it will reflect my personal perspective, while other parts will be informed by my professional life. I am a public servant with the Government of Canada, a bureaucrat, and my work is about implementing, creating, and sometimes changing policies and procedures. On May 20, 2014, I began my first day of work as the senior assistant deputy minister (senior ADM) for Treaties and Aboriginal Government (TAG) with what was then the department of Aboriginal Affairs and Northern Development Canada. This department was dissolved in 2018 and replaced with two new departments: Indigenous Services Canada, with a focus on delivering programs and services and Indian Act administration, and Crown-Indigenous Relations and Northern Affairs (CIRNA), responsible for negotiating treaties, self-government agreements, and other instruments of reconciliation with Indigenous Peoples in Canada.[6]

As the senior ADM, my job is to represent the interests of all Canadians in partnering with Indigenous Peoples to recognize and implement their inherent rights and treaty rights and to accomplish their visions of self-determination. My work is about making real the promises of the United Nations Declaration on the Rights of Indigenous Peoples and section 35 of the Constitution Act, 1982. In many ways, my work is about confronting the reality of Canada's past and ongoing relationships with Indigenous Peoples, what that says about who we are as Canadians and, importantly, what future we want as a nation. For me, the government's commitment to renewed nation-to-nation, government-to-government, and Inuit-Crown relationships highlights the need to change how I, as a public servant, work with Indigenous Peoples. To get to this vision of a relationship, I needed to change how the government approaches the negotiation of treaties and self-government, moving away from imposed solutions to working in true partnership to co-develop solutions.

My knowledge of Indigenous people's experiences is recent and primarily a result of my current position. I have many fond memories of growing up in my home province of New Brunswick. I remember Grade 7 social studies and learning the difference between a tipi and a wigwam and the role of various Indigenous nations in alliances with the French or English during Canada's early colonial period. I was taught that Louis Riel was a rebellious traitor, and that Inuit were in the North, hunted seals, built igloos, and helped European "explorers" survive harsh winters. In law school I took the single course on "native law" that was offered. I was a very good student, diligent, curious, and dedicated to learning, but my learning about Indigenous people was extremely limited.

In my job I have now learned that I knew nothing about residential schools. I had never heard of the Indian Act, the pass system, or the efforts of prior governments across Canada to assimilate Indigenous Peoples through policies oriented toward the destruction of their culture, language, and relationship with the land. I was not taught anything about the Peace and Friendship Treaties with the Mi'kmaq and the Maliseet, or about the Robinson Treaties, the Numbered Treaties, the Douglas Treaties – I was not taught that we are all "treaty people." I did not know the story of the Métis Nation, or the long history of Inuit and the Innu. I had learned little about section 35 of the

Constitution Act, 1982. I didn't know that Indigenous Peoples have inherent rights, and that some have treaty rights. I was mystified by the resistance to the Charlottetown Accord. I am fairly certain that for Canadians who finished high school in the late 1980s or early 1990s, this is fairly typical.

I think teachers did not teach these lessons because Canadians do not want to learn the history or current circumstances confronting Indigenous people and the role of our government in the dispossession of Indigenous Peoples from their land. Also, teachers are the products of the same education system that I am. While change has been happening, there is much more to do. In some ways, it is easy to do a land acknowledgment and say, "I appreciate you because my family and I live on your land"; it is much harder to learn the history of how it came to be this way. Harder still is making the decision to actually take action to dismantle the systems of colonialism and racism that confront us to this day.

My own journey to becoming aware that I did not know much of the history of Indigenous Peoples and their treatment by the Government of Canada begins on June 11, 2008. I remember driving to work in the morning, my car radio tuned to CBC. The reporter was talking about the apology the then prime minister, the Right Honourable Stephen Harper, was going to be delivering in the House of Commons later in the day. The reporter explained why the apology was going to be made and its significance. It was not without controversy; as I recall, the reporter noted that at least one member of Parliament felt there was no need for an apology. I remember being struck by the fact that the prime minister was making an apology for something I knew nothing about.

I feel shame today knowing that the apology did not spark an immediate quest for information. I watched further coverage and listened to and read the Statement of Apology to former students of Indian residential schools. At the time I thought, "Okay, the government has apologized and now we move on," and I went back to my life of work, family, and friends and thought little more about the intergenerational trauma inflicted on so many Indigenous people by the government and churches. In this I do not think I am alone among Canadians. I think it is simply too easy to sidestep the difficult work of confronting awful truths about public institutions and society when those truths have not directly impacted you. My reality is that I only started paying attention once I started in my current job. On reflection, I think this is an example of how institutional racism thrives: the indifference of the majority who enjoy privilege do not see the issue, and even on seeing it respond with complacency. I do think education is the key to helping people see their privilege, to overcoming this complacency and developing a sense of wanting to create change. I am not sure education alone is enough, but I can say with some certainty that without it we will not make any real progress. The impact of decades of wilful ignorance and bad public policy have resulted in a society in which settlers have a perspective on Canada and Indigenous Peoples that is deeply entrenched in colonialism and racism.

One thing I hope my story makes clear is that it is never too late to educate yourself. Without any real awareness of the history or the complexity of the issues, I ended up in a job that has about as direct an impact on confronting these systems of colonialism and racism as any job can in the Government of Canada. While others will judge whether I have been successful in contributing to the dismantling of systems of colonialism and institutional racism that Indigenous people continue to face in Canada, the point is that I work every day to broaden my understanding of these issues and to find ways to contribute to the dismantling of these systems of privilege. I also recognize that the opportunities this job has provided and continues to provide have had a profound impact on shaping my understanding.

My mindset going into the job was that I needed to learn and understand so that I could support the development of a vision and strategy to transform how the Government of Canada approached the relationship with Indigenous Peoples. The early days and months are a bit of a blur for me now. I know that when I started, I asked many "why" questions. Everything was new to me and so complex, given the centuries of history that structure the relationship with Indigenous Peoples. Unlike most Canadians, I had the vast corporate memory of the department at my disposal and countless experts who would brief me on anything I wanted to learn and would answer all of my questions. It became clear early on that the people working in the department are dedicated. Most want change. They want to do something to address the failures in the relationship and the socio-economic consequences for Indigenous Peoples of our policy failures. It was also clear that from the government's perspective there were no easy answers or identifiable pathways to reform.

I am not proud of my mindset during the first few months in the position. I was misinformed about Indigenous Peoples, whether through school or my own life experience. What I knew did not reflect the underpinnings of Indigenous perspectives as deriving from their relationship with the land and the significance of that relationship to identity, language, culture, and ways of being. I had mistakenly understood the relationship to be about economic exploitation. I did not understand the complexity of the relationship to the land that defines Indigenous identity.

In those early days I had many experiences of "white guilt," and at times the feeling of shame was overwhelming. I made use of a defensive mental brush, telling myself that these horrible acts were not done by my ancestors, or that I could avoid these truths as I am only a second-generation Canadian. It does not matter whether our relatives are directly connected with the legacy of residential schools, the pass system, or any number of the racist policies imposed on Indigenous Peoples; it *does* matter that we settlers directly benefit from those policies. It matters that I enjoy privileges built on foundations of colonialism and racism. Grappling with this truth will be my journey for the rest of my life. I do not have any specific insight as to how to get over shame. I know that shame can be a corrosive and dangerous feeling that all too quickly turns to anger and resentment. That statement feels somewhat hollow as I look at the world around me and recent events; this is not just about the legacy of the past.

The recent discoveries of the unmarked graves of Indigenous children across the country is a sharp reminder to Canadians of the horror that was the Indian residential school system. And while the legacy of that system and intergenerational trauma are matters that still need to be addressed, we should not be complacent in believing that colonialism is the stuff of history. There is an urgent and immediate need to address matters raised through the National Inquiry into Murdered and Missing Indigenous Women and Girls. We need to do the work to address why Indigenous people are overrepresented in prisons. There is a need for urgent and pressing action to ensure that the

Indigenous children of this generation are not the victims of the same traumas as were committed against past generations. Too many Indigenous children are living in poverty and being removed from their families and communities and placed in care facilities with no connection to language or culture. There is a continued need for urgent action to address the colonialism and systemic racism that underlie the relationship with Indigenous Peoples in Canada.

I can say that after six months in the position, my perspective did change, and my understanding broadened and deepened. Much of that change is attributable to spending time with Indigenous leaders. Shortly after I arrived at CIRNA, I started travelling to Indigenous communities to meet with those with whom we had negotiation tables. There were many conversations with many different leaders in those early months, and in the summer of 2015 I travelled across the country and met with provincial government officials and Indigenous leaders to hear their perspectives on what reforms were needed to the Government of Canada's approach to negotiating land claims and self-government. The time I spent doing this work of listening and seeking to better understand was invaluable.

I remember being in Nova Scotia and meeting with Mi'kmaq leaders who explained to me why the approach to negotiations at that time was viewed as extinguishing or terminating their rights. I listened as they explained that for a decade they had been discussing moose harvesting with us and our approach to the negotiations would require them to sign an agreement that set out forever the scope of their right to hunt moose, including how the hunt would be regulated. Aspects of those regulations meant certain traditional harvesting practices could never be used again. For them it was an example of extinguishing part of their right.

I asked whether there could be another way to approach this – for example, rather than setting out a final and forever agreement on the scope of the right, establishing a process by which we would develop together a harvesting plan that could be adjusted over time. They told me they had tabled this exact approach at the start and were told by Canada that the approach could not be discussed. I recall feeling shocked, and noted that the government had changed its position and was open to this discussion.

I have had many opportunities to visit Indigenous communities throughout the country. The hospitality shown to me has sometimes been truly overwhelming. Far too often, I was the most senior government official to have ever visited. On one occasion, I was blanketed by the two hereditary Chiefs who were participating in a meeting I attended in their community. The blanketing symbolized that they were undertaking to take care of me. It was an emotional moment for me. I kept thinking that all I had done was to show up for a meeting; I realized that having someone show up to hear and respond to your concerns can be worth celebrating. For me, the idea that just showing up and listening would attract this kind of response was a call to action for me to do more than just listen; I needed to be an active partner in using what influence, knowledge, privilege, and authority I had to change these systems of colonialism and racism. On reflection, maybe that is exactly what the hereditary Chiefs were teaching me: they were taking care of me, which included making sure I understood my responsibilities.

I have tried to understand what it must be like to have had generations of your family subjected to governments, churches, schools, police, and hospitals all treating you as a stereotype – and worse, having the very things that define you – your language, culture, traditions, and way of life– result in your being treated as inferior. How and why should Indigenous people trust public institutions to actually cease doing harm? I do not actually know what experience required me to ask myself, To what extent are the greatest privileges I enjoy the product of institutional racism? Public institutions should work to support all people, regardless of race, class, gender, sexual orientation, dis/ability. Public institutions should support and celebrate our humanity, not diminish it. As I begin to understand the scope and extent of this privilege that I enjoy, it also builds within me a sense of urgency and imperative to, within whatever sphere of influence and power I may occupy, change the very institution that I have worked in for my entire professional life.

In understanding the extent of this privilege, a second key understanding became clear to me: public institutions need to work in full partnership with Indigenous Peoples in order to redefine our relationship. We have all been conditioned by the Indian Act to think in certain ways about the relationship between Indigenous Peoples and settlers.

I think often about a trip I made to British Columbia in June 2016. I was in Vancouver for meetings to check in on various negotiation tables and to give a speech at a forum on nation rebuilding organized by the British Columbia Treaty Commission. While waiting somewhat nervously for my time to speak, I listened to presentations given by various Indigenous leaders. A young councillor from the Huu-ay-aht First Nations spoke about his community's experience in getting out from under the Indian Act and implementing their own system of government. This man talked about how his daughter was the first member of his family since his great- or great-great-grandmother who will never know life under the Indian Act. He talked about all the work they had to undertake within their community to unlearn the Indian Act. He spoke with pride about the potential future for his daughter, knowing she would have the opportunity to grow up grounded in their language and culture. The work to overcome colonialism was not finished, but this young leader talked about how long and hard they had to work as a community to unlearn oppression. As he succinctly put it, they had to unlearn the Indian Act. This truth then struck me: *all* Canadians have to "unlearn the Indian Act." I say this because unlearning the Indian Act is, in some ways, a proxy for undoing institutional racism. This is a shared journey for all Canadians, and in particular federal, provincial, and territorial governments. I look forward to the day when my children's children or their children will grow up in a country where there is no one left to unlearn the Indian Act.

I have come to view his point and my subsequent understanding as leading to this conclusion: whether you know anything about the Indian Act or the history of how public institutions regarded Indigenous people or not, your perceptions of Indigenous people have been influenced by them. Those of us who are settlers have an obligation to educate ourselves about this history and these facts because our failure to do so means we are contributing to the perpetuation of the colonial relationship ascribed by the Indian Act and the institutional racism that has pervaded our country since that piece of legislation was enacted, or even before.

My journey over the past six years has been about confronting the truth about Canada. Seeing it. *Understanding it. Wanting to change it.* If someone like me can overcome their own ignorance, feelings of shame, and work to make real change to address institutional racism, then you can too. I invite you to take this journey with whatever means may be at your disposal. I have been fortunate. I am indebted to the colleague who nudged me to consider this job, helping put me on a path that has changed who I am as a public servant and as a person. I have a lifetime left on my journey.

One suggestion I have for those who undertake this work is to understand that no matter how well-intentioned anyone may be, if settlers seek to impose solutions, the effort to undo centuries of colonialism will fail. Partnership is about understanding that we need to design solutions together through a process of collaboration that is built on respect and trust. Collaboration is worth little if power imbalances perpetuated by centuries of institutional racism are not addressed. The first step is acknowledging that these imbalances exist, and having identified them, committing to not continuing them. Indigenous traditions of governance and decision making, Indigenous laws and legal systems, Indigenous languages and cultures are of equal import to the fabric of our nation as the Westminster system, common and civil law, English and French, and multiculturalism. Every public policy and every action taken in accordance with public policies needs to reflect this. To me, this is the truth behind what section 35 of the Constitution Act, 1982 is all about. The differences between all of these things is the strength of our nation. Past – and some would say ongoing – attempts to eradicate these differences were and are wrong and only serve to weaken us as a society.

People across the country gather at their kitchen tables to celebrate, to mourn, to solve problems, to argue, and ultimately to hear and learn from each other's experiences. I started my story with an invitation to sit at my kitchen table and listen. It was somehow easier to tell you my story if I imagined you here. All of us who are settlers to this country need to start having conversations around our kitchen tables. We need to share our experiences of learning. We need to engage each other in difficult conversations. We need to invite and learn from and with Indigenous people. We all have a role to play in dismantling colonialism and racism to achieve justice. If we want to embrace our identity as proud Canadians, the land acknowledgment has to mean something; it has to be a first step in our learning. After all, we are all treaty people.

Whiteness, Settler Colonialism, and Relationship

Recognizing that they are implicated in colonialism, each of the settler storytellers describes the ways in which their learning put into question their knowledge and understanding of themselves, their understanding of Indigenous people, and their understanding of themselves in relationship with Indigenous people. Rather than turning away, they turn toward. They ask questions, listen, seek out opportunities to learn more, and put their learning into action.

Libby writes (page 37), "Facing inherent racism in our culture is a challenge I accept both personally and professionally. My goal is to be stronger than I have been, to engage in conversations that I wouldn't otherwise have had, to seek to understand the perspective that others may have because, like me, they just didn't know." As an educator, Libby is in a position to share her learning with others. She asks principals and teachers to think seriously about what they are teaching and how they are teaching about Indigenous people. She starts gently but does not shy away from insisting that educators be informed and responsible in their teaching about Indigenous people. She continues to see herself as a learner with responsibilities to investigate education's role in colonialism and how educators can change their practice.

Learning from her friend and colleague Lynda Powless, Sheyfali describes her own process of coming to understand (page 54): "I wanted the same opportunities that all my white, able-bodied colleagues enjoyed, and I resented the notion that non-Indigenous people ought not to cover Indigenous issues. What I didn't know, and couldn't fully concede, was Lynda's view that mainstream news coverage overlooked – sometimes astoundingly – so many important issues and nuances of Indigenous society, politics, and experience." Looking back on her experiences, Sheyfali now recognizes that she was collapsing difference. Based on a shared experience of being a brown-skinned woman whose family was directly impacted by colonialism, she acted on the understanding that she knew what it was like for Indigenous people. Importantly, she did not stay in this position but instead challenged herself to reconsider Lynda's argument. She did additional courses to expand her knowledge and understanding.

In his position as senior assistant deputy minister of Crown-Indigenous relations, Joe Wild has learned a great deal and describes a complex understanding of what has informed past relationships between the state and Indigenous leaders. Taking the opportunities offered, Joe invested time and energy in learning from and with Indigenous people in community. He emphasizes the need to listen, and to be willing – real change requires a willingness to do things differently. He identifies the role of power and racism in the relationship:

> The number one lesson I have learned in my job is the importance of listening to what Indigenous Peoples say about their rights and taking action in support of accomplishing their vision. The voices of Indigenous Peoples on their past and current lived experiences and their visions for the future are the foundations on which reforms must be built ...

> ...Collaboration is worth little if power imbalances perpetuated by centuries of institutional racism are not addressed. The first step is acknowledging that these imbalances exist, and having identified them, committing to not continuing them. (59, 70)

Expressing appreciation for Indigenous Peoples' right to govern themselves in their own way, Joe recognizes that this requires change on the part of the Canadian government. He also knows that these changes are ultimately in the best interests of all Canadians.

When invited to share their stories, each of the storytellers wanted to contribute to the dialogue in service of accomplishing change. Sharing their stories opens them to critique. Some readers will be critical, will see insufficiency in the stories, or in the storytellers' actions. Informed by Indigenous storytelling practice, my role is to hear their stories, to reflect on them, and to pass on the learning. I have purposefully included their stories, recognizing the significance of dialogue in the learning process, and Libby, Sheyfali, and Joe are all in agreement – ask questions, challenge, and speak back to their stories. Accomplishing justice in the relationship requires change in systems of education, journalism, government. It is an ongoing process that requires participation, and while many are frustrated with the slow pace, we are hopeful that change is taking place.

3

THE HISTORICAL TIMELINE
Refusing Absence, Knowing Presence, and Being Indigenous

From September through June, on the third Tuesday of every month, people gather at the Toronto District School Board Urban Indigenous Education Centre. Elder Joanne Dallaire opens the circle with a song, a smudge bowl is brought around, and the Urban Indigenous Community Advisory Committee begins its work. Our community includes Elders, Knowledge Keepers, parents, students, teachers, school board trustees, academics, and representatives from Toronto-area urban Indigenous community organizations. This committee advises the school board on issues of concern to urban Indigenous families and advances Indigenous education across the system. This gathering is not unique: Indigenous people have established advisory committees in education, health care, and policing systems, and even some municipal governments, across the country. We are working to address our priorities and concerns, identify and tackle anti-Indigenous racism, and create responsive, respectful systems.

When I was attending public school, my parents could not have imagined the existence of an Indigenous community advisory committee. For me, school was, as it continues to be for many Indigenous students, a place of alienation. As a child, I was haunted by a recurring nightmare. It always started the same way: I was in the field behind the school running, trying to get away from people who were chasing me. I was running to escape. I would look back to see if it was safe and could see the painted faces of tomahawk-wielding people who were after me. I would look again, and as they got closer, I could see the faces of my aunties, uncles, and cousins. They were the "wild Indians" trying to catch me. This nightmare rooted in stereotypical representation of Indigenous people is a significant marker of a gap in knowledge. Like many Canadians, I grew up knowing that a long time ago all the land in the Americas was Indigenous land. At school I was taught that explorers, missionaries, fur traders, and settlers came and took the land. I knew about reserves and the Indian Act. I did not know how it happened; how did Indigenous people go from having all the land to having so little?

In this chapter, I tell the history of Canada in broad strokes, weaving in my story of learning about the relationship between settler Canadians and Indigenous people, and documenting my process along with the historical details. This history challenges the dominant narrative of Canada and consequently constitutes difficult learning. That is learning that will "provoke a crisis within the self – it will be felt as interference or as a critique of the self's coherence or view of itself in the world."[1] For Canadians, learning about Indigenous people, history, and culture from the position of respectful admirer or patronizing helper is easy and familiar. Learning that requires recognition of implication in the relationship and a responsible response is not easily accomplished.[2] Following an Indigenous storytelling ethic, I am responsible for sharing a story and sharing in such a way that listeners/readers can find their own path to understanding. Before the story, I reflect on what it means to take a story usually told orally and commit it to print.

Telling/Writing Story: Making Meaning in the Space between Oral and Written Literacy

> For centuries our stories were passed in oral tradition ... with written language came the task of learning how to hammer the words onto the page with these little nails called "alphabet."
>
> – Diane Glancy[3]

Relying on the technology of my voice and my faith in the oral tradition, my preference is to tell the story in person. I have written it down only after serious consideration. I was getting far more requests to tell the story than I was able to meet. In choosing to write it down, I am adding my account to the broader dialogue that is taking place about Indigenous people's experiences and perspectives. Indigenous people are increasingly taking up the practice of recording our stories on paper, in film, in podcasts. For some, motivation is fuelled by exasperation with reading non-Indigenous experts whose writing was and continues to be valued over our Indigenous voices. In exchange for letting my story loose in the world is the ability to reach wider audiences, but it comes at a price.

The decision to share in print and video format meant confronting my fear over what would be lost in the relationship between myself as storyteller and listeners. I questioned the possibilities and considered the different relationship that exists between the worlds of readers and writers and the worlds of listeners and speakers.[4] I had resisted for a long time, choosing instead to protect the relationship that I establish with the story listeners as a critical component to the meaning-making process. My decision to share the story in print and video format was informed by the shift I experienced in audiences. The increased demand for the story was an indicator of an increasing number of people who recognize their responsibility for learning from Indigenous people. The growing demand became an indicator and a source of trust.

Embedding the story in a larger text that would create a broader meaning-making context added to my sense of trust: "Each telling of the story, whether in speech or writing, generates another story, a story of relations between people and their worlds."[5] A story of relations between people and their worlds – the timeline story is about my relationship to the world. I asked myself if the readers would know enough to understand the story in the spirit in which it is being told. I realize that whether a story is told in person or written down, it is not possible to ensure identical understandings. I was giving up the relationship between storytellers and listeners for the relationship between authors and readers. I was opening up new possibilities.

My trust in the process was further enhanced by the broader social and political context within which the story would be read. Increasingly, people were coming to my storytelling sessions with a demonstrated openness to hearing, and awareness of their need for, this story. My resistance was in part due to the experience of Indigenous people having our words misconstrued – or at least reconstrued with other people's interests in mind – in the treaties, in court decisions, or through the damaging effects of having our songs and histories reduced to quaint fairy tales or parables.[6] The judging of our literature, experiences, and perspectives as "less than" was reason enough to resist writing the story down.

My willingness to accept the risk and have the story published meant enduring the editing process, which was, at times, disconcerting as editors requested changes. It is troubling when someone wants to change your narrative: "Talking on the page involves a delicate balance between fixing and un-fixing words and meanings. It involves a cooperative venture between writer and reader, nearly the same magnitude as the one that existed between speaker and hearer."[7] Through the process, I came to see the editor as a stand-in for you, the reader. Editors and reviewers take up the reader's responsibilities – telling me what you would need to make sense of the story. The result is a negotiated text written with you in mind.

The story is here for you to read and reread; it is also available for you to hear. Sometimes it is good to listen to a story told aloud to see and be seen by the teller, to hear the cadence, tenor, and tone of the teller's voice. Although I won't be able to see you – you can listen to an oral telling of this story online.[8] The glossary in this book contains links to websites, articles, podcasts, and films helpful in responding to questions the story generates and to support further learning.

Refusing Absence, Knowing Presence, Being Indigenous

Nii ellongoomahtiik. K'winga-newulohmow. Nii Ndushiinzi Sheshkoohaaluwees Dion.
 Noonjiiyayii naahii / waak Toronto. Nii Ndulaapeewi / potwatomay. Niiha nish minito. Anushiik

Anushiik to the Elders and Knowledge Keepers for taking care of our teachings, for sharing their wisdom and for doing the work to protect, learn, and teach, often during difficult times. I introduced myself in Lenape. We greet each other with an acknowledgment of relationship with the land, water, and air, and all of our brothers and sisters, the four-legged and two-legged, winged and finned creatures that share our home on Mother Earth. These words acknowledge our place in relationship, remind us of our responsibilities, and reflect our worldviews.
 I am grateful to be able to speak even a little bit of my language; it is not something I ever expected to learn. I remember my mother telling me that when she was little, she did not hear the language often. On occasion, very late at night, she would wake up to the sounds of drumming, and looking out the window she would see her father and his friends gathered far out behind the house, sitting around the fire; she could hear the sound of drumming and singing in the language. That was the only time she heard Lenape, songs sung in the night when children and the Indian agent were asleep.
 My mother's parents were residential school survivors. She had three older brothers who also went to residential school. My mother was the first in her family who did not go; by the time she was old enough to attend school, there was a school on the reserve. In many ways it is impossible to document the impact of residential schools on our family. I do know that our language is one of the things that we lost. In truth, we did not lose it – it was taken from us. Today people are working hard to recover our language and cultural practices, and the knowledge embedded in language and practices.

My mother, Audrey Angela Dion (née Tobias), was born at Moraviantown, in Ontario. Born in 1930, she was in many ways a survivor of the state policy of forced assimilation. She could not teach my brothers and sister and me the language or ceremonies, but she did teach us about love, about pride and the confidence that comes from doing "a good job of work," about loyalty and responsibility, and about taking care of each other. When we went to school, our teachers taught us lessons about the Indians of Canada. These lessons reproduce what I call the discourse of the Romantic, Mythical Other – stories about native people who lived a long time ago, hunters, fishers, and gatherers who travelled by canoe, carried tomahawks, and wore war paint. Lessons that position the "real Indians" as a people of the past. These stories about our ancestors are essential; they need to be told, but they cannot be the only stories Canadians know.

My work in the field of Indigenous education is grounded in both my personal and my professional experiences. I started my professional life as an elementary school teacher, and I am sharing my stories today because I am shehshkoolhaaluwees – teacher. A teacher committed to transforming the representation of Indigenous people in classrooms, with a profound faith in the power of education and a firm belief that as educators we have a responsibility to work for justice in the relationship between Indigenous and non-Indigenous people.

I was living and teaching in a city north of Toronto when questions that had plagued me as a child resurfaced. I was teaching in the primary division but always knew when teachers in the junior grades were doing their People of Native Ancestry lessons. Some of you might remember teaching or participating in those lessons. They were conducive to group work and included lots of hands-on activities.[9] Teachers would divide the class into groups, and one group would be assigned the people of the plains, another would do the people of the woodlands, another the people of the west coast, and another the people of the north. Teachers and students loved those lessons. Within each group, one student would research and report on shelter, one would do clothing. Another student would focus on modes of transportation, and still another would learn about how people sustained life – were they hunters or gatherers? I would take my Grade 1 students to the library and see the villages on display, the longhouses made out of popsicle sticks, tipis made out of toothpicks, and sugar-cube igloos. When it was time for gym, we would pass the school foyer and see totem poles made out of cardboard boxes.

I was disturbed by it all, and questions that bothered me as a child re-emerged, nagging questions about what it means to be an Indigenous person in Canada, and new questions about how and why we continue to teach about First Nations, Métis, and Inuit in such limiting and often dehumanizing ways. There was something so familiar about these units, and I realized that we were teaching in the same way teachers did when I was in school. As time went by, every year I dreaded the arrival of those lessons. When my eldest child was in Grade 4, he did his first People of Native Ancestry lessons. I saw him participating in the activities and was compelled to act. As a mother and educator, I recognized my responsibility to address the representation of Indigenous people in the school curriculum, in museums, at historic sites, in product advertisements. I left my teaching position and went to graduate school. I wanted to understand what stories are told about Indigenous people, what is not told, and how to tell different stories.

In graduate school, one of the first things I did was a survey of history textbooks. I wanted to know why most Canadians, and specifically most teachers in Canadian classrooms, were so comfortable teaching about Indigenous people before contact with settlers and so uncomfortable teaching about the history of relationships. In schools, teachers were good at talking about shelter, clothing, and transportation. The majority were much less comfortable and less knowledgeable about the Indian Act, the reserve system, and treaty rights. Indigenous people have lived on the land we call Turtle Island from time immemorial. We have our own ways of governing, caring for, and educating ourselves. Moreover, we are working to recuperate Indigenous knowledge that informs our pedagogy, health care, governing systems, and spiritual practices. An increasing interest in Indigenous knowledge is expanding the ways we teach about and with Indigenous people and knowledge. However, for most of us, this content is not what we learned in school.

Explorers, Missionaries, and Fur Traders
In classrooms and history books, stories about Indigenous people prior to contact are followed by stories about encounters with explorers, missionaries, and fur traders. In these lessons, Indigenous people are friends and helpers to European newcomers, sharing knowledge of how to survive on the land, engaging in trade, and being willing subjects to missionary efforts. While teachers might introduce topics including disease, Christianity, and automatic weapons, they do not necessarily address the degree to which contact with Europeans impacted Indigenous people. Little, if any, attention is given to the "Doctrine of Discovery" or "*terra nullius*," or how these false and racist doctrines were used by kings and queens in Europe to legitimize the claiming of Indigenous lands. Few educators teach their students that European nations relied on declarations by the Pope made in the 1400s to justify colonialism. These declarations called on Christian monarchs to "invade, search out, capture, vanquish and subdue" pagans and other "enemies of Christ" and to "reduce their persons to perpetual slavery" and seize lands and possessions for the king and his successors.[10] Students are provided with few opportunities to investigate how this thinking continues to inform current government policies.

Contact with explorers and the ensuing fur trade brought benefits but also restructured our economies, ultimately disrupting traditional ways of sustaining life. Teachers do not seriously consider how the claiming of our lands devastated Indigenous families, communities, and nations. The more research I do, the more I learn about the significance of the lessons taught and not taught in schools. Consider, for example, the story of Shawnadithit, who is known as the last survivor of the Beothuk Nation. We teach the story of "the last"; we do not talk about how she came to be thought of as the last.

The Historical Timeline

Shawnadithit's Story

Beothuk territory (named Newfoundland by settlers) was home to a thriving nation of people who lived inland during the winters and travelled to the coast during spring to gather eggs from seabirds that nested on the coastal islands. In early spring, these eggs were a critical source of food protein that sustained the people.

While John Cabot is said to have discovered Newfoundland, prior to his arrival fishers from France, Spain, and Portugal returned year after year to this region to access the abundant cod stocks. They arrived every spring and set up fishing camps along the coast. Their presence blocked Beothuk access to the coastal islands. Cut off from an essential food source, the Beothuk became particularly susceptible to disease. Tuberculosis hit hard, and the population was decimated. However, the story does not end there. With their ships filled with salted cod for people in their home countries, at the end of the fishing season the fishers packed up and went back to Europe. They left their camps stocked with gear they would need the following spring. When the fishers left, Beothuk would visit the abandoned camps and take whatever useful items they found. When the fishers returned and discovered camp supplies missing, the Beothuk were seen as thieving savages, and a threat to prosperity. A bounty was issued, and people were paid for every Beothuk killed. By the early nineteenth century, the Beothuk were eradicated. There is historical evidence supporting stories of survivors who left the island and joined with the Innu of Labrador or the Mi'kmaq in Nova Scotia, but as a nation they no longer existed. The story we tell is of the last known survivor, a gentlewoman who drew pictures, told stories, and gave gifts of thanks to the settlers who cared for her as she was dying.

Questions about whose stories are told and not told are revealing. As a child I pressed my mother for details about our family history. She told me we were called Delaware and our traditional territory was on the east coast of the United States. She said we were the grandfathers because we were the first to greet the sun. Disease and Christianity affected our nation, and when the American War of Independence broke out, the Delaware were pushed off our traditional territory and moved north to land along the Thames River in what is now southern Ontario. Moravian missionaries were active in our communities, and that is why our reserve is called Moraviantown. In our language, we call ourselves Lenape and our home territory Lenape-hoking. I was in graduate school before I learned that Delaware was an English name the settlers imposed on us. It was the Americans who renamed the river and the people after a British nobleman.

Learning the name of my nation was significant. I knew that there were different nations, but I did not understand or appreciate the significance of recognizing difference. I want to pause here and talk about terminology because sometimes we get caught up in language, and there has been a lot of change in the language that we use to describe ourselves. For a time, the word *native* was used and, in some contexts, continues to be in use. For example, in the Ontario curriculum there are still curriculum guides titled "Native Languages," and in the United States, *Native American* and *American Indian* are recognized terms. However, anybody who is born in Canada is native to Canada. *Native* is not specific enough. When Columbus got lost and landed on Turtle Island, he called us all Indians, and this had an impact because it collapsed all of our differences and made it as if we were one people. But we are different nations. I use the term *First Nations* purposely. Whereas the word *Indian* conjures images of people of the past, *First Nations* acknowledges our nationhood, recognizes our differences, and acknowledges us as the first nations. The "s" signifies a diversity of nations – we are not all the same. *First Nations* is specific to Canada and is a particular response to the narrative of "the two founding nations." Quite a difference when you say *First Nations* rather than using a word like *Indians* or *native*, right? The term is political: if your ancestors signed a treaty with the British Crown or the state, your nation is considered a First Nation. However, the term excludes Inuit and Métis. In Canada, we now use the word *Indigenous* to be inclusive of the First Nations, Inuit, and Métis. If you are talking about or teaching about one of the nations, use the word that people use to describe themselves, and if you are talking about all of us, use the word *Indigenous*.

Now back to our shared history. Putting the details together, I could see the difference between how colonialism was experienced and how it was taught. For example, stories about missionaries emphasize their desire to Christianize people they judged in need of salvation. These lessons ignore the strength and wisdom embedded in Indigenous people's spiritual practices; they also do not address the divisive force that in many ways Christianity continues to be. At the time disease was decimating our nations, some people converted and others did not. Historians estimate that 90 percent of the Indigenous population died as a result of disease, including smallpox, measles, influenza, and tuberculosis. In combination, disease, Christianity, and the fur trade, which disrupted our traditional ways of sustaining life, made us vulnerable, and while our communities were under immense stress, the power of settler communities was also increasing as more and more settlers left Europe and came to these lands looking for better lives for themselves and their families. Before contact, we were different nations, and we battled with each other; but we did not have automatic weapons, so the numbers of people that died in our wars were much smaller numbers. Wars among the settlers also impacted the First Nations. During this period, settler populations were not only competing with Indigenous people but were competing with each other. As we know, settlers came from different parts of Europe, and they fought with each other, drawing Indigenous Peoples into the conflicts. Indigenous nations allied with European countries, depending on established relationships and promises for improved conditions once the battles were won. Drawn into the fighting between the French, the British, and the Americans, Indigenous people were ultimately fighting to protect their land and their ways of life.

The Métis Nation came into existence during the fur trade as a result of unions between French and Scottish men and Indigenous women. These unions, sometimes thought of as exploitive of Indigenous people, were just as much a reflection of the power and agency of Indigenous women who used their knowledge and skills to support the fur trade and their nations. The Métis developed their own distinct language and culture and established their own territories. Sometimes people get confused, collapsing mixed-race with Métis. To be Métis means having ancestral roots to place and time – the time of early contact between fur traders and the First Nations.

People are most familiar with the dominant story of Canadian history, told as a progress narrative that positions real authentic Indians as a people of the past who either died off or assimilated into the settler population. It is often presented as a tragic tale, a tale many people are comfortable telling. In that version of the story, Canadians celebrate the coming of settlers, the building of the railroad, and the building of a nation but fail to examine how the increased demand for land and resources by settler nations structured the relationship between newcomers and Indigenous people. Ignoring the strength, wisdom, and collective effort it took to survive, the dominant telling is an attempt to erase Indigenous people.

Increasing Settlement, Treaties, Reserves, and the Indian Act

As the settler population was increasing, Indigenous people were working to cope with the impact of contact on our communities. Indigenous people's specific experiences were determined to a certain extent by geography. Colonization started in the east and moved west. Explorers and settlers followed the water routes known to Indigenous people. If you look up the history of towns and cities across the country, you will find that most of them were significant places for Indigenous people. Settlers did not drop their bags wherever they felt like it. They were led through and followed the waterways, building their cities and lives among and over top of Indigenous ones. People whose traditional territories are on the east coast encountered pressure from settlers first. For the most part, Indigenous people were pushed north, west, and south, forcibly removed from traditional territories to make room for the increasing settler populations. Increasing demand for land, control of resources, and the wealth that came from extracting resources led to the signing of treaties and the reserve system.

Indigenous people along the Atlantic coast and the Great Lakes regions have made wampum beads out of the whelk and quahog shells for thousands of years. The beads were woven into wampum belts that served as mnemonic devices recording treaties, historical events, and personal social transactions. Long before the arrival of Europeans, Indigenous Peoples had an established practice of recording treaty agreements in wampum. The first treaty between Indigenous and newcomer nations is Kaswhentha. An agreement between the Haudenosaunee and the Dutch in 1613, it is recorded in a wampum belt known as the Two Row Wampum. The belt has a white background and two parallel lines made from the purple quahog beads. The belt represents the peaceful coexistence of non-interference: Indigenous people would travel the river of life in their canoe, settlers would travel in their boat, we could exist side by side, respecting each other's right to govern themselves and to determine their well-being. In Canada, treaties were signed with the French and the British Crown. After Confederation, the Canadian government continued the practice of negotiating treaties. In exchange for land, the state promised to provide housing, education, health care, and economic support for the transition to a sedentary way of life.

By the early 1800s, Indigenous Peoples were in a precarious position. Having survived disease, war, and the divisive effects of Christianity, patriarchy, and the fur trade, our traditional ways of supporting life were for the most part no longer possible. When lines between settler nations were drawn, Indigenous people were no longer of use as guides, partners in trade, or allies in war. We were no longer friend or ally; instead, we became the "Indian problem." Moreover, to solve the problem, the state adopted a policy of forced assimilation. I think the experience of the Cree and other Indigenous Peoples whose traditional territory is on the plains is helpful in understanding the impacts of colonialism.

When I was in graduate school, I continued to teach in the public school system and moved from the primary division to teaching English as a Second Language. One day I was sitting in on a Grade 8 history class when the teacher introducing the unit announced to his class that the Canadian government wanted to build a railroad to connect Upper Canada with the west: "There was nothing out there but some buffalo and a few hundred Indians." I retell this story not to demonize the teacher but instead to demonstrate the ease with which educators dismiss the experiences of Indigenous people. People in Canada today cannot understand the relationship unless they know the history of that relationship.

Mistahimaskwa's Story
During the mid-nineteenth century, buffalo hides were in high demand in European markets. Buffalo-hide blankets, hats, and coats became a fashion symbol reflecting high social status. Buffalo were hunted and killed for their hides. The bones were taken for use in the making of bone china, but the carcasses were left to rot. The decimation of the buffalo herds put the Cree, Assiniboine, and Blackfoot Nations into a state of crisis. Without the buffalo, their source of food, shelter, and clothing was eliminated, and the people were starving.

This was when the Canadian government sent agents to negotiate treaties. Concerned with moving settlers west and establishing a claim to the northern plains, the Canadian government wanted control of the land for the building of a railroad. Government agents were sent to negotiate with the Chiefs. Agents were authorized and pressured to get treaty agreements signed. In exchange for land, Chiefs were promised food, housing, health care, education, and assistance to transition to a farming way of life. While some leaders signed immediately, Cree leader Mistahimaskwa did not trust the state and did not believe that signing away the rights to Cree territory would ultimately serve the interests of his people. For years he resisted, and with a small group of followers he travelled across the Prairies in search of buffalo and in search of evidence. He wanted to know how those bands that had signed treaties were faring. Instead of a successful transition to an agricultural way of life, what he saw was ongoing suffering. Starvation and disease were ravaging his nation, the promised food was insufficient, and the promise of a transition to agriculture was inadequate. After years of resisting, it was no longer possible for the Cree to keep living without the buffalo, and even Mistahimaskwa was forced to sign and move his people onto a reserve.

At Confederation, Indigenous Peoples were positioned as childlike and in need of protection; the Canadian government took over fiduciary responsibility for them from the British Crown and in 1876 passed a series of laws regulating the relationship. While the Indian Act documents government responsibilities and Indigenous rights, ultimately it is an act in service of accomplishing the government's policy of forced assimilation. But in spite of the pressures, many Indigenous people refused to be assimilated.

Similar to what happened to the Cree, across the continent Indigenous communities were surviving the pressures of colonialism, and this was when the state sent Indian agents to meet with the leaders, enticing people to sign treaties and relocate to reserves. The settler population was increasing, and the government wanted to bring more settlers from Europe to establish and build the Canadian nation. Indian agents offered promises: if you sign a treaty, if you agree to give up your land and move to a reserve, we will provide you with housing, education, health care, a transition to a farming way of life. Some leaders resisted, but in the end they had to sign treaties and agree to live on reserves. The reserve system was initiated to ensure control of land and access to resources. Our ancestors signed those treaties with us in mind. They were conscious of and acted with consideration of the current and future need for housing, education, and ways of sustaining life. They negotiated treaties that offered long-term protection to Indigenous people, our rights and responsibilities.

I came to understand the significance of teaching treaty history during a conversation with Indigenous students. I was working on a research project in northern Ontario, interviewing a young Indigenous student about her school experiences, when she stopped mid-sentence and asked, "Miss, why do we have reserves? The town kids can get up at 8:30 and get to school on time. I have to get up at 6:00 a.m. to get the bus if I want to get to school on time. Like, why, why do we even have reserves? And why do natives have to live on reserves?" Indigenous students are living the legacy of this history, but they do not know the history because teachers often don't teach it. Students want to understand the context of their lives. They are trying to make sense of their lives without access to knowledge and the history that impacts their lives.

Indigenous and settler Canadians need to know and understand the treaty processes, the reserve system, the Indian Act and Indigenous resistance. If we hope to establish new and better relationships, we have to know the history of colonialism that structures our current relationship. Indigenous students tell me about getting hassled by their peers: "I am in Grade 12. I am going to university next year, and I get so much flak from my classmates because they say, 'Oh, you get free tuition. You are so lucky you get free tuition.'" The provision of education is not free – it is a treaty right.

The reserve system was not supposed to last into the twenty-first century. Indigenous Peoples were removed from our traditional territories to land reserved for Indians, with the expectation that people would either die off or assimilate. In many ways, the reserve system failed to accomplish the intended outcome. While Indigenous people were isolated, the isolation actually resulted in family and community ties being maintained and even strengthened. For many Indigenous people, reserves continue to be places of home, recognition, and belonging. However, reserves are also colonial places where laws are imposed on us, regulating and disciplining our actions and interactions. Many of our treaty rights are administered through the band council on the reserve. There is often competition for limited resources, competition between reserves in adjacent areas, competition among neighbours and within families. The reserve system created a strange place that is simultaneously comfort and conflict. The policy of forced assimilation was intended to ensure the elimination of Indigenous people and government responsibility for treaty rights. Reserves accomplished the goal of removing people from the land, restricting our participation in the economy, and created deep divisions between Indigenous and non-Indigenous people.

The Period of Forced Assimilation

> The great aim of our legislation has been to do away with the tribal system and assimilate the Indian people in all respects with the other inhabitants of the Dominion as speedily as they are fit to change.
>
> – Sir John A. Macdonald, 1887[11]

An Act of Parliament initially passed in 1876, the Indian Act regulates how reserves and bands operate and determines who is and who is not a status Indian. The act originally controlled every aspect of Indigenous people's lives, establishing where they could live, where their children went to school, their access to health care and social services – and even their religious practices. There were laws regulating travel off reserve and preventing political organizing and the practice of traditional ceremonies. According to the original Indian Act, a woman's status was determined by her father's or her husband's status. If a woman married a non-Indigenous man, she lost her status, meaning she lost access to her treaty rights, including the right to live on the reserve. If status Indians joined the army, got a university degree, moved off the reserve, or wanted to vote in a federal, provincial, or municipal election, they lost their status. Ultimately, the goal of the Indian Act was to control and assimilate Indigenous people.

Indian agents were assigned to each reserve to ensure that the laws of the Indian Act were followed and to document how the policy of assimilation was being accomplished. At the end of every session of Parliament, agents were required to prepare and submit a report to the Minister of Indian Affairs detailing how the reserve community was progressing toward assimilation. These reports are in the government sessional papers and document how many families were successfully farming, and how many families had adopted Christianity and were attending church regularly. The missionary program continued, and many churches were active within reserve communities, working with the state to Christianize the population and advance the project of assimilation. Churches were competing with each other, and many operated small on-reserve schools. In their reports, Indian agents described the situation. Children on reserve were going to the church-run schools, but at the end of the day they went home to their families. Their mothers, fathers, grannies, aunties, and uncles continued to speak with them in their Indigenous languages, to teach them their ceremonies, to raise them as Cree, Mi'kmaq, Ojibwa, Potawatomi, or Stó:lō. The minister read the reports and concluded that removing children from their families was necessary. In 1879, the prime minister at the time, Sir John A. Macdonald, authorized the practice of separating children from their parents as an adequate education and assimilation strategy. Duncan Campbell Scott, superintendent of Indian Affairs at the time, was determined to find a "final solution to the Indian Problem." He explained, "I want to get rid of the Indian problem. Our objective is to continue until there is not a single Indian in Canada that has not been absorbed into the body politic and there is no Indian question, and no Indian Department."[12]

The Indian residential school system started in 1879, and the last school closed in 1996. Almost immediately after the first schools opened, parents and Indigenous leaders brought serious concerns to the government's attention. The teachers were under-qualified, and the curriculum emphasized religious teachings and manual labour.

Allegations of physical and sexual abuse were frequent. These concerns were of no consequence to the government. Under the Indian Act, all Indigenous people were by legal definition wards of the state. Federal legislation made it mandatory for every Indian child to be sent to residential school, and school principals became the legal guardians of the children. In a report completed as early as 1907, a medical inspector for the Department of Indian Affairs stated that the appalling conditions in the schools were "a national crime ... the result of inadequate government funding, poorly constructed schools, sanitary and ventilation problems, inadequate diet, clothing, and medical care."[13] Dr. Peter Bryce calculated mortality rates among the children as ranging from 35 percent in some schools to as high as 60 percent in others. His calls for improvements were denied, his report suppressed. Instead, the superintendent of Indian Affairs proceeded to formalize agreements with the churches for the provision of education to forcefully civilize and Christianize Indian children.

Indigenous students in schools today are the children, grandchildren, and great-grandchildren of residential school survivors. Consider for a moment what school means to you and what it represents to the parents of Indigenous students. In her film *Muffins for Granny*, filmmaker Nadia McLaren interviews survivors. I have watched the film countless times, and each time I learn from the survivors' stories. The simple phrase "I guess they did not like us very much" stays with me, and I think about what it means to learn within a system aimed at erasing you and what it means to survive that system.

The passing of the Indian Act launched what is referred to as the salvage period. Anthropologists and archeologists, often accompanied by RCMP officers, went into our communities and removed our sacred items. Masks, shakers, ceremonial regalia, and even totem poles were taken away from families and communities. Some ended up in private collections, some in museums, locked under glass in cupboards and storage bins, stolen from our people. The Indian Act made it illegal to practise our ceremonies, and our sacred items were stolen to ensure that the ceremonies were no longer possible. The reason my grandfather only drummed late at night was that it was against the law. You could be imprisoned. Just like you could be detained if you refused to send your children to residential school.

Traditional leadership practices were outlawed, and the elected chief and band council system was an imposed and compulsory method of governance in all reserve communities. Band councils are not our way of governing ourselves. It was a part of the assimilation plan, aimed at assimilating Indigenous people into the settler population. If the RCMP heard that people were gathering, they would go into the meeting and arrest people. We were not allowed to practise our traditional forms of government. There was a time when the Indian Act stated that no more than three Indian men could gather at one time because the state was worried about political activism and resistance.

The Indian Act is an oppressive set of laws aimed at forcing assimilation. It has resulted in violence and harm. Our ancestors signed treaties accepting the reserve system with the promise of education, housing, health care and support through the transition to an alternative way of sustaining life. These promises were broken, and our lives have been controlled by a set of laws aimed at eliminating our existence.

Increasing Resistance

The reserve system, broken treaty agreements, the Indian Act, residential schools – knowing this history, hearing these stories gives me some perspective. It allows me to make sense of my family's history and Canadian history. Yet I still have questions. What changed? The government's plans to assimilate First Nations, Inuit, and Métis were not accomplished – despite the aggressive assault, we survived.

Although the Indian Act continues to impact our communities, there have been changes. Indigenous people have a history of resistance. In the late 1970s to early 1980s, Indigenous women were successful in protesting and partially eliminating sexual discrimination from the Indian Act. During this time, in the early 1980s, Sandra Lovelace

Sappier (now Senator Lovelace Nicholas) lost her status when she married a white man. When her marriage ended, Sappier took her son and returned to her home community, only to discover that she was no longer allowed access to housing on the reserve. After months of struggle, working alongside the Tobique Women's Group, Lovelace eventually took her case to the United Nations, and as a result Canada was pressured into changing the law. I have status today because Indigenous women resisted, fought, and successfully challenged the Government of Canada. Along with my mother, brothers, and sister, I applied for reinstatement of my Indigenous status and was successful.

To move forward, I look back and see a circle of Indigenous people who, from the time of initial contact, asserted Indigenous rights and acted to protect our ways of living and being. In particular, the resistance movement during the second half of the last century laid the groundwork for what I see as the contemporary movement. Oddly enough, once again war among European nations played a part. During the first and second world wars, Indigenous people enlisted in record numbers, and when they returned from fighting on behalf of Canada, they were confronted with their position as second-class citizens. Because they had joined the army, they were required to relinquish their Indian status, and without status they had no access to their treaty rights. During the 1950s and as part of the broader civil rights movement of the 1960s, Indigenous people formed national organizations, including the National Indian Brotherhood (the precursor to the Assembly of First Nations), the Native Women's Association of Canada, and a national Inuit association now known as Inuit Tapiriit Kanatami.

When my grandfather returned from the war, he took his family back to the reserve. They had been living and working on a farm that was located close to the training camp where he was initially stationed. After the war, they went back to the reserve and lived with my mother's grandmother for a while. However, the house was too small, and they could not stay. Like many Indigenous people in the postwar period, they moved to the city. In our case it was the city of Hamilton. My mother has distinct memories of that experience: "We were not, according to the government, we were no longer Indian, but we were not welcomed in the cities either." She told me about trying to get a job and having to pass by opportunities when she saw signs stating, "No Indians allowed."

The National Indian Brotherhood was a political organization originating in British Columbia, where people organized and pressured the government to reinstate fishing rights. When the national organization formed, one of the first issues they took on was education. Our leaders knew that re-establishing strong families, communities, and nations required control of the education of our children. In 1970, the National Indian Brotherhood published their first policy paper, titled *Indian Control of Indian Education*; in 1972 the Government of Canada adopted that policy, returning to Indigenous people the right to provide education for their children.

In response to Indigenous activism in 1969, Prime Minister Pierre Elliott Trudeau asked questions: Why does Canada have reserves? Why are there status and non-status people in Canada? Why aren't all Canadians equal? These are important questions, rooted in our colonial history. Trudeau asked then minister of Indian Affairs Jean Chrétien to write a policy paper calling for the elimination of the Indian Act. Somewhat ironically, policy papers are called White Papers. The 1969 White Paper galvanized Indigenous resistance across the nation. Trudeau's proposed policy would eliminate the Indian Act by doing away with reserves and status and erasing treaty rights. In response to this proposed policy, Indigenous people collectively and loudly said *no*. The Indian Act is outdated and oppressive, yet it is the only legislation that protects Indigenous rights. Our ancestors signed treaties with us in mind and we are not about to give up the rights our ancestors fought and sacrificed for on our behalf.

During presentations of this story, people often ask me why having "status" and a status card matters. Sometimes Canadians get confused about the status card, saying "Why do you need a card to prove that you are Indigenous?" I do not need the card to know my Indigenous identity. I do need a card documenting my status number to access my treaty rights. In 1969, when the Canadian government proposed doing away with the Indian Act, it failed to offer an alternative. Indigenous people will not agree to elimination of the Indian Act until alternative legislation is passed protecting our rights. Our goal is not assimilation; it is to re-establish self-determination. Our worldviews and knowledge systems continue to inform who we are, our rights and responsibilities to each other and the land. We were successful in resisting the 1969 White Paper and continue to fight for our rights to govern ourselves and for jurisdiction over our land.

Land and treaties are at the root of the resistance movement. To understand current conditions, it helps to circle back to the time of contact and the initial relationships established between Indigenous people and newcomers. Although colonizing states relied on the Doctrine of Discovery and *terra nullius* to legitimize their actions, Indigenous people did not ascribe to these doctrines. Our ways of being in relationship with the newcomers were premised on living in responsible relationship – with the land and with each other – and abiding by our treaty agreements. Indigenous people never agreed to give up our ways of being, our worldviews, spiritual practices, or control of our land. In spite of all the attempts at eradication and forced assimilation, we endure and maintain our right to be self-determining people.

In the years following the 1969 White Paper, resistance has continued, sometimes at the local level and increasingly at national and international levels. This includes, for example, Elijah Harper's 1990 defeat of the Meech Lake Accord and the seventy-eight-day stand-off at Kanehsatà:ke that brought international attention to Canada's oppression of Indigenous Peoples and the country's failure to fulfill its treaty agreements. The Idle No More movement in the winter of 2012/13 was particularly successful in mobilizing significant participation and support from Indigenous and non-Indigenous people. It started with four women in Saskatchewan who held a meeting to educate people about Bill C-45, the Canadian government's proposed legislation that would have serious impacts on Indigenous people's rights and the environment, including water and fish habitats. The first "teach-in," organized by Sylvia McAdam, Jessica Gordon, Nina Wilson, and Sheelah McLean, inspired a continent-wide movement with hundreds of thousands of people participating in sharing sessions, protests, blockades, and round dances.

Across the continent, from Haida Gwaii to Nunavut to Mi'kmaq territories, resistance is aimed at acknowledging Indigenous people's right to govern ourselves and re-establish sovereignty over our lands and our lives. This resistance is not new. Our leaders – starting with Chiefs Pontiac, Tecumseh, and Mistahimaskwa – have been organizing united resistance movements against encroachment almost since the time of first contact. However, more recent protests are garnering support from non-Indigenous people who are finding it increasingly impossible to ignore the contradictions between the dominant narrative, which positions Canadians as good, justice-seeking people, and the realities of Canada's actions against Indigenous Peoples. The release of the Truth and Reconciliation Commission's final report and its Calls to Action, in 2015, was a watershed moment, exposing the depths to which Canadians are implicated in the violent oppression of Indigenous children and youth and its devastating and long-term impacts on families and communities. These documents, together with the final report of the National Inquiry into Missing and Murdered Indigenous Women and Girls, released in 2019, have helped keep our experiences and government responsibility within the public consciousness.

This shift in public support is due to increased capacity of Indigenous people to have our voices heard, using both traditional and social media campaigns to amplify Indigenous perspectives and to facilitate organizing. As families and communities recuperate from the violence of the residential school era, youth – partly through their expert use of social media – are becoming more aware of their rights. Greater awareness is leading to change. In school boards, arts and cultural institutions, and post-secondary institutions, programs addressing Indigenous people's experiences and perspectives are being created and supported. Growth in Indigenous studies programs, and Indigenous streams in medicine, law, and social work, are all having a positive impact.

The road to recuperation is long. History has impacted our communities, and there is an immense amount of work to be done. Regaining control of our education system meant that we had to educate teachers to teach in our schools, to bring Indigenous knowledge and languages into our classrooms, and to do the work of resurgence. In our communities, we are working at all levels in education, health care, housing, policing, and the judicial system. We are working on behalf of our people, whether we live on reserve, in urban communities, or in suburban communities; we are accomplishing change. While the Canadian government never expected us to survive, I have come to understand that as difficult as the reserve system is, reserves are also places where we have survived. We have always been people capable of adapting to change, and we did adapt. In many ways, we were put into conflict with each other by having to compete for limited resources, yet there is strength in our communities because the knowledge of living in relationship with the land and each other keeps us alive. As urban Indigenous populations increased, we created Friendship Centres, schools, and health care centres where we gather, celebrate, teach, and learn. In post-secondary institutions we established Indigenous student centres, providing spaces and places where we locate each other. Drawing on our ancestral teaching in these contemporary times, Indigenous artists, filmmakers, musicians, and writers are telling our stories. Indigenous scholars, educators, artists, and activists are doing the work, contributing to resurgence.

Resurgence, Restitution, and Reconciliation

I do not claim to know all the stories. This is my telling, and each time I tell it my understanding of and appreciation for what our ancestors survived and the actions they took on our behalf deepens. I have come to understand that what allowed Indigenous people to survive is everything the anthropologists did not see, looking at us from the vantage point of Western superiority. They did not recognize Indigenous knowledge and how living in relationship with the land and each other supports a sustainable way of life. They could not see that our ways of being would support us through their attempts at assimilation. They underestimated the power of Indigenous women, of our Elders and Knowledge Keepers to protect our languages, stories, and traditional teachings.

Establishing new and better relationships asks something of all of us, and Canadians do not necessarily like it. Many would prefer to keep the past in the past by insisting that this history has nothing to do with the present. But Indigenous people are not going away; our ancestors survived, and we will continue their legacy. We are moving from recuperation to resurgence.

As explained in the introduction, when I give this talk in person, audience members say, "But Susan, I do not know anything about Indigenous people. I did not grow up on a reserve, I do not have any Indigenous friends, I am a *perfect stranger* to Indigenous people." I spent a lot of time thinking about that position, wondering what the allure is, the enticing nature of the Perfect Stranger position, and have come to understand that it gets people off the hook; it alleviates responsibility. If you are a stranger to Indigenous people, you do not have to be accountable for what you know or don't know. My position is that if you live on this land and accept the benefits that come with being Canadian, whether you realize it or not, you are in a relationship with us, and you have a responsibility to know. In recent years I have witnessed an incredible shift in peoples' attitudes and responses: rather than being comfortable with not knowing, people are uncomfortable, they want to know about Indigenous people, they want to hear our perspectives and learn from our stories.

In Chapter 4, I write in response to the work of contemporary Indigenous artists, to show how Indigenous people understand and respond to history in the present.

4

LEARNING FROM CONTEMPORARY INDIGENOUS ARTISTS

I teach a first-year university course called Indigenous People, Identity and Education that brings together Indigenous students from across a large urban centre and introduces them to university. I start the course with an images exercise. I spread an array of images on a table and invite students to choose one to write about. One year, a student chose a *National Geographic* photograph of people wearing grass skirts and loincloths and carrying spears. Beneath the image, the student wrote, "I don't know about you but sometimes I feel like I belong in a museum."

During a recent graduate course, I shared some of the art from this chapter with my class of mainly Indigenous students. We talked about the artists, their work, and what we learn from the art. As the class was coming to a close, a student expressed appreciation for the discussion, saying "I never like art. I can never figure it out; I don't feel connected to it. I don't think art is made for Indigenous people."

These responses reflect students' experiences with visual representations *about* Indigenous people. Their comments are not surprising to me. Youth are immersed in the task of identity construction and do so within a system that fails to provide a space for Indigenous self-representation. Well into the middle of the last century, representations of Indigenous people were bound up in colonial domination, a practice in which dominant cultures seek to control the telling of

Indigenous experiences. As the objects of other people's representations of us, Indigenous people were not the subjects of art, and the work of our artists was confined to the archive, the museum, and documentary film. The National Gallery of Canada was established in 1880; it was almost 100 years before it included art created by an Indigenous artist. The purchase of Carl Beam's work, *North American Iceberg* (1985), signalled an initial shift within the existing hierarchical system that privileged European and Western art. Although the inclusion of Indigenous art continues to be the exception rather than the norm, a growing community of Indigenous artists is working to create change.[1]

Indigenous Art by Indigenous People

Through creative practice, artists share their gifts of insight, interpretation, knowledge, and understanding. They create, and as viewers we are invited into their meaning-making experiences. Engaging with their work creates the possibility for our own thoughtful and sometimes emotion-filled learning. The artists whose works are included in this chapter are exploring themes of community, land, family, relationship, and resurgence. Together they are recreating the stories of our place and presence, illustrating that our teachings are alive and, as Louis Riel predicted, contributing to giving back spirit.

Indigenous art is rooted in the social-political realities and lived experiences of Indigenous people. It is informed by the past while simultaneously providing new ways of thinking about the future. Artists are contributing to the work of recovering from the profound and lasting impacts of colonialism, a process that is both arduous and exhilarating.

> Contemporary Indigenous artists in Canada and around the world are continually interpreting, portraying, and recasting Indigenous histories and knowledge teachings through their art; they pass on ancestral stories depicting the knowledge gathered along pathways

of family bloodlines, community histories, and across generations. These stories are not fixed in the past but are told in the present, being continually regenerated, weaving their way in and out of our narratives.[2]

Drawing on ancestral teachings, Indigenous artists are illuminating ways of knowing and being. Through their artistic creation, they access and pass on teachings, thereby bringing forward and translating knowledge for use in the making of a contemporary Indigenous world. It is about looking back, not returning to the past but rather recreating, and living our interpretations of the teachings in support of a new emergence.[3] This process of recovering and rebuilding requires an enormous amount of energy. Ancestral knowledge is accessed through relationships with family, through community Elders, and from oral and written documentation. It is also recuperated through participation in ceremony and traditional practices. Following pathways not always easily found or traversable, contemporary artists create work that is informed by the past and of use in understanding our Indigenous selves in the present.

From time immemorial, art has been woven through every aspect of traditional Indigenous life, yet in many Indigenous languages there is no single word for art. Rather, concepts of art contained in ancestral languages describe process and movement. Today the definition of Indigenous art continues to expand and evolve; in contrast to images created about us, Indigenous art is made *by* Indigenous people: "Art is not separate from the community – it is of the community and includes participation and interactivity – we come to know through observing and then joining-in, listening and looking, and take up our responsibility to participate according to our own capacities and gifts always with respect and in service of knowing self in relationship with community and nation."[4] Today Indigenous arts occupy the full spectrum of practices – sacred and ceremonial, community-based, amateur and professional, traditional and contemporary. Art continues to be a part of everyday life.

It is through the practices of self-representation that we tell of our survival, our presence, and our resistance. Artistic creation is both evidence of and means of cultural survival and resistance. I consider the work created by the artists included here within a historical and political context. In my responses to their work, my purpose is not to limit analysis; it would be a disservice to Indigenous artists to understand or analyze their art solely as a function of "righting wrongs" or speaking to a colonial world order. Instead, I appreciate that making art in an Indigenous context can also be understood as "participating in creation. It is making oneself available to the spirit, the vision, the invisible, the imagined."[5] In the search for ways to translate, transform, and reinvent Indigenous perspectives, knowledge, and worldviews, artistic production by contemporary artists provides access to Indigenous ways of knowing. Artists are equally conscious of the appropriateness of withholding knowledge. "Long ago her mother had to sing this song and so she had to grind along with it. The corn people have a song too. It is very good. I refuse to tell it."[6] Sometimes the art conceals more than it reveals in service of protecting knowledge from abuse and oversimplification, and to acknowledge that some knowledge is not translatable.

With a pedagogical purpose, I chose the artists for this chapter with intention. Their work is meant to initiate conversations. I hope that readers will reflect on and share comments and questions the images prompt – including, for example, What do you want to know about the image? What do you want to ask the artist? What are you learning from your engagement with the art? Educators wishing to display the work in colour for in-classroom use may find copies of the work, with the permission of the artists, on the following webpage: http://hdl.handle.net//2429/80924.

Questions of Representation

Rosalie Favell, Métis (Cree/English) | Facing the Camera, 2008–2018
Rosalie Favell created *Facing the Camera* in response to the dominant representation of Indigenous people by non-Indigenous people.

Adrian Stimson, Banff, AB, 2011.

Patricia Deadman, Banff, AB, 2008.

Pierre Aupilardjuk, Rankin Inlet, NU, 2017.

Ursula Johnson, Winnipeg, MB, 2017.

For a long time, painters, photographers, and filmmakers, including Edward S. Curtis, George Catlin, and more recently Disney, produced images contributing to dehumanized representations of Indigenous people as Romantic, Mythical people of the past. Along with images, literature defined, described and depicted us according to the observations, motivations, and desires of people outside of our community.

The title of this work, *Facing the Camera*, recognizes the fraught history of Indigenous people as objects of representation. Favell explains, "By emphasizing the individuals' gaze towards the camera, I gave subjects agency to challenge a history of misrepresentation."[7]

This documentary project has received broad support from the Indigenous art community. Artist Vanessa Dion Fletcher[8] explains her response:

> The first time I met Rosalie Favell was in Winnipeg, where she was conducting a *Facing the Camera* photo shoot. I was thrilled to learn that there were no strict rules about who could be included. "Are you a member of the Indigenous arts community?" was the only question I was asked. With this project, Rosalie affirmed my presence. This kind of acknowledgment of belonging and contribution from within the community stands in stark contrast to my experiences of exclusion from the Indian Act and Canadian government definitions of identity and belonging.[9]

Favell exemplifies a strong relational component in her artistic process and practice. Although she is focusing on singular identities (through the individual portraits), the growing breadth of this body of work as a whole speaks to the notion of individual in the collective. This is reflective of an Indigenous worldview that acknowledges the importance of a strong sense of self, and our own gifts as the basis for strong and healthy community. Giving broad representation to the community, Favell complicates identity, showing how it is constantly shifting, worked and reworked. The portrait convention gives agency to the individual providing space for the expression of self in all its complexities.

Learning from Contemporary Indigenous Artists

John Gadsby Chapman and Edward S. Curtis

John Gadsby Chapman,
The Baptism of Pocahontas,
1840. Oil on canvas, 12' × 18'.

Edward S. Curtis, *Lucille*,
circa 1907. Photograph.

> When I was eight years old, Disney's *Pocahontas* was released. I didn't know about the story of Pocahontas; I remember being a little excited to see a native person and story in the movies. But my mom was angry, and I remember learning why she was upset and why I was not going to be watching the movie.
>
> — Vanessa Dion Fletcher[10]

In presenting an Indigenous woman as a princess and the object of an Englishman's desire, as if she were an object for consumption and ownership, Disney produced for another generation of children an image of Indigenous people as caricature. The romanticized representation of the story rewrites the history of this young woman from a colonial perspective. Disney's portrayal was not the role model many Indigenous mothers wanted for their children.

In a 2002 university art class, Richard Hill expanded Dion Fletcher's understanding, pointing out that Disney was not the first to corrupt the representation of Pocahontas. In the Disney image, John Smith is steering the boat, while Pocahontas sits idly in the front singing for his and the viewer's entertainment. This history of misrepresenting Indigenous woman generally and Pocahontas explicitly dates much further back than the 1995 film. John Gadsby Chapman's painting titled *The Baptism of Pocahontas*, from 1840, is an early example. In this painting, which hangs in the rotunda of the United States Capitol, Pocahontas is kneeling at the feet of the priest, a light glowing all around her connoting the moral positives of converting to Christianity, while on the right side of the painting her Indigenous relatives are left in the shadows. Photographs taken by Edward S. Curtis continued the construction of the Indian Princess. In the early twentieth century, Curtis travelled across North America, producing some forty thousand negatives, of which more than twenty-two hundred were published. He was fascinated by the idea of the "Indian" and was determined to capture the image before it vanished. Wanting to represent the romantic dying Indian, he took along boxes of paraphernalia, including wigs, blankets, painted backdrops, clothing – in case he ran into Indians who did not look as the Indian was supposed to look.[11]

Making sense of how these types of images inflict harm can be challenging. For some, Pocahontas is a warm childhood memory, and many Indigenous people are devout Christians and appreciate the Chapman painting. As an Indigenous woman, I cannot see these images as innocent. But they are useful in helping me understand why so many people have limited and constricted knowledge of Indigenous women. Their way of knowing us is often based on these stereotypical representations.

After hundreds of years of outsiders telling our stories, making images of us, constructing a truth that is not our truth – and after hundreds of years of outsiders gazing at those representations of us – people are finally looking and listening to Indigenous people, hearing our truths, engaging with our self-representations.

Creation Stories: Reflecting and Informing Worldviews

Mary Anne Barkhouse, Kwakiutl / Dominion, 2011

I am drawn to the self-determined strength in this wolf's stride and feel a shared sense of resistance to the idea of dominion over. People's creation stories reveal their values, beliefs, and ancestral knowledge. Thomas King explains that "contained within creation stories are relationships that help to define the nature of the universe and how cultures understand the world in which they exist."[12] In her photograph titled *Dominion*, Mary Anne Barkhouse juxtaposes an excerpt from the Judeo-Christian creation story over the image of a wolf. The image conveys a clash of worldviews: an Indigenous worldview that positions humans in relationship with all of creation against a Western hierarchical worldview that positions man as superior to all of creation. Engaging with this image, viewers are invited to reflect on the confrontation.

In her artist statement, Barkhouse writes,

This image is no longer available for this printing.

Mary Anne Barkhouse, Kwakiutl, *Dominion*, 2011. Photograph, 91.4 × 121.9 cm.

> Notions of authority and control are prominent in considerations of Dominion. The quote, super-imposed over a wolf in mid-stride, is derived from the Book of Genesis, a portion of the Bible which delegates to man the right to rule over the earth and all of the animal kingdom. Many have interpreted this as a call to responsible stewardship, and with it a quest for knowledge and understanding ... others have taken it as their carte blanche to do with the planet as they wish.

Barkhouse does not assume to know or attempt to provide a singular interpretation of the Book of Genesis; rather, she offers interpretations, leaving the viewer to make their own meaning from the image she has created. Barkhouse goes on to say,

> The wolf featured in the photograph was the alpha female of a pack that resides at the Haliburton Wolf Centre in Ontario. Counter to

some depictions of the wolf as a ravening menace or a noble savage, she maintains a somewhat contemplative demeanour. Secure in her position as a sovereign entity, she continues on her way ... a path that is marked by self-determination and strength, characteristics she has both learned, and earned, as the matriarch of the pack.[13]

The care Barkhouse takes to introduce the wolf creates the possibility that viewers will see themselves in relationship with it. She draws attention to dominant stories about wolves and uses specific words, including sovereignty, self-determination, and strength, to establish the grounds on which the relationship might be established.

In a capitalist, profit-driven world where one's value is determined by the capacity to amass personal wealth, recognizing the need for conservation, stewardship, and appreciation of biodiversity is nearly impossible. *Dominion* provokes questions that are simultaneously hopeful and threatening. Admiring the strength and beauty of the wolf is insufficient. Our lives and the lives of future generations depend on more than admiration: we must be willing to learn. To what extent is it possible to learn from the wolf, to hear and learn from Indigenous creation stories, and to shift our understanding of what it means to live in responsible relationship with all of creation?

Joseph Jacobs, Cayuga | Creation, *1986*
Joseph Jacobs's work titled *Creation* is featured on the western wall of the members' entrance to the Centre Block in the Canadian Parliament Buildings. Every member of the House of Commons passes the sculpture when they enter; do they notice it, appreciate it, think about its meaning?

The five-panel limestone frieze depicts the formation of the earth and the establishment of the Haudenosaunee Confederacy. It is a complex piece that reflects teachings about responsibility and the significance of relationships, respect, and balance in accomplishing peace. In reference to Jacob's work in general and this sculpture, specifically, Bruce Fisher writes, "Haudenosaunee iconography is specific,

Joseph Jacobs, Tuscarora,[14] *Creation*, 1986. Frieze, Indiana limestone, 132 × 409 cm.

complex, and connected to extensive oral narratives that pierce European boundaries between religion and history."[15] Its presence in the House of Commons is noteworthy. It draws attention to the spiritual and governing practices of a people and culture that continue to thrive and whose understanding of themselves is informed by a set of distinct teachings originating on these lands.

There are different versions of the creation story about Sky Woman. Common in each telling is that the woman's fall from the sky is softened by the wings of geese and that she lands on the back of a turtle. In turn, various animals dive into the vast water, each trying to bring back mud. Finally, the muskrat is successful, and Sky Woman spreads the mud, creating the earth by dancing the shuffling dance, a dance that Haudenosaunee women continue to perform today.[16] I am most familiar with a version of this story shared by Thomas King.[17] It is his analysis that I find most useful. King draws attention to the co-operation that was required to create the earth; the actions of the creatures are motivated by generosity, care, and concern. He emphasizes individual skills and contributions. No single person is responsible for all things. We all have skills and capacities, and when we work in collaboration, we are our most creative and productive. Thus, each of us is responsible for developing our gifts and using our skills in service of family, community, and nation. Our survival is dependent on strong individuals committed to serving the well-being of all – this is what I hear in the story of Sky Woman.

I am less familiar with the story of the Peace Maker and the formation of the Haudenosaunee Confederacy. In *Creation*, Jacob incorporates vital references to the story of Sky Woman. Still, he centres Tadodaho and the founding of the Confederacy. I do know that it is a long and detailed story about a time when five nations had forgotten their teachings and were at war with each other. Pain and suffering were widespread. The Great Peacemaker, Dekanawidah, and his ally Hiawatha, working with Jigonsaseh, negotiate with the leaders of each of the five nations to make a commitment to the Confederacy. A fierce leader, Tadodaho initially refuses but is finally convinced to join. Jigonsaseh combs the snakes from his hair, and the warriors bury their weapons of war under the roots of the Great Tree of Peace, create a fifty-member governing body, and commit to a 117-article constitution documenting each members' responsibilities and rights. The Tuscarora joined in 1722, making it a Six Nation Confederacy.

Without the narratives, it is hard to make sense of the sculpture, which is I think the artist's point. We need to know our own and each other's creation stories. If we do not know the Peace Maker, Hiawatha, and Jigonsaseh, we cannot make sense of the man with snakes in his hair. Stories about Sky Woman and the Peace Maker get told in the recitations of the great law, and if we live on this land, we would do well to learn from the stories created from this land. "Jacob's sculptures penetrate deeply into the ancestral knowledge and teachings of his people," Fisher writes. "His rationale for his work was this: 'I want to give permanence in stone to the legends of my people.'"[18]

Colonialism and Its Impacts

Ruth Cuthand, Plains Cree, Scottish, and Irish | Trading Series, 2009
At first glance, the splashes of bright colour on black are perplexing; something about the organic nature of the patterns calls for attention.

Ruth Cuthand, Plains Cree, Scottish, and Irish, *Smallpox*, 2009. Beads and acrylic on suede board, 61.0 × 45.7 cm.

On closer inspection and after reading the title, it becomes clear: smallpox and other diseases, including typhoid fever, tuberculosis, and influenza, introduced by European explorers, missionaries, and settlers had devastating impacts on Indigenous people. From early contact to contemporary times, disease has played a role in colonialism. Historians estimate that the introduction of diseases – initially smallpox, measles, and typhoid fever – hit our communities hard. The spread of tuberculosis in Inuit communities during the 1950s contributed to the disruption of families and communities. Influenza and pneumonia were responsible for high rates of death among children in residential schools. Indigenous people's susceptibility to disease was, and continues to be, exacerbated by the lack of access to adequate food, clean water, and health care.

In *Trading Series*, Cuthand explores the relationship between beauty and the grotesque. It is precisely the discomfort created when confronted by a beautiful work of art that is communicating a grotesque reality that provides viewers with the opportunity for new learning. Cuthand explains her fascination with the attractive and repellant subject, the simultaneously beautiful and abhorrent:

> This dichotomous relationship between appearance and content, or between style and subject creates a cognitive schism; it is that gap that creates a space for contemplation about the work and what it means ... I have found that making work which confronts the most difficult truths about Canadian society and the impacts of colonization on Aboriginal people are made remarkably palatable when delivered in a strikingly seductive package.[19]

While many of us have heard references to the impacts of disease on Indigenous people, few of us are aware of the severity of those impacts. I am not a scientist or a health care professional, but having read the stories of the Cree, the Beothuk, and the removal of Inuit to sanatoriums in the south, I feel a strange attachment to these images. Is it because the images are so beautiful that viewers can get close to the story of smallpox? Does the image initiate questions? Knowing their horrible impacts, what would make an artist want to represent those diseases so beautifully?

Beading, as an act, provides an experiential understanding of relationship with time – with every stitch you reinforce, simultaneously reflecting back and projecting forward, over and over and over again in a cycle. Additionally, beading tells the story of colonialism: beads were used for trade, introducing questions about the economic relationship between Indigenous people and fur traders. Multiple lessons can be learned through beading: patience, self-regulation, problem-solving, relationship with yourself; a beautiful picture on top is secondary to the craftwork/skill of strong, resilient, thoughtful, intentional stitching underneath; stories explicitly told through image; stories implicitly told through talking with people you are beading alongside.

I have seen countless stunningly beautiful beading projects, but this one stays with me, each tiny bead reminding me of the beauty and generosity of my ancestors, who welcomed and traded with newcomers – and the price we paid and continue to pay.

Adrian Stimson, Siksika | Sick and Tired, 2004
Adrian Stimson is a multidisciplinary artist, who lives and works in his home Siksika community. Stimson's father attended residential school, and Stimson himself attended a residential day school.

This installation includes three Old Sun Indian Residential School windows, filled with feathers and backlit, and an old infirmary bed from the same school with a bison robe folded into a human shape placed on its springs. The bed is illuminated from the top to create a

Adrian Stimson, Siksika, *Sick and Tired*, 2004. Installation.

shadow beneath, similar to a stretched hide. The installation speaks to history, culture, genocide, absence, presence, and fragmentation. It creates a space of contemplation and challenges our relationship to the past, present, and future. Residential schools were instruments of genocide; they created isolation, disorientation, pain, and death.

The objects are imbued with weighted memory. *Sick and Tired* also tells us that this history is not long in the past. Contemporary artists can still find and use physical pieces of buildings in their work, just as the memory and experiences of residential school lives with survivors and families. In his artist statement, Stimson reflects on the installation:

> I can imagine many children peering out of these windows, longing to be home with their families. Their reality, however, was confinement similar to being smothered by a pillow. Sickness and disease were and still are a reality for First Nations—a legacy of illness represented by the infirmary bed. How many people lay sick, tired, dying or dead on this bed is not known, yet I feel the heaviness of its presence, a state that exhausts me physically, mentally, emotionally and spiritually.[20]

Drawing on his knowledge and understanding of residential school experiences Stimson creates the possibility for viewers to experience themselves in relationship with these experiences. We are a part of, yet separated from, knowing what it was like to lie on that bed. Knowing that children, specific children, Indigenous children, lay on that bed, the installation compels the question, Who are we and what is our relationship and responsibility to those children and their descendants?

The buffalo robe bundled and placed on the bed like a child's small body is for me one of the most striking elements of the installation. It visually connects the life of the buffalo and the life of the child. Much of Stimson's work is related to the buffalo and its decimation. In *Sick and Tired*, Stimson makes a clear parallel between the colonial project of hunting buffalo for settler profit and Indigenous decline and the deaths of Indigenous children in residential schools. The phrase *sick and tired* evokes exasperation. Stimson draws our attention to the exhaustion of surviving genocide, while drawing us in, inviting us into his story and the statistics of the story. Yet I feel the heaviness of genocide's presence, creating a state that exhausts me physically, mentally, emotionally, and spiritually.

Nadia Myre, Algonquin / Indian Act, 2002

Looking at Nadia Myre's installation titled Indian Act, viewers are confronted with fifty-six pages that they cannot read. Myre taped a copy of each page of the Indian Act onto a piece of cloth. She invited friends, colleagues, and strangers to assist her in beading over the words. The project involved over 230 people and took three years of

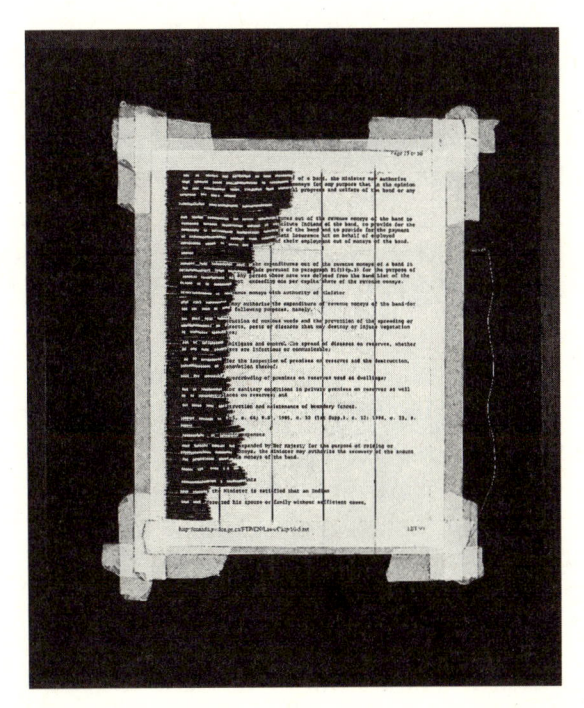

Nadia Myre, Algonquin, *Indian Act*, 2002. Installation.

Learning from Contemporary Indigenous Artists

collective effort to complete. They used white beads to sew over the letters and red beads to fill in the negative space. The result is a strikingly beautiful and powerful statement – some would say a powerful Indian Act of resistance.

Replacing letters with beads obscures the English words and creates the potential for new meaning making. Many of our ancestors, those who were initially removed to the reserves and whose lives were directly impacted by the Indian Act, did not have access to the text. It was not written in our languages, and many Indigenous people did not read English. We, on the other hand, understand what it means to bead, to gather, to participate in a shared act of resistance. The communal element is significant. Bringing people together to complete this work reflects the strength and resilience within many Indigenous communities. The collaborative beadwork creates new meanings, gesturing toward the action taking place in communities where combined efforts are aimed at replacing the current legislation with sovereignty and self-determination informed by our original teachings.

Primarily, the goal of the Indian Act was to accomplish forced assimilation in service of solving the "Indian problem." Indigenous people who were removed to reserves were supposed to either die off or assimilate into the settler population. The 1876 Indian Act was a series of laws aimed at controlling life on reserves in Canada by governing who was and who was not an Indian, where people were allowed to live and travel, what ceremonies and languages were permitted, where Indigenous children were allowed and required to attend school. The act imposed the chief and band council system in our communities, replacing our ways of governing ourselves with imposed policies. While changes have been made, the Indian Act continues to regulate the lives of status First Nations people in Canada. It fundamentally structures the relationship between people and the Canadian government.

Participation in the project changed people's relationship with the Indian Act. The practice of beading over the words provided opportunity and time for people to collectively engage with and reflect on words and sentences, making meaning of the act and its impact on individuals, families, and communities. The use of red beads adds to the effect, reminiscent of fire and blood; it provokes associations and contradictions with joy, passion, violence, and rage. The beadwork literally and concretely puts an Indigenous lens over a Western one. The beads traversing the page, some farther than others, reflects resistance and recuperation taking place in communities across Turtle Island. There is a sense of progress as well as a growing awareness of the ongoing work of resistance and resurgence.

Reclamation, Resurgence, Relationship

George Littlechild, Plains Cree / Indian Foster Boy, *1996*

George Littlechild, Plains Cree, *Indian Foster Boy*, 1996. Mixed media.

Reflecting on this image, Vanessa Dion Fletcher writes:

> I was introduced to this image, titled *Indian Foster Boy*, during an undergraduate art history class and I've never forgotten it. The background creates a colourful chaos. Littlechild points himself out with the red marker. An obvious sign that is not necessary because most of us see the difference. Gorgeous brown skin, dark hair and eyes stand out against the light skin and blond hair of the other children. He looks toward the camera. Written in all caps, "INDIAN FOSTER BOY." An aesthetic also employed by Gerald McMaster, Jane Ash Poitras, and George Longfish. It was popular in the 1990s. The institutional language further alienating the boy, drawing viewers' attention to an experience all too familiar within Indigenous families, the Sixties Scoop, which has only recently become a part of the national consciousness.[21]

Another policy in support of forced assimilation and cultural genocide. Some Indigenous organizations estimate that upwards of 20,000 Indigenous children were taken from their families and communities and fostered or adopted out to mostly white families, most commonly in the Prairie provinces during the 1960s. Some experts say the number of Indigenous children in the care of child protection services today is evidence that little has changed since the closing of Indian residential schools.

In 2017 Littlechild resurrected work from his 1996 exhibition, *Displaced Indians: The Sixties Scoop*, to be part of a major exhibition at Urban Shaman in Winnipeg. *A Place Between* was a groundbreaking project featuring the work of twenty Indigenous artists addressing the experience of being torn from family and community, the resulting trauma, and the energy required to recuperate from the experience.

"We all knew displacement, shame, hurt, abandonment and cultural loss," Littlechild writes in his artist statement. "We especially lamented the loss of home, our parents and loved ones, some we knew, some we only imagined, and some who peered through a fog as the memories of our past, before we were taken." He says feelings of shame are common among survivors. "We were taught to be ashamed of our Indian-ness. We craved love and acknowledgement." But he says all his work deals with social and political issues. Art is his tool for resistance – and transformation.[22]

Joi T. Arcand, Muskeg Lake Cree Nation | **Northern Pawn, South Vietnam**

As with creation stories, language embodies worldviews. The late Anishinaabe writer and philosopher Basil Johnston says there is a literal and conceptual meaning behind every word in Anishinabemowin. Words are encoded with Indigenous ways of knowing and being and include high-end intellectual, sophisticated, and philosophical theory. Many artists use language in their work or as the subject of their work. Whether they are language speakers or language learners, their artistic creations bring Indigenous languages into the present, contributing

Joi T. Arcand, Muskeg Lake Cree Nation, *Northern Pawn, South Vietnam – Here On Future Earth,* 2009. Inkjet print, 50.8 × 66 cm.

Learning from Contemporary Indigenous Artists

to resurgence and making space for our voices and words to be in our lives.

Joi T. Arcand is a photo-based artist from Muskeg Lake Nehiwawenin (Cree) Nation, Saskatchewan Treaty 6 Territory. In her work *Here On Future Earth,* Arcand reimagines her Prairie home. Photographing streetscapes and businesses, combining her knowledge of photography and typography, she works with a language speaker to translate all the text into nêhiyawêwin syllabics. The results are images that are benign and familiar; many will recognize the storefront and signage of small towns. However, the syllabics provide a twist. It is an imagining of an earth or perhaps future earth where nêhiyawêwin proliferates in our daily lives. Often using bright neon colours, and with strategic positioning, she is making the language "hyper-visible" in seemingly mundane spaces. In doing so she challenges our ways of looking at the world and how colonial presence is maintained through the dominant languages made accessible on the land in what is now known as Canada. Most often her work does not include immediate translation for viewers, which speaks to the emotional and mental labour involved in language recovery and reclamation.

Prior to contact, at least sixty different Indigenous languages were spoken in the territories that now make up Canada. All of them are currently critically threatened. Children in residential schools were punished for speaking Indigenous languages in an attempt to disrupt the transfer of Indigenous cultures and knowledge systems and erase Indigenous presence. Access to Indigenous language learning has not been made available to most people in this country and, most glaringly, in the education systems that are responsible for their current state of fragility. For many people living in urban settings, there is often an emotional impact when attempting to recover their Indigenous language, as it becomes a reminder of the dislocation of our peoples from our lands and systems of knowing.

I come from a community of very few Lenape speakers. There are only a handful of Elders who still speak fluently. For me, colonialism made a world alive with the sounds of Indigenous language unreal and unattainable. I can only imagine this world, and for me it is a kind of utopia. It is a place where I would feel welcome, comfortable, and affirmed by language. When I look at the images of *Here On Future Earth*, I see a visual representation of my utopia. Indigenous families, communities, and nations, in addition to artists, are working to develop strategies to relearn the languages taken from us. Arcand's "presencing" of syllabics and language in everyday places gestures toward the notion of future possibilities of recovery, reimagining, and hope.

Bonnie Devine, Anishinaabe / Battle for the Woodlands, *2014, 2015*

Recognizing the importance of land and water to Indigenous ontologies, Bonnie Devine expanded an early nineteenth-century map of Upper and Lower Canada. Painting directly on the gallery wall, she

Bonnie Devine, Anishinaabe (Ojibwe) and member of Serpent River First Nation, *Battle for the Woodlands*, 2014, 2015. Installation; acrylic paint, graphite, paper, felt, and beads, 5.5 × 2.4 m (approximate).

Learning from Contemporary Indigenous Artists **123**

used beaded lines to represent treaty boundaries that were, like so many others, ultimately ignored. She painted the rivers red and the Great Lakes as spirit animals, illustrating the bloodline between Indigenous people and Mother Earth. In response to the map, Indigenous student, educator, and activist Nicole Meawasige wrote, "In Anishnaabemowin, nibiikaa means a lot of water. Looking at this image I feel a deep connection to nibi (water), I am reminded of my responsibility to take care of the waters."[23]

The map is part of a larger piece included in the exhibition, titled *Before and After the Horizon*. The *Battle for the Woodlands* installation comprises several components and was constructed on site at the Art Gallery of Ontario in two separate six-week terms in 2014 and 2015. Throughout the installation, images of American and British soldiers mark historic battles and the militarization of the Great Lakes. With reference to leaders Tecumseh, Pontiac, and Crazy Horse, Devine reminds all of us that Indigenous warriors fought to protect our lands and the knowledge that informed our understanding of what it means to live in responsible relationship with land, water, and all of creation. The installation includes clothing for the warriors and images of Indigenous people and animals fleeing from the land damaged by colonization and industrialization. In the map, Devine portrays the lakes as images of spirit beings: "I painted them in red oxide and depicted them as animals: a buffalo, an otter, a turtle, a rabbit and a leviathan. I pictured them as spirit beings, for that is what they are." These images encourage relationships and remind viewers that everything is living and breathing, and in different ways we are all connected to each other, to the land, and to the waters.

Devine is also sharing an ancestral teaching, as she explains in her artist statement: "It's very deep and old. It hasn't got a lot of words. I don't have the words for it; all I have are these images and these figures. It's my way of talking about this very very ancient consanguinity, which means having the same blood, it means that the water running in the lakes and rivers runs in us."[24] Acknowledging our connections with spirits, animals, plants, and waterways, Devine is ultimately reminding us about the role we have in taking care of our relationships with all of creation. This teaching reminds me that I am responsible for *all my relations*. This includes self, family, community, water, land, and air. The health and well-being of one is tied to the health and well-being of all.

We're at a moment right now where we have a chance to make some changes because the rest of the world is finally confronting the need to understand the ways in which all life is interconnected, and humans do have responsibilities to the earth. Those issues and concerns resonate with Indigenous people, and others are turning to us for answers.

Vanessa Dion Fletcher, Lenape and Potawatomi | Relationship or Transaction, *2014*

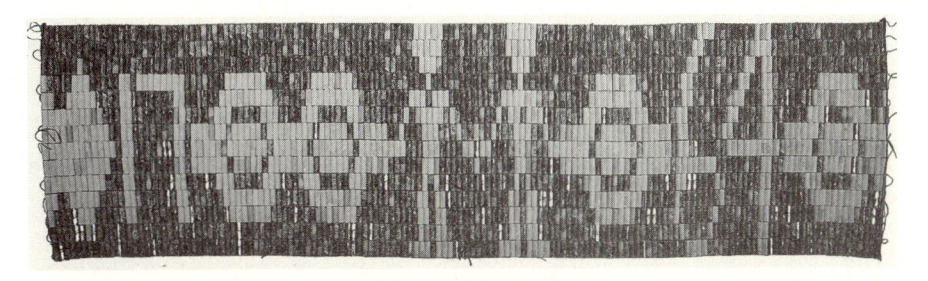

Vanessa Dion Fletcher, Lenape and Potawatomi, *Relationship or Transaction*, 2014. Canadian five-dollar bills, screen prints, jute twine, and leather, 1 × 4 m.

Detail from Vanessa Dion Fletcher, *Relationship or Transaction*, 2014.

Learning from Contemporary Indigenous Artists

For thousands of years, Indigenous people on the Atlantic coast and in the Great Lakes region made wampum. A wampum belt is a belt-like object woven together with two kinds of beads, made from quahog and whelk shells. Belts served as mnemonic devices for recalling treaties, historical events, and personal and social transactions.

Understanding colonialism requires attention to land, treaties, and relationships. Reflecting on the spirit and intent of the treaty-making process, *Relationship or Transaction* is a reproduction of the Western Great Lakes Covenant Chain Confederacy Wampum Belt. The belt depicts two figures holding hands in the centre, flanked by pentagons and the date 1764. This reproduction is made using five-dollar bills as the quahog (purple) beads and replica five-dollar bills as the whelk (white) beads. *Relationship or Transaction* emphasizes opposing understandings of treaty – as building relationships between nations or as a transaction in power and monetary terms.

The replica belt questions the concepts of value ascribed to the relationships between Indigenous nations and colonial governments. Dion Fletcher explains that while making the beads from the five-dollar bills, the value of those objects changed. The shift in meaning suggests that value is a shared responsibility, a process of investment by the people who negotiate its terms and physical manifestations. A significant aspect of this responsibility is the transmission of knowledge. The symbolic language woven into the belt tells the story of valuing the relationship, a relationship that was purposefully negotiated and represented in the wampum belt. From within Indigenous ontology the process of making represents a repository of this process: the terms of engagement are embedded and shared through reading the talk contained in each belt.

This piece is a good example of Indigenous art that is actively challenging a singular colonial narrative and worldview. The wampum belt and its lack of prominence in the Canadian historical narrative illustrates the deep clash of worldviews – one that is generative and rooted in relationships, and another that is transactional, consumptive, and extractive. Dion Fletcher's wampum belt challenges viewers to reflect on their knowledge and understanding of treaty history and their relationship with treaties. Engaging with this history can be unsettling, its complexity intimidating. Questions about comprehensive land claims, specific land claims, and unceded land are not easily understood.

5

THE BRAIDING HISTORIES STORIES

Co-written with Michael R. Dion

> We want to tell our own stories, write our own versions, in our own ways, for our own purposes.
>
> – Linda Tuhiwai Smith, *Decolonizing Methodologies*

During long summer afternoons at libraries around Toronto, we researched and wrote about the lives of our ancestors. We read about their struggles and triumphs and were overwhelmed by pain, sorrow, anger, pride, and joy as we immersed ourselves in their stories. Sitting at desks piled high with books, we would frequently interrupt each other, saying, "Listen to this." Our need to pass on what we were experiencing was immediate. We spoke back and forth about how these stories of injustice and resistance weighted us down and forged our commitment to our project. We found our desire to (re)tell their stories entwined with our own story. In the moment of (re)telling, we are both witness and testifier, bearing witness to the stories of our ancestors and giving testimony as survivors of the policy of forced assimilation. For us, history "is woven in stories, and storytelling provides a customary framework for discussing the past."[1] These stories are connected with our present and the future we are working to create.

We started writing the Braiding Histories stories almost twenty years ago, and three of the stories that are included in this book first appeared in my (Susan's) first book, *Braiding Histories: Learning from Aboriginal Peoples' Experiences and Perspectives*.[2] We always intended to write more stories and publish them as a collection. Our lives got busy with other tasks and we did not return to complete the project until a few years ago.

We are (re)telling the stories, conscious of our pedagogical and political responsibilities. Rather than thinking only about transmitting information, we tell the stories in such a way that the power the stories have for us will become a part of the story. Walter Benjamin writes, "In every case, the storyteller is a man [*sic*] who has counsel for his readers. The storyteller takes what he tells from experience – his own or that reported by others. And he, in turn, makes it the experience of those who are listening to his tale."[3] In our (re)tellings, we hoped to translate the meanings the stories have for us into a form that readers will recognize. While writing the stories, we kept three critical questions in mind: (1) Can we tell the stories in such a way that readers will have a sense of what the stories mean to us? (2) In what ways will our stories impact the story our readers tell themselves about Indigenous people? (3) Will our (re)tellings give readers what they need to recognize and act in regard to the alterity[4] of Indigenous people's experiences?

Indigenous people have always been involved with cultural production, representing ourselves and our worldviews in various texts, including stories, art, and ceremony. We wrote the Braiding Histories stories and think of them as (re)tellings. We take the stories people tell about themselves, or we take the stories that are written in books, newspaper articles, and so on, and write our re-telling of the person's story. Our purpose is, as Linda Tuhiwai Smith explains, to write our versions, in our ways, and for our purpose. We aim to tell a story that the people we are writing about would recognize as their own. In our (re)telling project, we are conscious of the stories non-Indigenous people hear about Indigenous people, and we purposefully disrupt dominant narratives. Our goal is to provide Indigenous representations of people's lives that show how colonialism has impacted the lives of individual people, and how people have survived, resisted, and recuperated from policies and practices aimed at eradicating Indigenous people, our knowledge, and our cultural practices.

The Braiding Histories collection in this book includes stories of people from different nations and different periods. Some of the people we write about are well known. Whole books have been written about the Beothuk woman Shawnadithit, the Cree Chief Mistahimaskwa, and the activist and now Canadian senator Sandra Lovelace Nicholas. Others are well known in their communities for their contributions, including Toni Goree, Oonig Paul Ward, Bernard Kerrigan, and Liz Hall. These stories feature subjects who stand out among their friends and families as people whose Indigenous identities inform their everyday lives in ways that are recognizable to insiders, those who see evidence of survival and presence. These people are not necessarily recognizable to outsiders looking for the Romantic, Mythical Other.

We are starting with our mother's story for two reasons. First, as stated earlier, the relationship between tellers/writers and listeners/readers is a critical component of the storytelling practice. We are telling our mother's story first as a way of deepening our relationship with you, the readers. And second, we start with our mother's story because for us it is the most important story. Our understanding of being Indigenous is rooted in our relationship with our mother, our family, and the broader urban Indigenous community.

We Wanted to Hear Your Stories[5]

What is dignity?
How do you learn self-esteem?
What is the value of your history?
and what happens when that history is denied?
Mom wrestles with her past
Like a pattern that would not go together
Stitching and ripping and stitching again

Not a single garment but a multi-layered gown
that becomes a baby's frock and a son's shirt.
The comfort comes not from wearing the garment
but from remembering
the hands that did the stitching.

Audrey Dion (née Tobias).

The blinds were open, and I (Susan) could feel the heat from the sun as it cast shadows on the kitchen table.[6] Standing on the inside, I had a deceptive impression of warmth on a cold February afternoon. I had just finished lunch with Mom, and as I cleared the dishes I found myself thinking back to family mealtimes when I was growing up. Including Mom and Dad there were seven of us gathered around the table, and when supper was finished we would stay at the table talking, listening, and telling stories. Many nights we would ask Mom and Dad to tell us about what it was like when they were little.

"How about some tea?" Mom asked, bringing me back to the present. She started to fill the kettle. I noticed that she was leaning against the sink – for support. As if she knew my thoughts, she asked, "Do you remember how when you were little we would sit around the table after supper drinking tea and talking? Sometimes we would still be sitting there at eleven o'clock."

"I was just thinking the same thing," I said, struck by the mystery of our connectedness. "You would tell stories about driving the coffee truck and dad would talk about people at his office. The news of the day was always a good topic to keep the conversation going longer. But the stories we liked best were the ones about what life was like when you were little. Dad was always telling us stories about his mother and growing up in Quebec." I paused for a moment to see if she would again continue my thought for me, and then, with a bit of hesitation, said, "Mom, you rarely told us about your life."

"I didn't know what to tell you kids, so I let your father do most of the talking."

I could tell from the sound of my mother's voice that this was a sensitive subject. These were not easy questions for her to answer. Feeling a need to go on, I asked, "Was it because you were so poor?"

"No, it wasn't that. Your father's family was poor too. But your father's family was white, and I was Indian. When I was growing up, being Indian meant being poor, being called nasty names, and being made to feel as if we were worthless. What kind of after-dinner stories would those have made? Remember, I always said, 'I'm Canadian.' I didn't want to be Indian."

I paused for a moment to think back. I could hear those words again. It was a disturbing memory. "I'm a Canadian! I'm a Canadian!" There was an insistence in her voice that made me feel uncomfortable and confused. I struggled with a word to suit the feeling. Her words were not an assertion of pride but a claim for self-respect.

I have lived with these words all my life, and only now am I beginning to understand what motivated my mother to make this claim. Mom always argued, "My father joined the army during World War II, and we gave up our Indian status – that meant that we were Canadians." I began to understand the contradiction. Being Canadian meant denying her Aboriginal identity. Other details started to come back to me. "I felt like you didn't want us to be Indian. Whenever anybody said something about our black hair you insisted that our hair wasn't black, it was dark brown. I always wondered what was wrong with having black hair. It was so confusing because we knew we were 'part' Indian, but we didn't know what that meant. The Indians we learned about at school and on TV were noble chiefs and pretty princesses who lived in tipis, rode on horses and carried bows and arrows."

"Those were not my stories."

"But Mom, we wanted to know, we wanted to know you. We wanted to hear your stories." As I spoke these words, I could hear a longing in my voice and recognized my desire to hear her story. I spoke again. "I remember you telling us a few stories about growing up on the reserve, and I remember that you took us to the reserve a couple of times. What was it like for you, Mom, when you were growing up?"

Audrey's Story
At the end of my day, I like listening to Aboriginal flute music. I turn out the electric lights, light a few candles and sink into my favourite blue chair. It is an old but sturdy chair, re-covered more than once. I can feel the new, soft, velvety material as my hands stroke the arms. I remember, when you children were young, walking into the living room and one of you would immediately jump out of the chair shouting, "Mom's chair, Mom's chair." I give the arm another soft caress and listen to the relaxing, even soothing sounds, of the flutes. The music evokes feelings of connection and I remember.

I was born on March 28, 1930, to Effie and Victor Tobias on the Moraviantown Indian Reserve and was named Audrey Angela. I never

Audrey's mother, Effie Tobias (née Dodge).

could figure out why my mother couldn't have put it the other way around. I always hated my odd-sounding name. I thought Angela would have been a much better choice. It sounded pretty.

Our house was set back from the dirt road, past a dried-out, scruffy lawn. It was a very small, two-storey, wood-frame house. The ground floor was one big open room. There was a table and a wood stove on one side and a bed for my parents and baby sister, Elizabeth, on the other side. I slept upstairs with my four brothers and other sister. There was a curtain dividing the girls' side from the boys' side. In the summer it was stuffy and hot, but the winters were cold. Lying in bed with my sister, I would try to ignore the cold, but the flimsy shingles rattling in the wind made it hard to sleep. The closest we came to insulation was the newspaper my brothers and I stuffed into the space between the walls and the roof. In the morning we would struggle, pushing the rickety old beds from one side of the room to the other. Stretching with all our might with fists full of newspaper, we tried to remember where the gusts of wind from the night before had blown in. The floor was just as bad. In the fall the whole family would work at collecting dirt to pack around the bottom of the house. This banking was supposed to stop the wind from gusting below the floorboards on cold winter days. But no matter how much newspaper and mud we packed in, it was impossible to keep the cold out of that house.

We grew most of our own food in a large vegetable plot out behind the house. In the spring, the ground had to be prepared and the seeds planted. One of my happy childhood memories is playing "Peter Cottontail" in the garden during the late summer. When the garden was in full growth, my sister Joan, who always played the part of Mr. McGregor, would try to catch me and my brother Ken sneaking food out of the garden. If she caught us, she would scare us, and we would run away. In the fall, the garden was a lot of hard work. We had to pick the vegetables and store them in the "dugout." We would be eating the potatoes, carrots, onions, squash, and turnips until just after Christmas, when the vegetables would run out and there was not much to eat. January and February were hungry months. For supper Mom would cook a pot of macaroni and mix it with a can of tomatoes. At breakfast we would sit around the table, watching her mix flour and water in a big bowl. She would take a wad of the gooey mixture in her hands, roll it into little strings, and drop them into a pot of boiling water. I called this stuff "slippery mush." With canned milk and sugar, it was good, but most of the time we had to eat it plain.

There were no jobs on the reserve. My father worked a few months of the year at a sawmill in town, and during the spring he fished, but there were many months when there was no work. During the winter I remember Mom was always busy weaving baskets. Dad would go into the bush and cut down a certain kind of tree. Then came the work of preparing the wood for weaving. I remember them cutting and pounding the strips of wood. The strips had to be soaked in the washtub for a couple of days, and then there was more cutting and splitting. When the strips were the right thickness, Mom and Dad would smooth the edges with sandpaper. Sometimes they would dye the slats to make fancy patterns in the baskets. Grandma taught Mom how to weave when she was little, and Mom taught us. We made laundry baskets, wastepaper baskets, and baby cradles. When we had a stack of baskets ready, Mom and Dad would go into town and sell them.

I knew that my family belonged to the Delaware Nation. What I did not know then was that Delaware is the English name given to my father's people. The original name of my father's nation is Lenni Lenape. My mother's family belongs to the Potawatomi Nation and she was from the nearby reserve on Walpole Island. I can picture my father and his friends sitting by the wood stove, singing in the Lenape language, but I never learned to speak Lenape. My father went to residential school, and when he became a parent he believed that it was best for his children not to know their own language and culture. He said that we needed to know the ways of the white world. My two older brothers went to the residential school at Muncey Town. I did not go to the residential school. We went to a small school on the reserve where the Anglican minister was the teacher. He was very strict and did not hesitate to use the strap. He taught us about the Europeans who discovered and conquered the Americas. We read stories about the white settlers who came and built a country out of nothing. The teacher and the lessons made us feel like nothing, as though we were nothing until the settlers arrived. It wasn't true. We had our own good way of living before the Europeans arrived. We knew how to take care of ourselves.

I was nine years old when I first moved off the reserve. Just after World War II began, my father and brother joined the army and were stationed in Petawawa. My mother took the rest of us kids and moved to a small town near Hamilton so that we would be closer to Dad and my brother Albert. There was work for Aboriginal people, doing manual labour on the farms in the area. Mom went to work on one of the farms and we kids went to a school in the town of Aldershot. The teachers at this school were not quite as bad as the minister on the reserve, but still we were made to feel that because we were Indians we were not as good as the white children. The white families owned the farms our parents worked on, and the tone of the teachers' voices let us know where we belonged on the social ladder.

When my father and brother joined the army, our whole family became enfranchised. This meant that legally we became Canadian citizens. Mom and Dad were eligible to vote, but we lost our Indian status and all treaty rights. At one point after the war had ended, we moved back to the reserve but stayed less than a year. As non-status Indians we were no longer entitled to a house on the reserve. We lived with Grandma for a while, but we really needed a house of our own. We moved back to Aldershot, and when I was nineteen years old, I left home and moved to Hamilton where I looked for work as a waitress.

After my family was enfranchised, I believed that I was no longer Indian. But being Indian was not something I could put on and off like a pair of shoes. Even if the Government of Canada no longer considered me Indian, the people I met in my day-to-day life were not willing to let me forget that I was. In those days there were places where I could look for a job and other places where I could not even consider applying. There were stores and restaurants I could go into, but there were many where I would not even think of going. Signs in storefront windows read, "No Indians Allowed"; in other places a look of disgust from the clerks was enough to send me back out onto the street. I finally found a job as a waitress at a restaurant owned by a

Lindy and Audrey Dion, Hamilton, Ontario, circa 1954.

Chinese family, and I worked very hard. I was determined to make something of my life. I wanted to be a part of Canadian society. I wanted to fit in. I needed to prove that I was just as good as or better than the other people I worked with.

I met your father at the restaurant where I was working. Lindy was a regular customer. He was kind and attractive, and he was white. The waitresses were scheming, trying to match Lindy up with one of their pretty friends. But Lindy often sat in my section and we would talk and laugh together while I served his food. I thought he was just being friendly. He was not Indian, and I never really believed that he would be interested in me. One night as I approached his table, Lindy stood up and said, "I have something to give you." When I asked, "What?" he kissed me. I think that our fate was sealed with that kiss. We started seeing each other regularly, and before too long we were married. I remember the Catholic priest who rather reluctantly agreed to marry us. When the brief ceremony was over, he mumbled, just loud enough for us to hear, "It'll never last."

But the priest was wrong. It did last. Life was not easy, but Lindy and I loved and supported each other for over fifty years. We lived in Hamilton until 1965, when your dad was offered a better job in a smaller city. We thought the move to a smaller town would be good for us, so in 1965 we moved to Sarnia. In some ways life in Sarnia was better, but in some ways it was harder. We were the only family of mixed race living in an all-white, middle-class neighbourhood. Some people were very friendly. Remember the couple who lived across the street? You kids always thought they were grouchy, but they always waved and said hello to us. Not like the family who lived up the street. They had two little girls about the same age as you, but those girls were never allowed to play with you.

Looking for a job in Sarnia was horrible. When I went to apply, lots of people just told me to get out. But I needed a job and I kept on looking. Finally, I got a job driving a coffee truck. It was hard. I felt like I was always working and always tired, but we had a home and a good life. I worked at that job for twelve years and drove a taxi for eight years before I retired.

I grew up at a time when Indians were considered savages who had no culture and nothing of value to offer me or anyone else. I was made to feel that to be successful I had to become a non-Indian. At home, at school, or at church I had no opportunity to learn about Indigenous culture. I knew nothing about Lenape language, history, and ceremonies. When you and your brothers and sister asked, "What was it like when you were little?" I did not know what to tell you.

The Braiding Histories Stories

Audrey with her brother George Tobias at Moraviantown, circa 1995.

But you wouldn't be discouraged. You and your brother kept asking questions. On Sunday afternoons, while I was in the kitchen baking with you kids at my elbows wanting to stir and pour and lick the spoon, you two would start again with the questions. My hands were busy stirring, measuring, and pouring, but my mind was free to think. Maybe it was the warmth and security in that kitchen, maybe it was the civil rights movement of the sixties and the rise of the National Indian Brotherhood. Whatever it was, while I prepared the cakes, cookies, and pies that you kids would devour, I began to realize that maybe there was something I could tell, that maybe it was important for you to know a little bit about what it was like for me when I was growing up.

It was hard for me, but that was when I began to tell you a few of the stories. When I look at you today, I see a commitment to family, a joy in the telling and hearing of stories, and a deep sense of responsibility to our ancestors. This is a part of our Indigenous culture that was not lost.

Today, I am a widow and live in Toronto, close to some of my family. Each night I listen to the music of the flutes and I know who I am.

Her Solitary Place[7]

Portrait of a Beothuk woman by William Gosse, 1841. Evidence suggests the portrait depicts Demasduit, but some experts believe it could portray Shawnadithit.

For five of the last years of her life
Shawnadithit lived with a family.
Was it her family?
Shawnadithit wore clothes.
Were they her clothes?

Shawnadithit learned a new language.
Whose language was it?
Shawnadithit was buried.
Was her body painted with red ochre?
Was she wrapped in birchbark?

Shawnadithit's Story

Shawnadithit spent the whole afternoon cleaning the Peytons' house. A couple of times she walked out the front door and sat on the steps, resting. Her energy was not what it used to be, and now there was this annoying cough that just would not go away. Shawnadithit had heard this kind of cough many times before; both her mother and sister had suffered with it until they died. Shawnadithit looked up to the sun; there was not a cloud in sight. She stared directly into the shining ball of fire and was momentarily blinded, but she found some pleasure in this forced darkness. *She could see herself in a canoe, paddling upriver, with her father in front. The banks of the river were lined with beautiful trees, interrupted only by grassy meadows. It was in one of these grassy meadows that Shawnadithit once lived with her family.* The vision disappeared as quickly as it came. As Shawnadithit stood up, maybe too quickly, she felt a little unsteady. Her unfinished chores waited for her inside.

Shawnadithit used all her strength to squeeze the rag dry; she watched closely as the dirty water slowly dripped into the rusted basin. The lye soap she used to scrub the floor made her hands burn and turned her skin to an ugly, blotchy mess. It was not the same colour as the beautiful red ochre that had once been used deliberately to coat her skin.

When she had finished her cleaning, Shawnadithit took one more long look around the house to be certain everything was in its proper place. She noticed that the wood she had put beside the fireplace had been toppled. Probably a mouse had disturbed the delicately balanced stack. It was a trick she had learned from her father, when she was a little girl. He taught her how to pile the wood awkwardly, so that if

Beothuk comb.

the wrong piece was chosen first, the entire pile would fall. This way you would know if some animal had been to your campsite while you were gone. It was a game she enjoyed playing with the children of the house. As Shawnadithit bent over to straighten the stack, the comb from her hair fell to the floor. She stared at it for a moment, remembering her mother, who had given the comb to her the first time she had braided Shawnadithit's hair. She picked it up and tenderly pushed it back into place. Feeling satisfied that her chores were complete, she left once again, out the front door, down the steps, not stopping to rest. She walked around the house to the back. The clearing behind the house stretched back at least thirty feet. Shawnadithit walked to the edge and began to gently spread the bushes apart as she stepped into the woods.

Shawnadithit knew that it was late in the summer. The cranberry bush that she knelt beside was full and ripe. Some of the berries had already fallen from its branches. Picking a few, she rolled them in the palm of her hand. She could feel their plumpness. She popped them into her mouth one by one, savouring the flavour. As Shawnadithit felt the burst of fresh juice she remembered a life from which she had been separated. *She was picking berries with her mother, little sister, aunt, and small cousins. They were searching for the ripe blueberries, partridge-berries, and marsh berries that grew in the fields. Together they worked to fill their birchbark containers to the brim. As they worked, Shawnadithit grabbed a handful of berries and as quietly and carefully as possible placed her full container down. She sneaked through the brush and, quiet like a fox, pounced on her little sister, squishing the berries into her hair. Shawnadithit looked to her mother expecting a scolding for playing when she was supposed to be working, and although she got the scolding, she also caught a glimpse of a smile. Mother had enjoyed watching the childish prank, but her protective spirit was constantly on guard. Shawnadithit listened to the scolding and recognized fear in her mother's voice. She was fearful that the noise of children playing might attract the attention of a white hunter. An encounter with the newcomers could mean capture or even death. Mother spoke to the children of the need to complete their work. Others in the village were depending on them to bring back an abundance of berries. While Mother spoke, she slyly took a single berry from her container. Turning back to her work, with a smile she tossed the berry to Shawnadithit, who caught it, rolled it around the palm of her hand and tossed it into her mouth.* Startled out of the daydream by the loud snap of a branch breaking under her foot, Shawnadithit had to think for a moment about where she was. The time of berry picking with her family was gone and she was alone.

 This pleasant memory of her childhood brought a small smile to Shawnadithit's lips, but it also came with an ache in her heart. Who would listen to her story of berry picking with her mother? Who would remember? This story, with the many other stories she had heard from her mother and father, would soon be lost, remembered by no one. Shawnadithit looked back at the Peyton house and decided to move on in search of her special place. The sun was beginning to set, but Shawnadithit didn't feel fear; she began to feel more at ease.

 Shawnadithit reached the clearing and could see the fallen tree with its huge trunk covered in a blanket of moss. Moving closer to the tree, she sat down, relieved to be in her favourite place. She felt

Beothuk canoe, cropped from John Cartwright's map, *A sketch of The River Exploits, the east end of Lieutenant's Lake and parts adjacent in Newfoundland*, 1768.

the damp coolness of the moss and then pulled the moss away to reveal the tree's bark. In Shawnadithit's mind, everything still seemed so clear. She missed collecting the bark from the trees and the work of moulding the bark into utensils and containers. Her hands were always busy. She had especially enjoyed watching her father use the bark to build canoes. Shawnadithit had an eye for detail, and her father would smile as she stood watching the canoes taking shape. Shawnadithit felt tired. Maybe tomorrow she would collect some bark and make a small canoe for the Peyton children to play with.

It was almost completely dark now. On a previous visit to this place, Shawnadithit had dug a deep trench beside the trunk. With the light of the moon guiding her, Shawnadithit began to remove the leaves and branches to reveal her precious sleeping spot. It was a space

Mamateek, cropped from John Cartwright's map, *A sketch of The River Exploits, the east end of Lieutenant's Lake and parts adjacent in Newfoundland*, 1768.

just big enough for her to lie down in. She curled up and pulled a blanket of leaves over her body to keep herself warm. The coughing started again and Shawnadithit could not sleep but lay thinking. Her eyes grew heavy and closed *and Shawnadithit felt the squirming of her little sister asleep beside her. She could hear the soft breathing of her parents and the buzzing of insects. She opened her eyes and saw the mamateek where her family slept. It was big and round, with long wooden poles bound together, covered with birch bark and deerskin. There was a fire pit in the centre. She shivered again and watched the curl of smoke from the fire rise to the opening at the top.* Shawnadithit heard the branches creak and felt a gust of wind blow through the trees. She closed her eyes again and waited a little anxiously for the voice of her mother to come back to her.

When Shawnadithit woke with the morning sun, she was hungry. Wearily she raised herself and found the spot on the tree where she had been peeling bark the night before. This time she dug a little deeper to get at the inner bark; she tore a piece, put it in her mouth and started to chew. The flavour of the bark was familiar to Shawnadithit. As she sat there quietly, Shawnadithit thought about the painful nightmares that had disrupted her dreaming. *There were no men asleep in the mamateek. Not her father, not her uncle. There was no food. She saw herself with her mother and sister, weak from hunger. They had left their camp and were walking toward the coast in search of food. Shawnadithit saw the terror in her mother's eyes. What was the price of survival? They had resisted with nearly every ounce of their energy, but sensing it was their last hope for survival, they gave themselves over to the white hunters.*

Shawnadithit could not escape her memories. She saw the faces of her aunts, uncles, and cousins. She recognized the face of hunger and disease and death. The newcomers had made these faces familiar to Shawnadithit. The stories that Shawnadithit heard around the fire changed from stories about her people to stories about the newcomers and the grief, hardship, and revenge they had brought. The men spoke about being robbed of their ability to move freely around their land in search of food. They talked about how the newcomers used their powerful weapons and hunted for more than was needed, stealing food from the Beothuk. The newcomers even used their weapons to kill the Beothuk. Shawnadithit remembered the blast of gunfire and rubbed her leg. She could sometimes still feel the pain from her own wound.

Shawnadithit dug for another piece of bark and remembered that when she was a little girl, there had always been food to eat. During the summer they had spent time on the seacoast. In a canoe her father had built, Shawnadithit and her mother would paddle to nearby islands to collect eggs from the wild birds that nested there.

The Braiding Histories Stories

Her father and uncle fished for salmon that would be dried on racks in the hot summer sun. In the fall, after the caribou hunt, the meat was hung to cure. She remembered visiting the storage mamateeks that stood along the banks of the rivers. Everyone worked together all summer long, filling them with food for the long winter season. There was even time for playing in the river.

The heat from the sun was beginning to get intense. Shawnadithit got up and began to cover her dugout with leaves. It was these trips to the woods, to her special place, that helped Shawnadithit live in a world that was not her own. Shawnadithit knew that she would go back to the Peytons' frame house. She understood that it was not hers. She would return to the family that was not hers, to a language that was not hers.

I Shared Their Anger[8]

Mistahimaskwa, in chains after his capture and the failure of the Riel Rebellion.

The charge was treason-felony and the verdict was guilty.
Mistahimaskwa, Chief of the Plains Cree, was sentenced
to three years in the Stoney Mountain Penitentiary.
Mistahimaskwa spoke in his own defence:
"I always believed that by being the friend of the Whiteman,
I and my people would be helped by those of them who had wealth.
I always thought it paid to do all the good I could.
Now my heart is on the ground."[9]
Mistahimaskwa fought for the rights of his people.
Why was he sent to prison?
Mistahimaskwa was not in my history book.
Why did I not hear his story?

On the morning of April 2, 1885, members of Mistahimaskwa's band went into the white settlement at Frog Lake and killed nine people. They then travelled to Fort Pitt and, after evacuating the fort, burned it to the ground. At his trial, Mistahimaskwa accepted responsibility for the actions of his warriors, saying, "Even as they rallied, I called to them, "Tesqua! Tesqua!" (Stop! Stop!). But they would not be stopped. They were angry and although I did not share their desire to shed the blood of the intruders on our land, I share their anger."[10]

When Mistahimaskwa spoke at his trial, he was not able to tell his story. But now, speaking to you, to Canadians who have come to inherit the land that once gave life to the Cree Nation, I (Susan) will pass on to you his story. It is the story that I hear Mistahimaskwa tell about his life and the events that led up to the attack at Frog Lake, in what is now Alberta, in 1885.

Mistahimaskwa's Story

Before going out on a hunt, I would go with my spiritual leaders to make an offering at the Iron Stone. At this sacred monument we would pray for a successful hunt, a hunt that would give life to our people. The Iron Stone was a protector of the buffalo and a guardian of the Cree because as long as there were buffalo there would be food,

Cree camp on the prairie, south of Vermilion, 1871.

clothing, and shelter for our people. But in 1866, the Iron Stone was taken away. Christian missionaries, who had no respect for our spiritual practices, loaded the Iron Stone on a cart and moved it 160 kilometres north to Victoria mission. When I saw that the stone had been taken away, I was angry. I heeded the words of my Holy Men, who recognized the removal of the stone as a sign of impending danger. Without the protection of the stone, our Holy Men prophesied that disease, starvation, and war would overtake our people. The prophecy of our Holy Men came true. Each year, more and more white people came to our territory, and their presence became a threat to our lifeways.

We were a hunting people, and our lives were tied to the buffalo. The buffalo was a gift from Manitou to the Cree, and we praised its spirit. We made use of every part of the buffalo: the hides became our clothing, the stomachs were used as bags, the bones and horns were made into tools, and the meat fed our people. I was a young Chief, but I had many lodges and people looked to me for leadership. I spoke with our Head Chief, Wihaskokiseyin, about the prophecy and the declining buffalo herds. We talked about the white hunters with their rifles who killed hundreds of buffalo, taking only the hides and leaving the carcasses to rot. Without the buffalo we could not survive, but for many of the white hunters, killing was nothing more than a sport.

Four years after the Iron Stone was taken, smallpox erupted in the Cree camps and spread like a prairie fire across the plains. Hundreds of our people died, and those that did survive were too weak to hunt. I was afflicted with smallpox when I was a child, and this time I did not get sick, but many people in my band died. When the worst was over, I sent scouts out in search of buffalo. When the scouts returned, they described what they had witnessed. Our land was desolate; entire families had been eliminated. They saw abandoned camps where the only signs of life were the wolves gnawing on the corpses of men, women, and children. I listened in horror to the stories of my scouts and the prophecy echoed in their words.

Fall came and we thought the worst was over, but because we had not been hunting through the summer, we could not move north to the protection of the woods. We were forced to spend the winter on the prairie in search of food. That winter, the herds did not come north, and we had to travel far to the south. There were a few scattered herds around the Hand Hills, and a large gathering of Cree had assembled there. Many council fires were held, and we talked about our conditions. We heard reports that the Hudson Bay Company had sold Cree land to the Canadian government, and there was a lot of talk about what we would do. I met with Chiefs Little Pine, Wihaskokiseyin, and Kehiwin. We did not know who or what the Canadian government was, but they must have heard about our meetings. They sent Missionary John McDougall with a message of friendship and goodwill. Head Chief Wihaskokiseyin expressed our response, saying, "We heard our lands were sold and we did not like it. We don't want to sell our lands; it is our property, and no one has the right to sell them."[11] He asked McDougall to tell the Canadians to come and meet with us. They refused, and our concern turned to anger. We were being ignored and our lands stolen from us.

The Braiding Histories Stories

In the fall of 1872, the buffalo disappeared, and we were once again forced to spend the winter on the plains, enduring harsh conditions with insufficient food to sustain our people. Some members of my band left in search of buffalo, hoping to kill a stray. Others returned to hunt and fish in the lakes north of the North Saskatchewan River. I moved the remaining members of my band into the South Saskatchewan River Valley, where we found some protection from the winter and a few buffalo. That year there was a frantic search for food. I can still see the thin, wasted bodies of my people, who were forced to eat their horses and dogs. There were times when we were so hungry that we tore our tipis and boiled the bits of hide to make a watery soup. I thought again about the prophecy of our Holy Men. We had known starvation before the white people came to our territory, but the buffalo had never before been so scarce.

We had lived side by side with the missionaries and the Hudson Bay Company men for many years. But this thing called the Canadian government was a mystery to us. Some of the younger Cree warriors wanted to fight. Many times, I had to speak to my warriors. I told them that we would not win against the white soldiers with their weapons and that fighting with the newcomers would not solve our problems. Each year more settlers were moving west, occupying our lands, killing our game, and burning the woods and prairies. We needed an agreement with the newcomers that would protect our land and the remaining herds of buffalo for our people. Again, George McDougall came to speak with us, and this time he had gifts to distribute. He told us that the government would meet with us the following summer, and in the meantime they wanted us to accept gifts of food, blankets, and ammunition. My people were starving, but I told McDougall, "We want none of the government's presents! When we set a fox trap, we scatter pieces of meat all around, but when the fox gets into the trap, we knock him on the head. We want no baits! Let your Chiefs come like men and talk to us."[12] It was not easy for me to walk away from food when my people were starving, but I would not be bought off with a few pounds of meat when our land and our freedom were at stake.

Cropped portion of *Treaty with the Saskatchewan Crees*, 1876.

    The following year, agents representing the Canadian government came to meet with us. But the agents had no intention of listening to our demands. They came with promises of food and medicine for those of us who would sign away our land and agree to live on what they called an Indian reserve. The agents said that the buffalo were disappearing and that Indians would have to give up hunting and make the change to an agricultural way of life. Our Head Chief Wihaskokiseyin had come under the influence of the missionaries, and he agreed to sign a treaty, but Chief Poundmaker was unmoved by the offers. He spoke for those of us who would not sign. He said to the government agents, "The government mentions how much land is to be given to us. He says 640 acres, one square mile for each family, he will give us. This is our land! It isn't a piece of pemmican to be cut off and given in little pieces back to us. It is ours and we will take what we want."[13] Conditions were desperate, but I was not prepared to accept the government's deal. I wanted a treaty that would protect the land and the remaining buffalo for the Cree. The treaty

The Braiding Histories Stories

that the Canadians were offering was no more than a rope around our necks. It would be the end of our freedom and turn the Cree into prisoners in our own land.

My band was growing. I had sixty-five lodges, more than five hundred men, women, and children. Wihaskokiseyin was still considered the Head Chief, and even though I had a larger following, I deferred to the elder. We were close friends and often consulted one another. Wihaskokiseyin would say that I was a dynamic and effective leader and that my band was destined to do great things. But the white newcomers had a different impression of me. The missionaries saw me as a pagan because I would not convert to Christianity. Government officials saw me as a troublemaker because I would not accept their gifts and sign a treaty. They were angry when I spoke to the Cree and warned them not to sign their treaties, but I was not afraid to voice my opposition to the Canadian treaty system. The treaties did not provide a fair exchange for surrendering our land and our freedom. We had no guarantees that we would escape starvation if we could not adjust to farming. I wanted something better. The buffalo were almost gone, and I knew that eventually I would have to deal with the Canadians, but as long as there were buffalo on the plains, I would not sign away our freedom. At the summer gathering, I told the government agents that I would wait four years, and during that time I would watch to see whether the government would faithfully carry out its promises to the Indians who had signed their treaties.

I met with the leaders in my band and told them that we would travel south in search of the remaining herds. We would wait four years and watch what happened with those bands that had signed treaties. I was not willing to give up our land until we had assurances that our conditions would improve. Again I had to argue for peace. My War Chief, Wandering Spirit, was anxious to fight. I had gained a reputation as a leader who would not give in to the whites and had attracted many young rebels to my band. My son Imasees was one of the most rebellious. He, like Wandering Spirit, was anxious to show the Canadians that the Cree would not give up easily. I managed to persuade my followers to hold back. I told them about a battle in my younger days when we were at war with our traditional enemies, the Blackfoot and the Peigans. Our enemies had been armed with rifles given to them by white traders. And again, the prophecy came back to me. War was the third element of the prophecy. It had been a warning. We had suffered great losses in our last battle with the Blackfoot, and I did not want to go up against the rifles of the Canadians. My warriors listened and we moved south.

Four years later, when the last of the buffalo were gone, pressure to sign a treaty was great. My people were starving, and many families had left my band and signed a treaty under other Chiefs. I travelled north to see for myself what the conditions were like for the Treaty Indians, and what I saw sickened me. "Two thousand Treaty Indians were camped near Cypress Lake, their skin tepees [*sic*] rotting and falling apart; families were living in makeshift shelters of cotton cloth and tree branches. Many people were emaciated and in rags, their moccasins worn out, their horses sold and even their dogs gone to make stew."[14] The transition from hunting to farming was not made easily, and the Canadian government had not yet kept its promises. As Chief I had to make a decision. Those bands that had signed a treaty received some support, but because I had refused to sign, my band received nothing. Tensions were rising, and still the consequences of signing weighed heavily. I was haunted by the words of the prophecy. I had taken the warning seriously and worked to prevent the loss of our freedom, but my people were dying, and my first priority was them. I signed my adhesion to Treaty 6 on December 8, 1882.

Signing the treaty increased the tension within my band. Many of my warriors were angry. They were angry at me for not signing earlier and for not arranging a better deal. They wanted to know why they were still starving. Many of my young followers again wanted to fight. I knew that we could never win a war against the newcomers and believed that the only way to pressure the Canadians into honouring their promises was to unite. I believed it would take the power

The Braiding Histories Stories

of a united Aboriginal assembly to force the Canadians to keep their promises. I travelled to other reserves, met with their Chiefs, and organized a grand council at Poundmaker's reserve, near Battleford. During this council, the leaders of twelve bands sent a message to the Canadian government protesting its failure to keep its promises. But the government continued to ignore us. We had agreed to sign treaties and live on reserves, but we were not willing to sit by and watch our people die from starvation. After the failure of the gathering at Battleford, many of my followers dispersed. I was left with a hostile core of young warriors, and their resentment smouldered through the winter.

In the spring of 1885, my people rebelled. I was away from the reserve on a hunting trip and returned late on April 1, 1885. Word had arrived only that day that Louis Riel and the Métis had been successful in a battle at Duck Lake. I knew nothing about the attack until after the first shots were fired at Frog Lake, and although I counselled peace, my War Chief was in command and I was unable to stop my warriors.

Mistahimaskwa at Stony Mountain Penitentiary.

After his trial, Mistahimaskwa said, "Even after the Iron Stone was taken, I always hoped that we could live in peace. We were not put here by the Great Spirit to shed each other's blood nor were we meant to control each other's lives. I believed that one day Canadians would recognize our rights to the land and respect our traditional lifeways. Did my faith in the newcomers cost me the trust of my people?"

I Am Wolastoqiyik (Maliseet) and No One Has the Right to Take That Away[15]

We were determined to seek our heritage.
We always knew what was happening was wrong
We just got to the point where we weren't going to take it anymore.

Acting in solidarity with the women in her community
Sandra worked to accomplish change.
She didn't do it for herself, she did it for all of us:
those who came before, those who are here, those who are yet to come.

When do you know that enough is enough?
What does it take to accomplish change?
What is courage?

Sandra Lovelace Sappier[16] headed for her uncle Louis's place, where people would be gathered for morning coffee. When she opened the door, heads turned but, rather than the customary greetings, the room fell silent. There were tears streaming down Sandra's face and it was impossible to tell if the news was good or bad. "It's over," Sandra said. "We are going to be reinstated." A holler of joy was raised and congratulatory words immediately spread around the room, directed not only at Sandra but at all the women who had worked ceaselessly to change the Indian Act. Caroline, Juanita, and Glenna were there, and so were Sandra's sister Karen and Eva Saulis. Eva was Gookum (aunt)

The Braiding Histories Stories   **157**

to most of the people in the room. She gave Sandra an extra-long hug and the look in Gookum's eyes was all the confirmation Sandra needed. It was June 1985. Parliament had passed a bill that was a first step in ending sexual discrimination against First Nations women.

When the celebratory hugging and patting of the backs was over, people rearranged their chairs and made space for Sandra at the table. Caroline's husband, Dan, poured fresh coffee for everyone and as the sugar and cream were passed around, the reminiscing began.

Sandra's Story

Looking out the window, Sandra watched the morning sun sparkling on the river. She grew up on this small reserve wedged between the Saint John and Tobique Rivers. Her ancestors called it Na Goot-cook – the river that flows swiftly. She breathed a long sigh of relief: all the years of fighting, all the trips to Ottawa, all the interviews. "Is it really over?" she asked. "Will I finally be able to claim my right to live here?"

Sandra relaxed in her chair and thought about that day seven years before, when Glenna Perley and Dan Ennis asked her to sign the official complaint against Canada that was being sent to the United Nations. She was so naïve back then – and scared. She looked across the table at her sister Karen and smiled as she spoke. "Remember how scared I was to sign that complaint? I thought it would get me into more trouble with the band council."

"Yeah, you were scared all right. But," Karen told the group, "she was more stubborn than scared!"

Laughter erupted around the table and Sandra replied, "Me stubborn? Whatever gave you that idea?" She went on more seriously, "But in the end, I realized that if it was going to help other non-status women, then I was going to have to do it."

The group gathered around the table settled back to listen as the two sisters told the story of the Tobique Women's Group and their working together to improve the situation for Indigenous women. Their struggle did not start out as a fight for reinstatement. It was about getting help for women and children in their community, and it had started as early as the mid-1970s.

"Sandra," asked Karen, "do you remember when we were kids, waiting for Mom to come back from seeing the Indian agent?"

"Yeah, the Indian agent was always giving her a hard time. One day it was freezing and there was no wood for the stove. It was December and we had no heat. Mom went to see the Indian agent about getting us some wood, and when she came back she was furious. I remember her saying, 'The men get all the help. The women don't get anything.'"

Sandra sipped her black coffee and winced as the scorching liquid reached her throat. "Before we knew it, we were the moms."

"And we were grandmothers," added Juanita.

"Yes," Sandra continued, "and the situation for women around here was worse than ever."

Sandra went on with her story. "When I came back home to the reserve after my divorce, I went to the chief and asked for housing for me and Christian, who was only two years old at the time. When the chief told me I had no right to a house because I wasn't Indian anymore, I was shocked. That was the first time I had heard of the status issue. No one told me before I got married that marrying a non-status man would mean I would lose my status. You should have seen the chief. He sat behind his desk and said, 'When you married that white guy, you became white.' I said to the chief, 'Look at me. You know who I am, you know I was born here and grew up here. What do you mean I'm not Indian anymore?' It was wrong. I knew it and he knew it!

"I lived with my sister for a couple of weeks, but an extra family created tension in her already crowded house. I took Christian and we lived in a tent, but when the weather started getting cold, I went back to see the band council about getting somewhere permanent to live. They only repeated what the chief had said: I was non-status and that meant I had no right to live on the reserve.

"I didn't know what to do, but this is my home and I wasn't going to let the chief or anyone else tell me I had no right to live here. I heard that the basement of the jail was empty, so Christian and I moved in there. There was no bathroom and no running water, but it was warmer and dryer than the tent. That was when the women occupying the band office approached me about joining the protest. I thought about it and said yes."

Glenna joined the conversation to explain how the Tobique Women's Group first got organized. "We took over the band office because conditions for women on this reserve were desperate and we were not going to take it anymore. That's how our group got started. It was because we were tired of the way women were being treated. Couples were always fighting, and men were always forcing women and children out of the family home because houses were always in the man's name. Elaine and her husband had been fighting on and off for a while. I'll never forget the night he told her to get out. Gookum and I went over to help her. Gookum stayed in the car and I went in. Her little girl was so confused. When we left the house, Jennifer looked up at her mom and said, 'Mummy, I don't want to go.' But that's the way it was. Houses were always listed in the man's name. And if a man felt like it, he could kick his wife and children out and there was nothing the woman could do."

Drawn in now to telling the story, Glenna went on, "We started to organize that very night. We talked to women and asked them to write out a description of the discrimination they had experienced. We sent these to the Department of Indian Affairs. We organized petitions and started protesting in front of the band council office. Next thing we knew, we were inside, occupying the office. We asked for a meeting with the chief, but he refused to meet with us. The chief and the band council hid behind the Indian Act and said there was nothing they could do because of the law. The men were happy to keep things the way they were and had no interest in helping women get better treatment. The Indian Act gave power to the men in the community, and the men had no interest in sharing that power."

Sandra started talking again and once she got going, people smiled and remembered the strength of her convictions. "A woman is not the property of her husband. That's what we were fighting against. According to the Indian Act, a woman's status is determined by her husband. If her husband is Indian, she is Indian. If her husband is white, she is white. The Indian Act erases a woman's ancestry. It doesn't matter where a woman was born, who her parents are, where she grew up, or what her experiences are. She is judged according to the status of her husband. That is what I could not accept. I was born Maliseet; I was raised in this community. Maliseet is my first language. This is where my family is. When my marriage ended, I brought my son home. I wanted to be close to my family, my community, my culture. Sure, I was scared when Dan and Caroline Ennis approached me about signing the complaint for the United Nations, but I said yes. By then I had realized how important the status issue was. Without status, I had no rights in my community. I could not get any help from the band. I couldn't even get a job – jobs were going to status women even if they were white women."

Karen's pride in her sister showed. She turned to face Sandra and said, "You may have been given the position of spokeswoman because you signed the official complaint, but you stayed spokeswoman because of your determination and commitment."

"Well," said Sandra, "it was like that for all of us. Once we started, our determination took over and there was no way we were going to stop. We had a lot of support in the community, but there were also a lot of people against us. When we started off with protesting, some of the women I'd grown up with would say, 'Hey, you don't belong here. Get out of here. You're non-status – a troublemaker.' It was hard to deal with the abuse, but I knew that what I was doing was right. I didn't care if they liked me or not."

"We had no experience organizing a protest," Glenna added. "We just learned as we went along. We supported each other and asked questions and kept working and working and working. We had to make Canadians understand what Aboriginal women were having to cope with. Our primary goal was to obtain better housing for women and children. We started out asking for a meeting with the chief, and when he refused we tried to arrange to meet with the Department of Indian Affairs in New Brunswick. But they wouldn't talk with us either. The Union of New Brunswick Indians met with us, but they wouldn't get involved. We felt like we were going in circles: Indian Affairs kept telling us that it was an internal issue and that they did not want to get involved, and Indian organizations either refused to talk or would tell us that their hands were tied because of the Indian Act."

"We were gaining public attention and support, but we weren't making any real progress!" Sandra said, frustration apparent in her voice. "Public support was great, but we wanted to see change. That was when Glenna got the idea to go to the United Nations."

Glenna nodded. "It was kind of strange, really. Everyone was over at my place talking one night when I thought of it. The idea just came to me. I asked, 'Why do we always just go to the Human Rights Commission? Why not go to the UN?' The next day a couple of us went to see Dr. Noel Kinsella, the chair of the Human Rights Commission of New Brunswick, for advice on what to do, and he helped us register a formal complaint. The United Nations accepted the case because we had no other legal recourse to follow in Canada."

"But we kept up the pressure at home," Karen said. "We continued our protesting, we began to lobby members of Parliament and even organized a protest march from Kanesatake to Ottawa. The march in July 1979 was a big event that increased public awareness, and it was during the march that Sandra really became a major spokeswoman for the group."

"Yes," Glenna added, "it was the reporters who focused on the status issue. Whenever any of us were interviewed, we were always asked about status. Reporters were surprised by the extent to which Aboriginal women were being discriminated against, and they continually wanted to talk to Sandra about the complaint to the United Nations."

Glenna continued, "Registering our complaint with the United Nations helped in a lot of ways. It brought international attention to our situation and put pressure on the government. Canadians were quick to condemn other countries for their failure to protect human rights but were not taking care of violations in their own backyard. It took a long time, but we finally heard from the United Nations in 1981. It found Canada to be in violation of the International Covenant on Civil and Political Rights. Canada was in breach of the covenant because the Indian Act denied Sandra the legal right to live in the community of her birth."

"It was a long time in coming, but we have accomplished change." Sandra's voice cracked as she spoke. Dan shifted restlessly in his chair. Others lowered their eyes as Sandra continued, "When we were kids, the nuns always favoured the fair-skinned kids. If you had light hair or blue eyes you got to do errands for the nuns, and stuff like that, you know. So I used to pray for blond hair and blue eyes. That was sick. We were ashamed of being Indian. It should have been the other way around. They should have taught us to be proud of who we are. When I first went to school, I could only speak Maliseet. I did not even understand English. But we were made to learn. We would get slapped for talking Maliseet, so you learned pretty quick to keep your mouth shut. We went to school on the reserve until Grade 6, and then we had to go to town. The town kids hated us. There was a lot of name-calling and a lot of 'go back to where you came from.' Even the parents tried to get all the Maliseet kids kicked out of the school and sent back to school on the reserve. That was when I quit school. I thought, 'If this is what the world is like, I don't want anything to do with white people.' I hung around for a couple of years, and when I was seventeen, I went over to the States to look for work. Some of my girlfriends were going and said, 'Why don't you come too?' So I left. I want things to be different for my children. If they grow up and choose to leave our community, that's fine, but I don't want them forced out and I want them to be able to come home when and if they want to. They are Wolastoqiyik (Maliseet) and I'm teaching them to be proud."

Note: On September 9, 2005, Sandra M. Lovelace Nicholas (Tobique First Nation) became the first Indigenous woman to be appointed to the Senate.

Good Teachers[17]

It was only a sign:
Indian Reserve
No trespassing.

But whose land is it?

With a quiet patience
Teaching and learning
he responds

Land is identity,
Land is strength,
Land is survival.

Jim was going to perform a smudging ceremony. He was in his backyard collecting small twigs and dried out leaves. It was a thoughtful process that had become a daily ritual for him. I (Michael) had not seen my brother for a long time and when he picked me up at the airport, I was immediately aware of a change. He talked excitedly about being back at school, where he was learning to carve and learning about his Indigenous history. I had never known Jim to be a reader or a carver and wondered about where his inspiration was coming from. Bernard Kerrigan was a friend and a teacher whose name kept entering into Jim's conversation. When I asked about the changes in his life, Jim replied, "I have had some good teachers. I think you should talk to Bernard. He'll tell you his story."

Bernard's Story
We sat at the table on the cement patio outside Jim's basement flat. Looking over at Bernard, I saw an imposing and dignified figure. I didn't feel intimidated by his stature but rather felt in awe of it. Bernard sat in the chair a little stiffly, his arms crossed in front of him, making his burly chest seem even larger than it was. His straight, dark hair

was tied back in a ponytail. Bernard knew why we were getting together for this talk. It was so that he could tell me his story. He was very serious; the story of someone's life is not taken lightly.

"Did you always know that you wanted to be a teacher?" I asked. Bernard smiled, "No, at one point I was sure that I would be a lawyer. I had a teacher at college who encouraged me, and I followed her advice. I graduated from law school at the University of British Columbia in 1987."

Bernard had liked the idea of being a lawyer. He saw it as an opportunity to help people in need, but there seemed to be too many incidents where his hands were tied and he was unable to help people change their lives. I sensed that he was frustrated with a system of justice that created situations in which justice is not served. Bernard spoke slowly and thoughtfully when I asked him to talk about the differences between his work as a lawyer and teaching.

"Law," he said, "is much like a manipulation game where you manipulate words and you manipulate people's lives. It felt to me like a big game with other peoples' lives and money at stake. Whoever can twist the words around the best wins. I didn't really feel that it accomplished much, whereas when I teach, I can actually see the students learning. When I'm working with a group of students, or sometimes even months after they finish classes, students come to talk with me about the different things that they have learned and what they are doing to improve their lives and the situation in their communities."

I reflected on the changes that I had witnessed in my own brother. Jim demonstrated a sense of confidence and strength that I had not seen before. I said, "Bernard, you get a lot back from your students, don't you?"

"Where I'm teaching now, I get a lot back." Bernard was teaching at the Institute for Indigenous Government. This school was started in 1981 by the Union of British Columbia Indian Chiefs to implement the principle of Indian control of Indian education. Bernard

The Braiding Histories Stories

taught at the school in Vancouver but also travelled to Vancouver Island once a week to teach a course called Fundamental Concepts of Indigenous Government and Nationhood at a reserve in Saanich.

Looking at his watch, Bernard said, "I have to pick up my wife, Lorraine, from work." We decided that I would tag along with him to the island on the following day. I could observe his class and we would have time to talk on the trip.

Bernard picked me up in the morning in his GMC four-by-four, a big vehicle for a big man, and he was right on time. We didn't speak much on the thirty-minute drive to the ferry terminal. The day was cloudy and there was a light drizzle falling, but still I was mesmerized by the beauty of the land. Shrouded in mist, the mountains held my gaze, and by the time we reached the terminal the sky had cleared and the sun was shining. After boarding the ferry, we headed to the cafeteria for breakfast. I had coffee and enjoyed the view while Bernard ate. There was a comfortable silence between us, almost as if Bernard was giving me time to appreciate this territory.

Arriving on the island, we had a twenty-minute drive to the reserve, and I asked Bernard about the course he was teaching. He explained that the students were encouraged to research and explore the meaning of Indigenous nationhood.

"The students need to understand Indigenous and non-Indigenous concepts of sovereignty," he said. "Right now, we are investigating the modern federal Indian Affairs policies and their impact on Indigenous communities." Bernard went on to say that the students at the Institute for Indigenous Government were learning about significant and immediate issues affecting their communities. For Bernard, the institute was about changing students' understanding of their role as leaders. "At the institute our objective is to prepare students for future leadership and students are encouraged to take what they've learned back to their communities."

Bernard began to talk a little about the other courses he was teaching, History of Colonization and Indigenous Resistance, and Decolonization and Self-determination. "In the course on decolonization, we talk about what it would mean for Indigenous people in Canada to be liberated," he said. "It is especially important to create a safe, supportive environment in this class. More than other courses, this class gives students the opportunity to talk about their personal experience of colonization. All the students agree that there is an overwhelming amount of pain when some of the social issues are discussed – issues such as alcoholism, physical abuse, suicide, and the mortality rate in Indigenous communities. Our students know that walls have been built around them on the reserve. Not concrete walls – something much stronger: walls of indifference, shame, and deprivation. There is a lot of anger and frustration when issues of Indigenous rights and Indigenous sovereignty are discussed. Our students are here because they want to help accomplish change. They are fed up with not getting any respect from the Crown, from history, and from both federal and provincial governments.

"Students come to the institute with lots of questions about why conditions for Indigenous people are so bad. Many of our students come to us thinking that the Department of Indian Affairs is doing Indigenous people a service by being there. Indigenous people in Canada have so much to learn about how the system works – about how the Department of Indian Affairs manipulates our lives and what our rights are and what we can do to take back control of our own lives. During my second and third years of law school, I studied different laws that affected my nation – the Haida. I looked at what the law stated and what the government has done. There are many instances when both the federal and provincial governments act in direct contravention of the law. As Indigenous people, we have to learn about our rights and know how to use the law to protect those rights. The Canadian government has not always acted in accordance with the law when taking control of Indigenous land. In the past, the Canadian government had control of education for our people. Teaching about the abuse of Indigenous land rights was not a priority. Indigenous control of Indigenous education was a critical accomplishment for the First Nations in Canada. Understanding how our land was taken and how we can take back control of our land and our lives is a major goal for Indigenous people.

"I really feel a sense of accomplishment when I'm teaching. My teaching technique might seem relaxed, but it is demanding of the students. I expect students to pay attention to what we're discussing in class. Students are expected to think about their own experiences and add to the discussion with comments and questions that make us all think about the topic. It might seem like we are only just sitting in a room talking, but there is work going on in that talk. I try to get my students to believe in themselves. I don't want them to memorize and recite theories. I want students who can think for themselves. That's why I like the open discussions we have. The thing about teaching is that you have a chance to change the world a little bit at a time. What is amazing is that I get the chance to help other people. I read somewhere that 'you can either make the world a better place to live when you're alive or a better place after you're gone.' I decided to work at making the world a better place while I'm in it."

I spent the day observing Bernard at work. He was right. On the surface, his class looked relaxed and easy. But following his suggestion, I watched and noted the way students listened to each other and asked questions, sometimes arguing with and other times supporting each other. On the trip back to the mainland I could see that Bernard was tired. I did not want to intrude, but still I had an important question. "Bernard," I said somewhat tentatively, "you've talked a lot about your commitment to teaching, and I saw it in the way you work with your students. Where does your commitment and strength come from?"

Bernard remained quiet and I thought that perhaps he was too tired to continue our talk. I looked out the window and watched the land. I was lost in my own thoughts and a little startled when he spoke. "I remember walking along the beach with my father when I was about six years old. I found a piece of black stone in the sand and holding it in my little hand, told my father, 'When I was big, I carved this stone.' My dad didn't question me. He just smiled and nodded. The Haida believe in reincarnation, and maybe my dad knew what I couldn't have known at that time, that carving would become important to me again. My grandmother knew for certain that carving would be important to me. Grandma saw in me her cousin Charles Gladstone. When I started doing my own carving, the dogfish became one of my favoured designs. It was only later in life that I learned it was also one of Charles's preferred designs as well."

When Bernard was seventeen, his Uncle Claude asked him if he would like to take a course in traditional carving. Art, especially carving, plays a significant role in Haida culture, and Bernard welcomed the opportunity to learn more about it. For Bernard, carving was simultaneously a source and an expression of his Haida identity. He still got most of his cedar from up on the islands; sometimes relatives would come back with gifts of cedar. Mostly he made masks, but had recently made a panel for the University of British Columbia. He had started working with silver about ten years before. "Silver," explained Bernard, "is a two-dimensional art, whereas the masks are three-dimensional."

Bernard comes from a long line of traditional carvers. He is the great-grandson of legendary Haida carver Charles Edenshaw and cousin to Robert Davidson, a master carver of totem poles and masks. In 1969 his family participated in a potlatch ceremony celebrating the raising of a totem pole in Masset carved by Davidson – the first pole raised on the Queen Charlotte Islands in over a hundred years.

"When missionaries invaded Haida territory, our identity, culture, and beliefs were replaced by Christian ideals. But with the raising of the totem pole, there was a re-awakening of our souls and our spirits. There was a reconnection with Haida values and beliefs." Bernard recalled the celebration. "There were certain songs and dances that had to be done, and the Elders told the young ones what our responsibilities were. Everyone was there to witness the raising of the pole."

This was an important celebration for the entire community, and it had significant impact on Bernard's sense of the nation and the rights of the people. During the time of the potlatch, another significant event took place. There were two lighthouses nearby, one metal and one wood, and some of the younger Haida cut the electrical wire that gave power to the lamps. It was the first time Bernard was aware of an act of civil disobedience on the islands, carried out in protest of the invasion of Haida land.

Bernard was born in Queen Charlotte City on the Queen Charlotte Islands (now Haida Gwaii). His family moved to the mainland when he was a baby. His mother was Haida; his father, who died when Bernard was eleven years old, was English.

"We visited the islands almost every summer and usually stayed with my grandmother," Bernard said. "I have a lot of cousins who seem more like brothers. They were responsible for keeping me entertained. I was responsible for keeping them busy and out of trouble. One day, when we were playing on the beach, we came across a sign that said **No Trespassing: Reserve Property**. My cousins were not concerned by the sign, but I was confused and deeply concerned. I wasn't even sure what a reserve was. I don't know, maybe it was a child's fear of getting into trouble. My mother's Indian status was taken away when she married my father. We were Haida but we did not have status – did that mean that I was trespassing? I couldn't be sure where the boundary was, but I tried not to cross that invisible line. The sign was a puzzle to me, and it stayed in my mind. Years later, I continue to think about and question the meaning of those words. Who put up the sign? Whose land is it? Who has the power to control the use of the land?"

Bernard's teaching was a response to that sign and the questions that it initiated. It was a response to our situation. "Haida lived on the land for thousands of years, and the land sustained us. Today multinational corporations are stripping the land of its wealth and taking that wealth away from the community of people who live on the land." Bernard acknowledged that there were many non-Indigenous people living on the islands and did not have a problem with this. He was, however, insistent that the wealth from the land stay in the community and support the people who want to live on the islands. Bernard had a deep love of the islands and the Haida traditions and wanted to see the communities prosper. He saw that the lumber companies were continuing to get rich from the land of the Haida. "Jobs are not going to the people in the community but to outsiders who come up and work and then leave," he said. "The lumber companies have no commitment to the community."

He spoke of his desire to be a part of a revolution that would see the lumber companies removed and the residents of the islands taking back control of their lands. His contribution to the revolution would be through teaching not only Haida but Indigenous people from across Canada who are part of the greater revolution that will see the rights of Indigenous people restored.

For Bernard it was not just that he was from the Queen Charlottes that kept drawing him back. "It's an incredible place," he said, as we neared Vancouver. "You have huge forests, huge trees and one of the beaches is over seven miles of sand. The mountains are on one side, water is on the other side." On his most recent trip to the islands, Bernard had experienced a feeling of belonging – not just to the people but to the land. A spiritual feeling – a feeling of affirmation. His people had been living there for over ten thousand years, and it was a place he would like to go home to.

> *Note:* Bernard moved to Haida Gwaii in 2000. He has retired from full-time teaching and continues his art practice, making jewellery and carving.

Who I Am[18]

I am strength.
I am love.
I am daughter, mother, partner.
I am a Black woman.
I am an Indigenous woman.
I am vulnerable, I am an educator, a seeker, a helper.
I am still learning who I am, still becoming who I am meant to be.

Toni Goree in front of her artwork.

In essence, storytelling is about who we are. I (Michael) had been tasked with interviewing Toni to ask questions and write her story. It was an honour to listen as she conveyed the experiences of her life to me. I don't know what I was expecting; some people find it difficult to tell their story, but that was not the case with Toni. She shared the details of her life with careful attention and love. In the telling she taught me about her resolve to know herself, to contribute to her community and in the process create a place of her own making.

The job of interviewing can conjure feelings of rigidity; lists of questions approved and double-checked, academic and work-like. Writing Toni's story was perfection; she is a woman of strength, tenacity, and honesty. A woman with humour – and, of course, no one is without complications. The account told here is *not* intended to evoke sympathy. Toni is a very strong woman who grew up Black in Halifax, Nova Scotia, and New Brunswick. Her Indigenous roots were revealed at an early age and set her on a path of discovery that eventually took her and her kids from coast to coast. Toni's story transcends the perceptions of many teenage mom stories. I tell her story not to make her shine but to show others how to see their stories in relation to where Toni is now.

The story, like Toni herself, is truthful. She did not shy away from telling about the hard realities of a Black/Indigenous woman's life. The story reflects complexity and reminds me why hearing a diversity of stories is a must. This is why getting to know Toni was so enriching. Her story added to the knowledge of life that I hold on to. In the telling of her story, Toni created moments when I could not say a word, when I knew it was time for me to listen, to hear, and to learn from and with her.

Toni and I had met briefly in a meeting of five or six members of a research team for the Listening Stone Project, perhaps four years ago; our interaction was minimal. For the Braiding Histories interviews, since Toni lives in Halifax and I live in Toronto, I would normally have made my way to Halifax for an intense, two-day storytelling session. Alas, it was not meant to be; it was 2020 and we were living in "COVID times." Toni and I had several long conversations on Zoom – *de rigueur* nowadays. As I listened to them a month later, I could feel a sense of camaraderie forming. There can be a fear of telling your life story; Toni was fearless. In addition, I began to feel the honour of the (re)telling of her story. During the sessions, questions were asked, and I listened, sporadically interjecting my thoughts, support, encouragement, and, of course, my humour, as I am wont to do. Hearing Toni laugh, or say "exactly," warmed my heart.

Toni's Story
Our first relationship is with our parents; from them we learn how to love and be loved. Lessons of sharing, contributing, being rewarded

with praises for a job well done, hugs and kisses, perhaps a new jump rope, or even a bike that you could call your own. My childhood was not picture-perfect; as much as I would like to paint that picture, it would not be accurate. I did know love. My mother taught me what it means to love deeply, and her love stays with me, inspiring me in all that I do.

I was born in Halifax, Nova Scotia, on March 2, 1955. I am sixth-generation African Nova Scotian, Mi'kmaq, and Maliseet. I also have Jewish ancestry.

When I was a girl, my mother did domestic work, cleaning houses of white families, really the only work available for a Black woman. Hands covered in sores from the abrasive cleaning supplies; I remember feeling such sadness, such helplessness. I was the oldest girl, so the way I could help was sharing some of her chores at home. This was not some joyful sharing experience of creating a "chore wheel" and taping it to a cupboard. This was the harsh reality of growing up poor and Black. I saw the sores. I saw that my mother was in pain. I remember feeling that twinge of anguish; I knew it must have been painful and yet she never spoke of it. I needed to help, and I felt as well that helping was a silent declaration of love. I began to feel that this created a connection, a special bond between me and my mom. I felt very close to my mom, a feeling of being in this together, creating a family together, providing and keeping a house together. On the other hand, I spent much of my childhood trying to get my father to like me. It never really happened.

Early on, I remember living in a really rundown house. I am not sure how my mom accomplished this, but she pushed every button she could to get us into public housing. That's one of the characteristics of my mom that I carry through my life – her tenaciousness to protect, feed, take care of family. I always remembered her ways and that helped guide me with my own family. Gratitude is not a strong enough word.

Our home was not always a happy place, my mom working so hard all day and my dad working nights and sleeping during the day.

We had to be extra careful not to awaken him; there could be no disruption of any kind. However, for some reason, birthdays were always celebratory: you got to choose your cake, and everyone sang "Happy Birthday" and you received a small gift. Christmas was another good memory. Mom always brought a tree home on Christmas Eve and we woke up to a decorated tree with presents and had a traditional turkey dinner. I love telling this story because it speaks to my mom's brilliance.

Growing up, I identified as a Black girl, and my mother and father identified as Black. I was born in Halifax, but when I was age four or five we moved to Spar Cove Road in Saint John, New Brunswick. When I was around age ten, we moved again to social housing – in what was then called the Rifle Range. School was okay; it was a place I could stay under the radar. Teachers paid no attention to you unless to scold or belittle you. It was in this period of my life that I started to feel the existence of God, and that feeling has stayed with me to this day. I started to go to church with neighbours, as my parents showed no interest in attending. I felt safe in the church.

I have early memories, maybe I'm ten years old, of us in the community being Negro and then Coloured and then Black. My mom and auntie were having rousing arguments around the kitchen table. Mom was very light skinned. She leaned to the radical side and was pro-Black. It was the height of the Civil Rights Movement. Muhammad Ali, Malcolm X, Dr. Martin Luther King Jr. Mom would say, "I'm Black," and her sister would say, "I'm Coloured," and the yelling would commence.

I believe my mother was a forerunner, claiming Black as her identity, and my auntie was staunchly conformist, "don't rock the boat," cautious. These boisterous evenings, when conversations went on for hours, were coming from a very politicized time in our community.

Some of these kitchen table conversations included my father saying to my mom, "Norma, why don't you go to the reserve and get a house?" He asked this in a playful manner, which was quite strange and not his usual tone. I always thought my grandmother (maternal) looked a bit different. I knew nothing about "Indian People"; we didn't learn anything at school. I did not ask any questions, but this did stay with me. I did not explore this curious illumination of my family history until later in my life.

I was very young when I became pregnant with my first child and my dad put me out of the house. I had to figure out how to survive on my own. My mom rented a room for me in a rundown house. I had my daughter, Dawn, on my own. At fifteen, I called a taxi and went to the hospital and delivered my baby. One of the scariest moments of my life. As a teenage mother, I depended on my mom and my siblings, who were looking after the baby more and more frequently. Taking care of a baby, living for, always having to give for a child, was difficult.

My life was in total disarray at this time. I was a troubled teen mom, poor and with few supports. My home environment had been abusive, and alcoholism was rampant; as a teenager I found myself floating, doing drugs, drinking, bouncing around trying to survive. By the time I was thirty I had six children. It wasn't some grand notion of sexual freedom. Looking back, I can see that I spent a number of years seeking acceptance, favour, comfort. I was looking for my prince, a man who would provide me with that picture-perfect life.

My difficulty in finding "place" was a constant companion, by my side for every decision I made. I wanted to be a success. I struggled to achieve a better life for my children, a life for them that had choices and possibilities. During this time, as I had done with my mom, my oldest daughter, Dawn, took on many responsibilities, and her immense help relieved some of the pressure on me. I know I can't make it up; my years of therapy taught me that. The responsibility I feel for the pain I caused my children resulting from my too-often thoughtless choices can be overwhelming some days. Also, poverty was part of my family's life for decades, but now something has shifted and we have worked our way out. I am not abandoning that part of my life, not running from it. I have no qualms about talking about it. I can't erase it. While I don't have much in the way of savings, or my own property,

I don't have to worry about rent or putting food on the table. My life today is a reawakening, independent working out, or working through, the many manifestations of my life. In my life right now, I strive to treat people with the highest respect.

I managed most of my young life as a single mom, struggling, regularly on some sort of assistance. I didn't have great expectations of my children's fathers; child support from them was practically non-existent. I found jobs as a server in restaurants and at night clubs, I worked long and I worked hard. In the late 1980s, I went back to school: Dalhousie University. This was a true challenge of resolve. Perhaps the "place" I had been searching for was school.

I always felt the presence of God in my life, and my spirituality helped me through some very difficult times. I felt I was not just put here randomly; I was supposed to do something. It was my academic career that enabled me to pursue some meaningful way of being, of contributing and finally breaking the cycle of poverty. I want to work with youth. I think the education system needs to step up. We don't appreciate how much we need to tell youth to keep them safe. It's not enough to get some sex ed in high school, because it's more than that. If you are a kid walking around with a hole in your heart from emotional or physical abuse and lacking self-esteem, you are going to gravitate toward certain situations, lifestyles, that are detrimental to your well-being.

It took me seven years to complete my bachelor of arts in international development studies. All of my children sacrificed so much for me to earn my BA. While we were going through it, I could not help but wonder if the benefit was worth my not being there for them. My mom came to the graduation ceremony, and she was very proud, and my kids came. I was attending one of my final classes when I met Lynn. She happened to live close to me and we started to walk home together. These walks included many questions, lots of smiling and laughing, really getting to know each other. We were having such a good time that I barely noticed she was white. But how was this going to fly with my kids? The community? I started to have serious feelings

Toni Goree with her mother at her graduation from Dalhousie University.

for this woman, and they were reciprocated. I allowed love into my life, and how could that be a mistake? These walks home turned into a twenty-five-year relationship. The twists and turns in my life are never-ending, right? Now I'm bisexual, ta-da!

There had been some very violent crimes in our neighbourhood and talk of abductions of young teenage girls. True or not, I was fearful for my girls. I decided to leave town and get far away. We moved to Vancouver. From coast to coast we went, much to the chagrin of my children. They were so angry. My oldest, Dawn, was living in Toronto and had a beautiful son. My next daughter, Jill, refused to go; she had her high school life and community in Halifax. I did finally acquiesce, and she stayed behind. Shortly after I arrived in Vancouver, I got a job at the Downtown Eastside Women's Centre as a legal advocate. At the time I worked there, in 1992, Indigenous women were *missing* and we were marching about it. But none of the authorities cared or did any-thing. It was a hard time.

While in Vancouver, I began engaging in ceremonies. I attended Hey-Way-Nogu Healing Centre. That was where I had a breakthrough in healing. I came to understand how my father's rage and abuse had shaped my perception of my self-worth. This was a turning point in my life. I finally felt I knew who I was. I am sixth-generation African Nova Scotian, urban Indigenous, Christian, Two-Spirit mother and grandmother. My time in Vancouver was a time of healing; through smudging, sweat lodges, and Elders' wisdom, my Indigenous spirituality has found a place beside my Christian spirituality. I am fond of saying, "Don't put me in a box, I can be many things." The box is a trap. Breaking out of the box gave me choices and possibilities. And believe me, you have to fight to get out!

We lasted three years in Vancouver, but we were all missing family, friends, and community in Nova Scotia. I missed my mom, and her health was not great. My kids missed their grandmother. So we packed up and moved back to Halifax. We landed back in the North End.

The younger kids were finishing high school. Now I had time for me, so I enrolled at Mount Saint Vincent, and in two years I had an education degree. I started working as a teacher in the public school system. It was not a long teaching stint. In order to fulfill my desire to continue learning, I applied to the master of education program at York University, in Toronto. I was accepted. This was an opportunity I could not pass up. I feel so strongly about this degree – not so much the piece of paper, but the learning, investigating, enriching my knowledge. I aimed to do it through an Indigenous lens; I wanted to understand Indigenous epistemologies and methodologies.

We moved to Toronto and I began my course work for the MA. We broke up, and I was emotionally devastated as well as economically busted. This prolonged my program. This time in my life was plain hard. I felt like I was blindfolded and spun around, just struggling so badly. But I managed somehow to regain control of my life. I was introduced to the associate dean at Georgian College, in Barrie, Ontario. They were looking for someone to teach a course in the Indigenous studies program. My résumé was a good fit, and I was hired, thank

Toni at her graduation from York University, 2015.

goodness. Here I need to mention my friend Arlene McKenzie. On one of my bleakest days, I dropped into the Barrie Native Friendship Centre, walked down the hall and sat in an empty chair outside an office. Arlene popped out of the office, took a long look at me, and said, "Come on inside." She lit a smudge bowl, we smudged and she said, "Okay, tell me the story." What a comfort and spiritual lift. We are friends to this day.

While teaching, I got a room in exchange for agreeing to do some work. I did some painting. To supplement my food, I joined the community garden. This got me through to graduation; it was 2015 and I had earned my master's degree. I made my way back to Halifax.

Today I'm doing my PhD in health at Dalhousie University and helping to coordinate a community-based health project with Indigenous youth in Halifax. I want to have a positive impact, creating policies in our schools for Indigenous youth, African Nova Scotian youth, and newly arriving immigrant youth. I've worked for the school board and I've worked for the Department of Education, and we've created all kinds of policies. However, I think that for the kid sitting at their desk on a Tuesday at eleven o'clock it just feels the same. We haven't accomplished the kind of significant changes that offer them a life of well-being.

The policies and changes that I hope to make include creating opportunities for youth to be free to claim all of who they are, their Indigenous, Black, French, Asian, and mixed ancestries and all their ways of knowing, being, and doing. I especially want African Nova Scotian youth to reclaim their Indigeneity and vice versa. Not for some government status but for their spirit.

Afterword

Today my kids have all reached high levels of success. They are teachers, administrators, managers, actors, and stay-at-home mothers, and several have university degrees. All are good and honest people who stand up for social and economic justice. They have families of their own and I have nine wonderful grandchildren and one great-grandson. I am grateful beyond measure.

What I Do and Who I Have Become[19]

Stories of friendship,
Stories of school, learning, and good teachers
Stories of family, community and being Mi'kmaq

I work hard
It is not always easy

I am always thinking
Talking to people, reading books,
putting myself out there
learning more.

You do life for yourself really
People say it is for someone else,
But it comes down to you
You decide

Oonig Paul Ward at Membertou, 2019.

Oonig Paul Ward is a cook, heritage interpreter, and Mi'kmaq Grass Dancer. His first home was in Metepenagiag, on the north shore of the Miramichi River, in New Brunswick. Oonig started visiting Membertou on Cape Breton Island when he was fourteen, and now lives and works in this close-knit, vibrant Mi'kmaq community.

 I (Susan) met Oonig in the gift shop at the Membertou Heritage Park. He had finished work for the day and popped into the gift shop to visit with his friend Andrea, who works at the shop, and to see who else was around. I visit the heritage park whenever I am in Cape Breton. My partner was born and raised in neighbouring Sydney, and we visit her parents most summers. I had met Oonig's brother Tyler and his dad, Jeff, on previous trips. It was nice to meet Oonig this time. I was taken by his welcoming spirit and positive energy, and especially his commitment to working at the heritage park. When I told him about our book project and asked if he would be interested in sharing his stories, he tried to put me off, saying his brother or friend, or maybe even his dad, would tell a better story. When I explained that no, it was his story I was interested in hearing, he agreed to give it a try. "Let's see how it goes," he said. "Let's see if we are comfortable with each other?" We agreed to meet the next day.

 On a very sunny August afternoon, we sat on a picnic table at the heritage park. We shared stories, laughed, and talked for almost two hours. We took breaks, Oonig got us some water to drink, and we shifted our seats around the yard, searching for patches of shade. We were both hot, but the conversation was lively, and neither of us wanted to cut the session short. At the end of the visit, Oonig decided it was working. He had stories to tell and wanted to be a part of the Braided Learning book. I was happy to spend time with this young Mi'kmaq man and to hear his stories, told with good humour and sincerity. He likes to laugh and joke, but his commitments to family, community, and nation are deep. He is outgoing and easygoing, but don't be fooled: he is serious about living a good life and making a contribution.

Oonig's Story

When I was a kid, my friends and I would ride our bikes to the woods, and we'd go searching for garter snakes and tadpoles. The woods were all around here. I wasn't the most popular kid in school, but I always had three or four good friends. We'd take a pail and see how many snakes we could catch in one day. We'd ride our bikes around and just kind of get lost in the woods. Not really lost, but lost in our own adventures. In the end, we would let the snakes and tadpoles go; the point was to see how many we could catch.

My earliest memory is of living in a house with my mom and my dad. We lived in Metepenagiag. When I was just a little kid, maybe four or five years old, my mom and dad separated. My dad had a house in Metepenagiag, and my grandfather moved in with us to help raise me. And then I was always travelling back and forth, weekdays with my dad and weekends with my mom at Esgenoopetitj. I started going to school in the city of Miramichi; it was between my mom's place and my dad's place. I went to school there for about four years. I have good memories of that time in my life when I was living with my dad and my grandfather. My grandfather was a loving caretaker, a hard worker, and he was always kind to me. He was a giving person who would always lend a hand.

New Brunswick is a bilingual province and the languages spoken are French and English. In a Mi'kmaq community from Grade 1 to Grade 3, you learned Mi'kmaq. You also learned at a very young age that once you go off the reserve, maybe to a town school, you're not going to get that anymore. Now in schools they will give you a Mi'kmaq course, but at the time when I was in school, when you were off the reserve, you were expected to speak French or English. Just as you were developing your language, you were cut off from it. As an adult, I'm still learning, and sometimes I get caught off guard by the young ones who can actually speak in sentences and recite our prayers and songs. They are just so great at speaking our language. It is a phenomenal feeling, you are so taken aback that they learned it, they earned it – good for them.

Nmultis

"See you again."

Pjila'si

A welcome mat with the word *Pjila'si* on it.

A traffic sign at Membertou. ▶

I learned to speak a bit of Mi'kmaq while I was going to school, but when I left school, I did not have much of a chance to speak it. If you don't have a chance to use the language, you start forgetting it. It takes time, focus, and commitment to relearn our languages. At Membertou we have classes, and we use the language as much as we can. We use the word *pjila'si* (it means "come in"), *nmultis* for "see you again," and of course *NAQA'SI* means "STOP." Some of our Elders say it is like our language has been sleeping and it is our job to wake up the language by using it. The more we use it, the more awake it becomes.

Being in school was good. I had some good teachers. In Grades 2 and 3, I always loved my Mi'kmaq language teacher. In Grades 4, 5,

Oonig in his regalia.

and 6, there was this one teacher who would always take all the Mi'kmaq students and tutor us. She was the teacher who always had that extra time for teaching and helping us. She was really good; she taught me Mi'kmaq, treaties, language, culture and – things that I would grow up with to use today, really. She taught us about the seven Mi'kmaq territories and history, and the Donald Marshall Jr. case that upheld our treaty rights to hunt, fish, and gather. The seven sacred teachings: love, respect, courage, honesty, wisdom, humility, and truth. We learned about the Peace and Friendship Treaties of 1760 and 1761. We still honour and uphold those teachings and traditions. It is such a good thing that we were taught our own history. Now when we see people with their drum, people with regalia, we know what it is about because they taught us in school and it is a part of our lives. I remember learning about leadership. The symbol on the drum is a teaching about government and leadership in Mi'kma'ki. The seven hills represent the seven districts; the seven crosses are the seven district chiefs; and the moon and sun in the centre are there to remind us of Kisulkw – Creator.

When I finished high school, my dad wanted me to continue my studying. He wanted me to have a solid education so that I could have a great start in life. I chose to study culinary arts at Nova Scotia Community College. It was a two-year course, and I did an extra year to bump up my grades. I decided on culinary arts because I liked cooking and I wanted to develop my skills. One of my favourite creations is the lavender blueberry sorbet. I learn from recipes in cookbooks and online and then try it out on my own. In the program, the hardest part was doing a menu. I was nervous because I had never done it before, and I was scared to mess up the entrée. The difficulty was that I lacked experience, but I grew into it and got better at it. Nothing about this was easy for me. It was a real challenge. The problem I encountered was that I couldn't get the entrée to my liking. My results were not matching my expectations. I overcame the problems with a lot of practice. The most rewarding part was seeing it through to the end and never giving up.

I started learning to dance when I was very young. I had a lot of energy when I was a kid. My aunts didn't even want to take care of me because I was a bit hyper. I enjoyed being on the powwow trail and getting to run around and visit. I still like meeting and talking with people; if you want to keep learning, it helps to address yourself to people and see what you can learn from them. If you don't take the risk, there is no reward.

I am a men's Grass Dancer. I used to be a boy's Fancy Dancer but don't specialize in that style now. I was four when I started going to powwows and learning about being a dancer. My dad used to take me. I loved travelling across our territories to different powwows to see other dancers and different styles, and learning how to craft my own style. But when you are at school, it is hard to keep that secret. You might quietly say to some people, oh, I do powwows, but most of the time you kept that part of your life separate from school. People are more open about it now, but when I was growing up it was best to keep it quiet. I used to do that, going to celebrations, being a dancer, and keeping it a secret.

To be a Grass Dancer you have to be physically strong and confident in yourself and be able to pay attention to the people you are dancing alongside. I dance to know myself. It is a way of building the fire within; it is also a way of passing on my knowledge. Grass Dancers go out first; we are like the young scouts. It is our responsibility to prepare the space. We pound down the grass, making sure there are no negative spirits, making sure there are no rocks so that everyone who follows will be able to dance safely. Being a dancer is excellent. It is beautiful. It is also serious. You have to love and respect yourself and respect that you are doing it. I enjoy sharing my craft, when people witness powwow dancing, they learn about our culture. People need to visit our communities to learn from us.

Of course, I have good teachers – my mom, aunties, and grandmother. It is difficult to put into words what they mean to me because they are life-givers and protectors. They taught me to be comfortable with myself, to accept myself, to take life one day at a time. I have so much love and respect for my father, for everything he does as a community leader; my goal is to be like him one day. I love learning about my culture, language, and teachings, and keep that at the centre of my being – learning for myself, to know who I am and also to pass my learning on to others.

Being part of the community and helping out is important to me. I don't have a car but get around and help out with whatever is going on, doing whatever needs to be done. If there is a Sacred Fire and someone needs help to watch it, I often step up to help out. A Sacred Fire is lit at the opening of a powwow, to honour someone's life, or for other ceremonial purposes. An Elder lights the fire and conducts

A sample of Oonig's beading.

the prayers, and we sing a song to invite the spirits to come to watch over us and protect us during the gathering. When the fire is lit, people offer tobacco to the fire with their thoughts and prayers. My role is to watch over the fire, to keep it going until the Elder's closing. The Sacred Fire is to honour our ancestors. It is sacred prayers and songs that start the fire, and once the gathering or ceremony is complete, we give thanks and send off our ancestors in a good way.

I remember when I was little and my mom was washing the dishes, I would get the kitchen chair and push it over to the sink and climb up on the chair so that I could help her. My mom would wash the dishes and pass them to me so that I could rinse and dry. I would stack the dishes on the counter because I couldn't reach the cupboards to put them away, but I liked that, standing on the chair, helping my mom. Grandmothers, mothers, aunties – I always have strong people in my life, teaching me about life. At a young age, I learned to appreciate who I am and to feel gratitude, love, and joy in my life.

People always say they are working hard for their mom or their dad, always wanting other people to be proud of them, but really when it comes down to it, you're doing it for yourself. I'm not going to lose my way; they will always be a part of me, no matter what. When you take a look at what you're doing, it's still a good thing, knowing who taught you what you learned. I learn in different ways from different people. I inherited my father's regalia, and it is my responsibility to take care of it and use it. Still, I am also thinking now about starting work on making my own regalia. I have many teachers and mentors, but mostly I learn by watching others, asking questions, and trying things out.

Oh Dear[20]

Oh dear – could be whispered under her breath.
Oh dear – could be said with a force that sent us running.
Oh dear – could be sighed with a hint of shame.
Oh dear – a familiar sound of exhaustion.
Oh dear – a beautiful dress, sewn to completion.
Oh dear – cannot be said without bringing back the memory of Mom.
Oh dear – braids our stories together, my grandmother, my mom, my children, and me.

Liz's Story

Algonquin Park. It wasn't always a park. It was simply a place where the Algonquin People lived in harmony with the land; no gates, no permits. I shall start my story there. My husband, Ryan, our son Caelan, and I were on a canoe trip. We couldn't have asked for better weather: a slight breeze was helping to push the canoe, and the sun was shining, highlighting occasional big fluffy clouds. Ryan and I would lay the paddles gently in the boat and just start drifting over the glistening water and ask Caelan, "What do you see in the clouds?"

This was not a new game – but still, a fun one for sure. Clouds bunched, clumped, dancing in the air, creating unique images as the wind altered the shapes. Caelan always saw our dog, always. I suspect he wished Indy were with us.

Our campsite was not far from the water's edge. Caelan suggested to me a stone-skipping challenge, and I was definitely up for it. After skipping a few stones across the calm, sleek water, I noticed a bird flying in circles above. I could hear a quiet little *click*, *click*, so I started to make gentle clicking sounds, and Caelan joined in. I held my arm up, and just like that the bird landed on my outstretched hand. I whispered to Caelan, "Put your arm up." Without fear, he raised his arm, and the bird flew to his hand. Caelan was quietly oohing and aahing; then the bird flew away. That was one cool nature experience for both of us. It is a story to tell and retell.

The experience stays with me. Recently, when I connected with a cousin back in Saskatchewan, I learned that the bird, a whisky jack, was my late grandmother's favourite bird. She called it Napuakan, loosely translated as her "spirit bird" or "dream bird." I like to think she sent that bird to us that day.

My name is Liz Hall, and I am a woman of mixed race. Other than the blood quantum that I have from my Cree family, I have very little that connects me to being Cree. I know very little, actually, and ask myself, am I truly an Indigenous woman? In a haze about what cultural and ethnic identity is, I feel different each time I am confronted with the question. Having to specify who and what I am initiates complex and sometimes uncomfortable emotions. Growing up, I recall my mom would often say, "that's the Indian way," especially about hospitality. She reminded me how Indian people love to laugh and joke, which seemed to be contradictory: my mom was not much of a laugher or joker. Yet, with all my mother's sternness and practicality, when she reminisced, I saw a hint of a smile. I live by these messages that she passed on to me. Therefore, am I Indigenous? I feel like a poser sometimes, not having lived the reserve life; therefore, I'm not.

However, if I listen to the drum, I feel it deeply; it speaks to me. Thinking about my mom and the life she lived can bring me to tears. Consequently, I am?

Life has many instalments, dividers, periods, even moments, each one with its difficulties – challenging, teaching, shaping us. There have been several significant phases in my life, and nothing can be recounted without a bit of history. My mother, Maryann, was born on Cree territory in Saskatchewan, December 27, 1923, at Stanley Mission. It was a community ideally situated for trapping, near water for transporting and fishing. A canoe was needed to get there from the nearest town, Lac La Ronge. As is the case for many, my story is intertwined with, braided with, my mother's and my grandmother's lives and experiences. The maternal line is strong, resilient, enduring.

The youngest of three, I have two older brothers; however, I was separated by more than fourteen years from my brother Donald and eighteen years from the oldest, Stephen. While I am the youngest of three, my mother was the eldest of twelve. She was my grandmother's firstborn, and she was born before my grandmother was married. My grandmother never told my mother about the man who was her biological father. It was never revealed and was never even a topic open for discussion. My grandmother did eventually marry. I think it was soon after my mom was born. My grandparents had eleven children together, and although my mother called him dad, she always knew that he was not her father.

At an early age, because of the Indian Act, my mom was taken from her home and community to an Indian residential school that was miles away. Mom remembers that she was young but does not know the exact age at which she was taken from her home. Memories of these early years are hard to recall, and even harder to share. She does remember thinking that her mother let her go because she was not wanted. As a young child, my mom could not comprehend that it was the government removing and isolating children, deliberately separating us from our real families, denying us our culture and traditions. My mother, like generations of Indigenous children, did not have the chance to learn from her family and her community. The trauma of being taken was something she would endure for her entire life.

Despite the hardships, or perhaps as a coping mechanism to survive residential school, my mom developed a charming personality. She told me stories about her classmates, who all called her "cutie." Eventually, my mom was adopted out of the school, along with three other children who were siblings from the same family. They were adopted by the Chief of Muskaday and his wife and were moved from the school to a farm on a reserve in southern Saskatchewan. It was a community even farther away from her home, and once again, my mom was on her own: one of four children adopted, but not really a

Liz's grandmother Betsy McLeod at the family summer camp. The people in the photo are identified (from left to right) as Adam Charles, Minnie, Rosie Charles, Jane (Charles) McKenzie, Mary Charles, Hannah Charles, baby (identity unknown), two children (identity unknown), Lydia Mirasty, Florence Charles, Betsy McLeod carrying Amy Milne, and Josiah "Joe" Mirasty.

The Braiding Histories Stories

Liz's maternal grandmother Betsy (outside the tent), with members of her family and members of the Kemp family en route to Stanley Mission to help repair the church's steeple in the early 1920s. Betsy nannied for the Kemp family.

Betsy with two of the Kemp children soon after she became their nanny.

sibling to the other three, who were connected by blood and birth. Her home at Stanley Mission seemed worlds away.

Mom spent many years on the farm with her new adoptive family. Later in life, she shared stories of life on the farm with a student who was interviewing people for a school project. I listened to the interview. My mom described the hard work, the endless chores, which were tedious and tough – fetching water from the well, washing, ironing, setting the table, doing the dishes, milking the cows, churning butter. They were the ordinary, mundane chores of farm life. Mom was a good storyteller, conveying the day-to-day details; her voice softened when she spoke about her love of the farm animals and then rose again, telling stories of the northern lights. She was fascinated and fearful of these celestial light shows. She described the lights cascading like a waterfall, bright blue, pink falling into white, sometimes feeling like they could envelop the house. Mom told and retold these stories over the years, always the most pleasant tales that served as proof that her childhood was a happy one. Her formative years passed by on the farm. My mother did reconnect with her biological family when she was a teenager, re-establishing a relationship, but I think it was kind of forever strained because of all of those lost years.

In 1942, my mom left the farm. The war was raging in Europe and was the topic of conversations in small towns all over the country. Mom, who had always had a strong sense of adventure, joined the military, expecting a whirlwind to follow. Posted to Kingston, Ontario, she was assigned to typing and filing, tasks that soon dampened her excitement. In the end, Kingston was as far as she got. The administrative work suited my mom, as she responded well to structure and discipline. "It taught me how to be a good worker and a hard worker." All the strictness and order of the farm years was paying off. She was not afraid of hard work. When the war ended, Veterans Affairs gave her an option: she could get a ticket back to Saskatchewan or be given some money to relocate. With a small pocket of funding for some vocational training, she chose Ottawa.

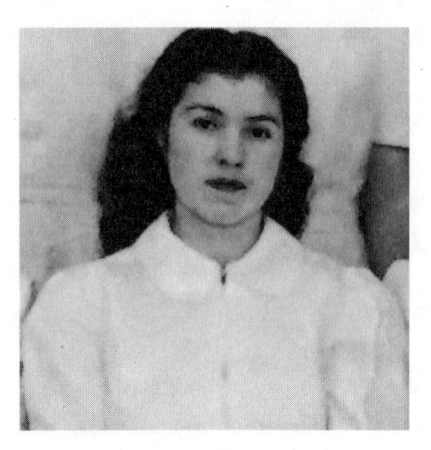

A portrait of Liz Hall's mother,
Maryann, in 1947, at age twenty-four.

When she arrived in Ottawa, my mom was ready to start her career and to make a home for herself. She used the funding to attend hairdressing school, and as soon as she finished her training, she started working and learning all that she needed to know. School taught her the necessary skills, but she would have to learn about taking care of her clients as well as the business side of running a salon. She worked long hours and was determined to make it. She met a French-Canadian fellow named John Legault, and in 1948 they got married and started a family. Baby Stephen arrived in 1951, and four years later, Donald was born. Those early years in Ottawa were busy and stressful. Her marriage did not last, and before long, Mom found herself alone with her two young children. Still, this did not stop her; she opened her own hair salon, took care of the little house she had managed to purchase, and focused on raising her sons. Life was about survival, fitting in, and making a comfortable home for her boys.

Mom was fair-skinned, which suited her just fine. In her mind, she looked white; this was an advantage that she felt contributed to her success. She raised Stephen and Donald with a lot of their father's heritage, and the boys identified as French-Canadian. Mom was committed to her family "passing" as average mainstream Canadians. She took on the ways of the colonizers, collecting fine bone china, learning the proper way to brew and serve black tea. She knew the history of Harris Tweed, strictly defined as "a tweed, hand-spun, hand-woven, and dyed by the crofters and cottars in the Outer Hebrides." This was the knowledge that mattered and contributed to her success.

Mom had exposure to this way of life because of her clientele. She became a very successful hairdresser, and her business prospered. She was a female entrepreneur in the 1950s. Her style of being was learned from observing her mostly middle-class Anglo clients. Mom did not finish high school back in Saskatchewan, but she did go back and do some upgrading when she was in her fifties. As a youngster, I could sense my mother's constant need for self-improvement, perhaps a little too much, leading to fatigue and causing her to be irritable and short-tempered. I know my mom's achievements are impressive; her self-reliance and determination were, I believe, coping mechanisms and survival strategies. She kept herself busy; she sewed, knit, crocheted, knew how to keep a house. She cooked three square meals daily; we ate like farmhands, because that was what she grew up cooking. Everything was made from scratch, just as she had learned. Mom worked full-time, ran a business, owned a car, owned a house; she did all of these things on her own.

As a child, I felt alone. Mom was so busy getting everything right, but she was emotionally unavailable. Her love was shown through all her practical efforts, which were plentiful, but she was not very warm or demonstrative. There was no appreciation for or acknowledgment of her Cree culture. Her time at residential school, followed by years on the farm, resulted in the loss of her Cree language and culture. The need for security, family, and home took priority, and there was no opportunity for maintaining or cultivating our Cree traditions, spirituality, and ceremonies. I often catch myself thinking, did she lose her Cree, or was it stolen from her? Is there a difference? Does it matter?

The Braiding Histories Stories

My mom was not a registered Indian when she was born. She became a status Indian when the Chief adopted her, and when she married John Legault, she again lost her status. My mother, my grandmother, and me – as Cree women, we share an intergenerational, intertwined story of surviving Canadian policies of forced assimilation, and then appropriated assimilation. In the move from Cree territory in Saskatchewan to Ottawa, Ontario, what did we gain, and what did we lose?

Despite all her successes, my mom was not successful in her relationships. With a fractured upbringing, she was disconnected from her biological family. She experienced the brokenness that happened to so many Indigenous children who were forcibly taken from their families and placed in the schools or taken into the child welfare system. My mom did not grow up immersed in her family; she did not have the opportunity to learn parenting skills or how to build loving, supportive relationships. Creating community, learning trust and comfort, experiencing feelings of belonging – all of this was absent for her. By the time my mom had a relationship with my father, who was an East Indian raised in West Indies culture, she was accustomed to – almost expected – failing in her relationships. It was a tangled, complicated partnership that I was born into. When my parents separated, I carried on seeing my father and have stayed in touch with my extended family.

I was proud of my mom for all the things she did, and of my grandmother, who spent her whole life living on the land and trapping, right up until she passed. My grandmother, who was also mixed race (her father was Scottish), was able to take her grandchildren into the bush and teach them how to trap and fish. My cousins grew up with nightly fires where our grandmother Betsy spoke in Cree and shared vivid stories of their ancestors. My brothers and I missed those experiences because our mom was adopted and taken away.

To this day, I struggle with clearly articulating or defining myself. The complexities of identity are ever present. Sometimes I feel like an imposter. I can remember, on occasion, in the shop, if a client were getting to know my mom a little better and would ask, "Mary, so what's your background?" I could feel her tightening up, and she would reluctantly say she was Indian. Her voice would go quiet, but if asked directly, that is how she identified herself: I am an Indian. My feelings about my mother's most awkward and vulnerable moments are imprinted on me forever. My mother went through life with a mask on; she could never show her true self.

When I was five, my mom (disconnected from her family, with a failed marriage followed by a second failed relationship) was vulnerable and in need of a sense of belonging, precisely what a religious community could offer. She connected with the Jehovah's Witnesses and never looked back; they became her everything. It is another twist in our life stories. That faith was our lives until I was in my early twenties: grade school, high school, Kingdom Hall, going door to door, spreading the message, and on the lookout for other folks in need of belonging – potential converts. I was a Jehovah's Witness. I married a fellow Witness and had two beautiful baby girls while I was still a member of that religion.

Then tragedy struck; my brother Donald got sick and died. Donald was my rock, my bee's knees. He was the one who took care of my spirit, my essence. He listened, he made me laugh, understood, and cared to soothe my soul. I was with Donald when he passed. Now, still, twenty-six years later, I continue to feel Donald's spirit around me, lifting me, guiding me, supporting me in making decisions. I feel his presence. Witnesses don't believe we have souls. It was a moment of truth for me – my worldviews collided, and I made a decision. It was time for me to leave that religious organization.

I left, but my mother stayed, and she continued to be an active member of the Jehovah's Witnesses for the rest of her life. She was a hard-working, strong, independent woman. She lived alone up until she went into a nursing home, which was only two years before she died. Until she was ninety-two, she was getting her groceries, keeping

Liz's mother, Maryann, with Liz's youngest daughter, Isla.

house, still walking every day. My strained, confusing, and sometimes tumultuous relationship with my mother is a constant in my life. Spending time apart, my own maturing, and especially death have allowed me to pause to think and learn. Reflection has been the liberator of memories, and reflection has healed my wounds.

Afterword
Liz is now married to Ryan Hall. They have two beautiful children, Caelan and Isla, and they live in Kanata, just outside of Ottawa, Ontario. Liz also has two grown daughters from her first marriage, Jasmine and Riley, and is also a grandmother of two boys.

Liz with her three daughters, Jasmine, Riley and Isla

When Liz left the Jehovah's Witnesses and divorced her first husband, it created a rift with her mother that would take a long time to heal. Eventually it did, and Liz reconciled with her mother. When her daughters started school, Liz went back to study, first at Algonquin College and then at the University of Ottawa. While she was in college, she did an internship at Indigenous Services Canada (the former Indigenous and Northern Affairs Canada). Liz has spent most of her career to date committed to advancing First Nations education, inspired by her mother's enduring efforts for self-advancement and to help ensure that all Indigenous children have access to quality education.

In November 2019, Liz received an Exceptional Dedication and Contribution Award from Paul Pelletier, Director General, Education Branch, Indigenous Services Canada.

CONCLUSION
Wuleelham – Make Good Tracks

Wuleelham is a Lenape word that means "make good tracks." I like the concept embedded in this word; for me, it inspires action and hope. I imagine taking careful steps in support of positive change, and in doing so making good tracks for others to follow. *Braided Learning* starts from the position that most Canadians do not know enough but are increasingly wanting to learn more about the history of settler colonialism.

My faith in the power of education is strengthened by the change that I have witnessed. When I first started telling the timeline story in the mid-1990s, I would be invited to present to groups of people, and the day before I was scheduled to give the talk, the organizers would call me saying, "We only have four people signed up for your talk – will you still come"? More recently, on the days leading up to my scheduled presentations, I still receive calls from organizers. But now I am being asked, "We have double the number of people we planned for – is it okay with you if we change to a bigger room and increase the size of the audience?" I appreciate that some might dismiss this as inconsequential, but I see it as a promising indicator of possibility. Although learning this history is arduous and the desire to resist remains strong, there is an increased willingness to recognize implication and to invest time in the work of learning. More and more

Canadians recognize that improved relationships are in the best interests of all Canadians, many people want to have a positive impact and are willing to take action in support of positive change. Engaging with this book is a starting point.

Speaking back to dominant narratives, the art and stories shared here engage readers in learning from Indigenous experiences and perspectives. They invite Canadians to reflect on how the policies and practices of settler colonialism impact Indigenous people, and to learn from our responses to the attempted eradication of our knowledge, our worldviews, and our ways of living and being. Exploring in detail Indigenous responses to government policies, these stories illuminate how the knowledge embedded in our art and stories nurtures our resistance. We keep our stories alive, and our stories keep us alive.

Additionally, the stories show that even as Indigenous people work to recuperate from the violence of settler colonialism, the violence continues. Most Canadians do not have to think about the ways in which assumptions about white superiority informs their relationship with the government. This book asks all readers to investigate and understand how the Doctrine of Discovery and the concept of *terra nullius* were used to legitimize the domination of Indigenous peoples. The reserve system that forcibly removed us from our lands, and the Indian Act that outlawed our spiritual and cultural practices, imposed systems of governance, education, health care, and social services – control over every aspect of our lives – and literally made us dependent on the settler government.

There is a desire to say "Okay, what our ancestors did was bad, but we know better now – we listened, learned, apologized, and now we move on." But change requires action in response to the ongoing implications of settler colonialism and specifically the inequitable distribution of wealth and power. It requires not only recognition but actions in support of Indigenous Peoples' right to be self-determining.

Listening to and Learning from Indigenous People

As the principal researcher for the Indigenous Education–Focused Collaborative Inquiry Initiative, I had the opportunity to learn from and with the Indigenous people participating in the project. Over the four years of the project, I spoke with Indigenous educators, senior secondary school students, and community partners, including parents, Knowledge Keepers, and Elders. They deepened my understanding of what and how schools and their broader communities need to change. They want to see an increased focus on Indigenous language instruction, increased integration of Indigenous content across the curriculum, ongoing support of Elders and Knowledge Keepers in the classrooms, and an increase in the number of Indigenous educators in schools, particularly in positions of leadership. The voices of Indigenous students draw attention to how their teachers' and classmates' lack of knowledge, understanding, and awareness of Indigenous histories, cultures, and perspectives are impacting their day-to-day school experiences. They attend school to learn and are increasingly frustrated by the lack of Indigenous content in their classes and by the racism and discrimination they encounter in their school communities. With access to social media, Indigenous youth are more informed and have an emerging awareness of what is missing from their education. They want access to Indigenous literature, the history of the land they live on, and access to language, culture, and Indigenous knowledge. In many ways, these students are living with the legacies of colonialism. They are aware of the staggering income disparities between Indigenous and non-Indigenous people, the lack of access to health care, inequities in the justice system, and the over-regulation of Indigenous bodies through child and family services, policing, and government policies. They want opportunities to develop the knowledge, understanding, and skills that will prepare them to work in service of their communities. They want to work toward the fulfillment of treaty promises, strategies for negotiating nation-to-nation agreements, access to land and resources, and representation for urban Indigenous people.

Working with people in school boards across Ontario over a period of four years, I have come to appreciate how people and systems contribute to creating change. I know for certain that it does not happen by accident: it starts with committed people. Actively working together, they

- make a plan for change, including identification of needs and commitments
- get involved, listening to and learning from and with Indigenous people
- locate allies, and organize people to work alongside Indigenous people
- review policies and practices to identify what kinds of systemic changes are required
- take responsibility for accomplishing transformation

Work at the grassroots level needs to be supported by the leadership within organizing structures.

I appreciate the demands for a faster pace of change, returning land, establishing Indigenous control – and I am impatient for an end to the colonial relationship. I do not claim to have the answers on how to do it; I do know that education is necessary and rely on my faith in education as a source of hope. Education for non-Indigenous people, to learn about the history and present circumstances of Indigenous people. And education for Indigenous students, to develop knowledge skills and understanding.

Recognize the Complexities of Creating Change

A few years ago, I attended the *Walking with Our Sisters* memorial exhibition. Traversing the ceremonial path, I was overwhelmed with sadness, feeling the violence of loss experienced by Indigenous girls and women, and their families, communities, and nations. Not surprisingly, I turned to my work as an Indigenous educator to make sense of the emotional turmoil. As an educator, I am daunted by feelings of responsibility to create educational experiences that will teach ways of knowing that honour the knowledge, strength, and creative capacities of Indigenous girls, women, 2SLGBTQ+ people. I strive to understand how educators can create trauma-informed classrooms that will provide safer spaces for Indigenous people to make sense of their lives and to experience well-being. I know the work required to engage all instructors, practitioners, and students across fields including social work, health care, law enforcement, public administration, and justice in learning from the history of the relationship between Indigenous people and settler Canadians. I also know that we will not understand each other until we understand the history of our relationship with each other and the land we live on.

During a conversation about Indigenous education, Paul Martin, former prime minister of Canada, told me that Canadians care about what is fair; when you talk to Canadians about settler-Indigenous relationships, you have to frame the discussion in terms of fairness. I did not disagree but added that equally significant is how people *conceive* of what is fair. The artists and storytellers in this book challenge readers to engage with Indigenous conceptions of fairness grounded in responsibility for the self in relationship with all of creation – taking care of oneself so as to contribute to balance and harmony with kin, community, and land.

As I sit quietly at my desk writing the conclusion to this book, thousands of people are in the streets across Canada and across the world, protesting, demanding, risking their lives for change. Some people, communities, and even some nations are much better at recognizing that living in balanced relationship, using your gifts and capacities for the well-being of the whole, is possible. I have faith in the power of art and story to teach. As Acoma Pueblo poet Simon Ortiz explains, stories are about creative action:

The storyteller doesn't just tell the characters, what they did or said, what happens in the story, and so along. No, he participates in the story with those who are listening. The listeners in the same way are taking part in the story. The story includes them in. You see, it's more like an event, the storytelling. The story is not just a story then – it's an occurring, coming into being.[1]

And so the responsibility of story-listeners is action, to take action in response to the stories you hear.

Through visual art and story, Indigenous people share our experiences and perspectives, reflecting the complexities and multiplicities of our lives, our enduring presence, and the ways in which we use ancestral teachings in contemporary times. This is a book filled with art and stories. Art inspired by agreements made between Indigenous people and settlers over a hundred years ago, and art that reflects a time in the future when Indigenous languages are once again alive and thriving. Big stories about broken treaties, stolen land, and forced assimilation, and tiny stories about whispering across the library table. The art and stories are shared with intention and expectation to inspire engagement and learning, and contribute to the making of good tracks.

GLOSSARY AND ADDITIONAL RESOURCES
Making Connections, Extending Learning

Relationships between storytellers and story listeners are key to meaning-making. Within Indigenous contexts, storytellers know their listeners and have shared knowledge and experiences. This chapter provides detailed information on key concepts addressed in the book. I introduce each concept with a quote from the book to support connections and extend learning. I have also provided links to additional resources so that readers who are interested in particular topics, or who have persistent questions, can learn more. I imagine this chapter as a kind of Q&A that would take place following an oral presentation of the art and stories found in the book.

Activism and Resistance

> Across the continent, from Haida Gwaii to Nunavut to Mi'kmaq territories, resistance is aimed at acknowledging Indigenous people's right to govern ourselves and re-establish sovereignty over our lands and our lives. (97)

Indigenous people have always been active in creating and sharing knowledge through art and stories, taking care of our land and each other, defending our rights to do so through negotiations and, when necessary, mobilized activities. Our actions are labelled *activism* when they interfere with the day-to-day lives of other Canadians. We do not choose to do this easily, and it is frustrating that change is accomplished only when our actions interrupt the lives of non-Indigenous Canadians. Activism and resistance is about drawing attention to unbearable conditions; it is a call to pay attention and learn. Protests in response to the 1969 White Paper were successful in defeating policy changes proposed by the state. Consistent and regular activism by Indigenous people has resulted in raising awareness of and increasing public support for Indigenous rights. It takes a great deal of our time, energy, and financial resources to support the movement. The following long yet incomplete list of protests, blockades, and occupations reflects the work of Indigenous activism and resistance.

Activism and Resistance Focused on Indigenous Rights

1979	Tobique Women's Group's 110-mile march from Kanesatake to Ottawa, marking 110 years of injustice for Indigenous women in the Indian Act
1980s	First Nations blockades in British Columbia aimed at putting a stop to resource extraction on Native land
1987	Innu occupation and blockade of the Canadian Air Force/NATO base at Goose Bay, Labrador, protesting low-level flight training
1988	Lubicon Cree boycott of the Calgary Winter Olympics and the associated Glenbow exhibit *The Spirit Sings* – The Lubicon Cree were living in poverty while oil companies made millions from their land.
1988	Temagami First Nation blockades of 1988 and 1989 to stop encroachment by non-Native development
1989	Algonquins of Barriere Lake's struggle to stop clear-cut logging within their traditional territories
1990	Defeat of Meech Lake Accord by Elijah Harper because Indigenous Peoples had been completely left out of the proposed constitution

1990	Seventy-eight-day standoff at Kanehsatà:ke to halt the expansion of a golf course on sacred lands
1992	First annual commemorative march in Vancouver for Missing and Murdered Indigenous Women and Girls – The march has grown into an annual nationwide event aimed at addressing violence against Indigenous women, girls, and 2SLGBTQ+ people, and serves commemorative, educational, and protest purposes. A national inquiry was finally launched in 2016, with a final report released in 2019.
1995	Ipperwash Provincial Park occupation in protest of the appropriation of the Stoney Point Reserve by the federal government for use as a military camp – Dudley George, an Anishinaabe protester, was killed by a OPP officer.
1995	Armed confrontation between RCMP officers and Indigenous people at Gustafsen Lake, focused on access to land for ceremonial purposes
1999–2002	Burnt Church Crisis, a conflict between the Mi'kmaq people of Esgenoopetitj (Burnt Church) First Nation and white non-Indigenous fishermen in New Brunswick and Nova Scotia
2008	Launch of the Truth and Reconciliation Commission (final report released in 2015)
2012	Beginning of Idle No More, a grassroots movement in support of Indigenous sovereignty and treaty rights
2019	Blockades and protests against construction of the Coastal GasLink pipeline in northern British Columbia by members of the Wet'suwet'en Nation, with ongoing solidarity protests taking place across the country, resulting in closure of highways, railway lines, and port terminals
2020	Nationwide anti-Indigenous racism and Black Lives Matter solidarity movement demonstrations against racism and police brutality

Glossary and Additional Resources

2020   Beginning of LANDBACK, a movement reclaiming Indigenous jurisdiction and bringing to life our rights and responsibilities – The goal is to show Canadians how their government dispossesses Indigenous Peoples from the land and what communities are doing to get it back.

2020   Disputes over the right to a Moderate Livelihood fishing in Atlantic Canada in response to the federal government's inadequate action on the Supreme Court's 1999 ruling in support of Mi'kmaq treaty rights

Resources

Noel Dyck and Tonio Sadik, "Indigenous Political Organization and Activism in Canada," *Canadian Encyclopedia*, Historica Canada, 2011, https://www.thecanadianencyclopedia.ca/en/article/aboriginal-people-political-organization-and-activism.

Rise Up! A Digital Archive of Feminist Activism, https://riseupfeministarchive.ca/activism/issues-actions/indigenous-womens-rights/.

Appropriation and Indigenous Cultural Appropriation

> And, of course, the images associated with sports teams that we all know. (38)

The appropriation of Indigenous cultural items and images of our people for use in advertisements, film, literature, sports, the fashion industry, and even in the construction of Canadian nationalism has been going on for centuries. Images associated with Indigenous people have been used to sell cars, trucks, butter, medicinal remedies, and even life insurance. As Libby Stephenson documents in her story, these images produce and reproduce stereotypical thinking about Indigenous people and contribute to the ongoing dehumanization of them. Many people refuse to recognize the proliferation of stereotypical representations as offensive, while others are confused by what counts as appropriation and find it difficult to know what makes an image offensive.

Appropriation is about power and power relations. When members of a dominant group control the representation of people and use those representations to their own advantage, that is appropriation, and it causes harm. The proliferation of stereotypical images of Indigenous people is especially harmful because these images are all that many Canadians know about us. In 2020, as a result of pressure from Indigenous and Black Lives Matter activists, the Washington football franchise agreed to change the name of its team, which put increasing pressure on other sports franchises to follow suit.

Concerns about cultural appropriation contribute to the fear non-Indigenous people experience when it comes to teaching about Indigenous people. Not understanding or knowing how to decide what is harmful, people are afraid of making mistakes. A useful guiding principle is to use a diversity of images produced by Indigenous people, representing the dynamic complexities of our people and our experiences.

Resources

Alootook Ipellie and David MacDonald, *The Inuit Thought of It: Amazing Arctic Innovations* (Toronto: Annick Press, 2014).

Ontario Arts Council, *Indigenous Arts Protocols* (Toronto: Ontario Arts Council, October 23, 2016), video, 10:07, https://www.youtube.com/watch?v=c6VuHJi6OoQ.

Ceremony

> Ancestral knowledge is accessed through relationships with family, through community Elders, and from oral and written documentation. It is also recuperated through participation in ceremony and traditional practices. (102)

Ceremony is a form of cultural practice, an expression of spiritual beliefs, and can be a source of belonging and connection. Ceremonies vary from nation to nation, and there are different kinds of ceremonies that serve different purposes – for example, when there is a new moon, when a child is born, when there is a need for healing, or when it is time to honour a community member. They are often led by an Elder, and there are specific protocols to be followed, with participants often having different roles, such as fire keeper or water carrier. Sacred medicines, teas, specific foods, and special items may be used as part of a ceremony. Teachings are sometimes shared with participants. In ceremony, Indigenous people attend to the spirit, strengthen their identity and connection to community, and access knowledge and understanding. Ceremony is a time and place where family and community members can be together, learn from and with each other, and practise their spiritual beliefs. For many artists, there is a connection between ceremony and the creation of art. Ceremony can inform art production, art making can be a kind of ceremony, and some ceremonial objects are artistic creations.

Some people refer to Indigenous ceremony as ritual. The word *ritual* has connotative meanings and associations with cults, the primitive, or the pagan. While the Catholic practice of baptism is called a ceremony, a vision quest is named a "ritual," reflecting judgment. Whereas pouring water over an infant's head is deemed a legitimate practice sanctioned by an organized religion, a vision quest or strawberry fast is categorized by some people as a ritual, or a primitive practice, delegitimizing it.

Ceremonies reflect peoples' belief systems and worldviews. For many people, participation in ceremony affirms relationship and shared commitment, and can provide access to ancestral knowledge.

Resources

Nikki Bayley, "Learning about Smudging with Old Hands, of the Shoshone First Nation," *Destination Indigenous*, December 14, 2017, https://destinationindigenous.ca/blog/smudging-101-with-old-hands-of-the-shoshone-first-nation/.

Gail Maurice, dir., *Smudge* (National Film Board of Canada, 2005), video, 12:17, https://www.nfb.ca/film/smudge/.

Circle

> Elder Joanne Dallaire opens the circle with a song, a smudge bowl is brought around, and the Urban Indigenous Community Advisory Committee begins its work. (74)

The circle is significant in most Indigenous cultures. It represents wholeness, interconnectedness, and the cyclical nature of life. The sun and the moon are circles, and their circular movement contribute to life cycles. Circles are present in many important concepts and items, including the medicine wheel, dream catchers, tipis, and drums. Powwows and round dances also happen in a large circle as dancers form and move in a circle. Many Indigenous nations use the talking circle as a form of respectful discussion or knowledge sharing. In the circle, there is no hierarchy; balance is established because each members' gifts, capacities, and contributions are recognized and appreciated equally. The circle does not collapse difference or suggest that everyone has the same gifts; rather, the circle emphasizes the importance of recognizing and appreciating difference and knowing that our strength and well-being is only possible when we honour each other. Talking circles can be used for any kind of discussion, from conflict resolution to personal story sharing. In some nations, participants in a circle will take turns speaking, going in the direction guided by that nation's protocols. Often, circles will begin with a smudge, participants will introduce themselves, and the circle will continue with the intended discussion.

Resources

Manitoba Education and Youth, *Integrating Aboriginal Perspectives in Curricula: A Resource for Curriculum Developers, Teachers, and Administrators* (Winnipeg: Manitoba Education and Youth, 2003), https://www.edu.gov.mb.ca/k12/docs/policy/abpersp/ab_persp.pdf.

"Talking Circles," *First Nations Pedagogy Online*, 2009, http://firstnationspedagogy.ca/circletalks.html.

Indian Act and Fiduciary Responsibility

> While the Indian Act documents government responsibilities and Indigenous rights, ultimately it is an act in service of accomplishing the government's policy of forced assimilation. (88)

Prior to confederation, laws affecting Indigenous people depended on local circumstances, treaties, and agreements with the British monarchy. In 1876, the laws were combined, expanded, and summarized in the Indian Act. This federal legislation provides a coordinated approach to Indian policy. It imposes a governing system and allows the Canadian government to control reserve land, education, policing, and access to housing, health care, and social services. It defines who is and who is not entitled to Indian status, and excludes the Métis, Inuit, and many urban Indigenous people.

The Indian Act is paternalistic and assimilative legislation that authorizes the Canadian government to regulate and control the affairs and day-to-day lives of people and reserve communities. It gives the government "fiduciary" responsibility – meaning the right to control the finances of Indigenous communities. Although the Indian Act is oppressive, it is also the only legislation that provides access to treaty rights, including housing, health care, and education. It cannot be removed without replacing it with new laws establishing self-governance, self-determination, and sovereignty over Indigenous lands, finances, and membership. The Indian Act has undergone various amendments and revisions since 1876, aimed at reducing the assimilative goal, yet it remains a powerful force in the lives of Indigenous people.

Resources

Falen Johnson and Leah Simone-Bowen, "What Do You Really Know about the Indian Act?" *The Secret Life of Canada* (CBC Radio, June 27, 2019), podcast, 44:41, https://www.cbc.ca/radio/secret

lifeofcanada/what-do-you-really-know-about-the-indian-act-1.5188255.

Bob Joseph, *21 Things You May Not Know about the Indian Act: Helping Canadians Make Reconciliation with Indigenous Peoples a Reality* (Port Coquitlam, BC: Indigenous Relations Press, 2018).

Indigenous Languages

> Why do our teachers think we know our histories, our languages, our teachings? And why do they judge us and ask us, "Do you speak your language, how Indigenous are you, what's your clan?" (26)

Worldviews and perspectives are embedded in language. It carries understanding, allowing speakers greater access to cultural knowledge. Recognizing the power of language, it is not surprising that colonial governments created policies to eliminate languages. And it follows that language revitalization is one of the most pressing concerns confronting Indigenous Peoples today. Statistics Canada confirmed that there are over sixty Indigenous languages spoken within Canada and that most are only spoken by a small number of people.[1] In residential schools, children were forbidden to speak their languages, and in on-reserve schools the language of instruction was English. Indigenous students today do not speak their languages because of the education imposed on their parents and grandparents. As the statement above explains, we are often judged as "less" Indigenous if we don't speak our language, yet colonialism is the very reason so many of our languages have been nearly eliminated.

There is promising work being done, and the 2016 census reported that the number of people who identified as being able to speak an Indigenous language had grown by 3.1 percent.[2] This suggests that more people are taking on the work of learning to speak their language. Recognizing the significance of language diversity, UNESCO declared 2019 the International Year of Indigenous Languages.

Glossary and Additional Resources

Resources

Lindsay Morcom, "A History of Indigenous Languages – and How to Revitalize Them," filmed February 2019 in Kingston, ON, TEDx video, 13:21, https://www.ted.com/talks/lindsay_morcom_a_history_of_indigenous_languages_and_how_to_revitalize_them/.

United Nations Permanent Forum on Indigenous Voices, "Indigenous Languages," *Indigenous Peoples, Indigenous Voices*, fact sheet, 2009, https://www.un.org/esa/socdev/unpfii/documents/Factsheet_languages_FINAL.pdf.

Land and Territory

> I ask people to learn about the land they live on: Whose traditional territory is it? When were Indigenous people removed from the land? How was the land used before and after contact? (28)

Lakota scholar Vine Deloria Jr. explains that Indigenous people "hold their lands – places – as having the highest possible meaning."[3] Sacred places are the foundation of all other beliefs and practices because they represent the presence of the sacred in our lives. They properly inform us that we are not larger than nature and that we have responsibilities to the rest of the natural world. It is this relationship *with* land that in many ways defines Indigenous people and positions us differently to those who claim power, control, and even ownership over the land.

Living in respectful relationship with land does not mean that Indigenous people do not have conceptions of territory. Territorial boundaries are recognized and protected. People are responsible for and rely on what the land within their territorial boundaries provides. We developed social, cultural, and economic structures to support ourselves and our people. In Canada, Indigenous nations have treaties that protect the rights of individuals and their territory. Indigenous people think of themselves as caretakers who live in a relationship with the land, rather than owners, or possessors, of it. Every gift of life comes from the land, including food, clothing, shelter, recreation, and creativity. Our ceremonies and teachings remind us to take only what we need and to use all that we take. Our worldview and perspectives are informed by our relationship with the land.

Resources

âpihtawikosisân, "Beyond territorial acknowledgments," *âpihtawikosisân*, January 25, 2017, https://apihtawikosisan.com/2016/09/beyond-territorial-acknowledgments/.

"Land and Rights," *Indigenous Foundations* (First Nations and Indigenous Studies, University of British Columbia, 2009), https://indigenousfoundations.arts.ubc.ca/land__rights/.

Métis Nation

> Word had arrived only that day that Louis Riel and the Métis had been successful in a battle at Duck Lake. (156)

Métis are distinct people with their own unique cultural practices, beliefs, spirituality, and traditions. They came into being as a result of unions between fur traders and Indigenous women. People who identify as Métis have roots in this time and place.

Section 35 of the Constitution Act, 1982 recognizes the treaty rights of the "aboriginal peoples of Canada," defined as "the Indian, Inuit and Métis peoples." The Constitution Act was a triumph for Métis people because, for over one hundred years, Métis had not been included within the definition of Indigenous peoples. In the 1990s, Steve and Roddy Powley were charged with hunting without a licence. They pleaded not guilty and went to court to defend Métis rights. They were successful, and the Powley case, in addition to acknowledging hunting and fishing rights, defined criteria for claiming Métis identity by establishing the "Powley test," which outlines ten specific criteria.[4]

The Métis have a specific and rich culture that is more than fiddling and jigging. Michif is a Métis language with influences from many languages, including French and Cree. The Métis sash is an identifying symbol of the people.

Resources

Matt LeMay, dir., *The Métis Nation of Ontario: Twenty Years of Achievement* (Métis Nation of Ontario, December 4, 2013), video, 48:25, https://youtu.be/WSniHvhnAaU.

Library and Archives Canada, "Métis Nation," September 29, 2020, https://www.bac-lac.gc.ca/eng/discover/aboriginal-heritage/metis/Pages/introduction.aspx.

National Indian Brotherhood and the Assembly of First Nations

> In 1970, the National Indian Brotherhood published their first policy paper, titled *Indian Control of Indian Education*; in 1972, the Government of Canada adopted that policy, returning to Indigenous people the right to provide education for their children. (95)

The National Indian Brotherhood (NIB) was incorporated in 1970 to represent status Indians, and was concerned with representing First Nations at the national level and advocating for self-government, treaty rights, health, education, and culture. In 1972, the NIB released a policy paper entitled *Indian Control of Indian Education*, outlining First Nations values for education, including strengthening of identity and harmony with the natural world.[5] The NIB organization grew into the Assembly of First Nations (AFN) in 1982. The AFN is a national advocacy organization representing over 630 First Nations, each given a seat in the assembly and holding the right to vote on the National Chief. The AFN and National Chief work to advocate for First Nations with the Canadian government and helped negotiate the Indian Residential Schools Settlement Agreement and the Kelowna Accord, a ten-year plan and $5.1 billion to improve life for First Nations people (although a change in government resulted in the plan not being fully implemented).[6]

Resources

"About AFN," Assembly of First Nations, https://www.afn.ca/description-of-the-afn/.

Chief Perry Bellegarde, National Chief of the Assembly of First Nations (Association of Municipalities of Ontario, August 19, 2019) video, 17:58, https://www.youtube.com/watch?v=kojWRWqVtAA.

1969 White Paper

> The 1969 White Paper galvanized Indigenous resistance across the nation. Trudeau's proposed policy would eliminate the Indian Act by doing away with reserves and status and erasing treaty rights. (95)

In 1969, the Canadian government and Prime Minister Pierre Elliott Trudeau proposed the "Statement of the Government of Canada on Indian Policy, 1969" which has become known as the White Paper. The policy intended to "abolish previous legal documents relating to Indigenous peoples in Canada, including the *Indian Act* and treaties ... [and] assimilate all 'Indian' peoples under the Canadian state."[7] Even though the Indian Act is discriminatory and paternalistic, it also upholds treaty rights and the Canadian government's responsibility to status Indians. The White Paper would have removed the Canadian government's financial obligations to Indigenous people and voided its commitment to the treaties. It would also have removed the distinctness of Indigenous Peoples as sovereign nations that should be consulted and considered in matters regarding Indigenous land and territories. The White Paper was vehemently opposed by Indigenous people and was withdrawn by the Canadian government in 1970.

Resources

Naithan Lagace and Niigaanwewidam James Sinclair, "The White Paper, 1969," *Canadian Encyclopedia*, Historica Canada, September 24, 2015, https://www.thecanadianencyclopedia.ca/en/article/the-white-paper-1969.

"The White Paper 1969," *Indigenous Foundations* (First Nations and Indigenous Studies, University of British Columbia, 2009), https://indigenousfoundations.arts.ubc.ca/the_white_paper_1969/.

Oral and Written Literacy

> Relying on the technology of my voice and my faith in the oral tradition, my preference is to tell the story in person. I have written it down only after serious consideration. (76)

In *The Truth about Stories: A Native Narrative*, Thomas King reflects on the relationship between oral and written literacy, explaining that written literacy is judged to be more valuable, more worthy, because books are quantifiable. Further, there is an assumption that in order to be complete, stories must be written down. For the most part, Indigenous people were judged as illiterate because our recording systems were not recognized as "writing." However, as King explains, "in the valley of Mexico, the Aztecs maintained a large library of written works that may well have been the rival of the Royal Library at Alexandria. Written and oral. Side by side."[8]

Hieroglyphics, petroglyphs, and pictographs were and continue to be carved or painted on a variety of surfaces, including wood, stone, birch bark, leather. They are created for practical and spiritual purposes, as well as to mark important events. These records can be found on wampum belts, totem poles, rock faces, birchbark scrolls, beadwork, and pottery.

Access to knowledge embedded in story is about more than the form of expression. It is about commitment to engaging with story as well as who has control of our stories, written and oral. For, as Thomas King explains,

> in the end, though, neither fared any better than the other. While European diseases and conflicts with explorers and settlers led to the death and displacement of a great many Native storytellers, superstitious Spanish priests, keen on saving the Aztecs from themselves, burned the library at Tenochtitlán to the ground, an event as devastating as Julius Caesar's destruction of the library at Alexandria. In each case, at Tenochtitlán and Alexandria, stories were lost. And, in the end, it didn't matter whether these stories were oral or written. So much for dependability. So much for permanence.[9]

King argues that "neglect is as powerful an agent as war and fire," putting the responsibility on us. Maintaining a literature depends on people telling/writing stories and people listening to/reading stories.

Resources

Barrie Carter, "Orality – Indigenous Knowledge through Oral Narratives," *ETEC540: Text Technologies*, October 3, 2010, https://blogs.ubc.ca/etec540sept10/2010/10/03/orality-%E2%80%93-indigenous-knowledge-through-oral-narratives/.

Peter Dickinson, "'Orality in Literacy': Listening to Indigenous Writing," *Canadian Journal of Native Studies* 14, no. 2 (1994): 319–40, https://pdfs.semanticscholar.org/0b89/3c1df4f7745acccca4d6a09e6787f65fd7a5.pdf.

Potlatch Ceremony

> This was an important celebration for the entire community, and it had a significant impact on Bernard's sense of the nation and the rights of the people. (169)

The Potlatch is a gift-giving ceremony practised by Northwest Coast First Nations to celebrate important events, including weddings, births, and deaths. One of the central tenets of the Potlatch is to redistribute wealth in the community. In Western society, wealth is associated with an abundance of valuable possessions or money. Contrary to this, the generosity of a host during a Potlatch is recognized as a sign of wealth. It is not how much you keep to yourself but how much you give away that reflects wealth. Traditionally, gifts included animal furs, copper, canoes, and oolichan oil. Contemporary gifts might include jewellery, food, or clothing.[10] The Canadian government considered the Potlatch a hindrance to assimilation. Potlatches and other ceremonial gatherings were banned in 1884 under the Indian Act.[11] During this time, the Potlatch did not stop; it was done secretly, and if participants were caught, they would be arrested and ceremonial items confiscated. The Potlatch ban was in place for seventy-one years – until 1951, when the Indian Act was amended.

Resources

Candice Hopkins, "Outlawed Social Life," *South as a State of Mind #7* [documenta 14 #2] (Spring/Summer 2016): 1–16, https://www.fondationprincepierre.mc/en/downloads/medias_upload/oeuvres/PDF_000609.pdf.

Andrea Spalding and Darlene Gait, *Secret of the Dance* (Victoria, BC: Orca, 2013).

Reserve System

> While Indigenous people were isolated [from settlers], the isolation actually resulted in family and community ties being maintained and even strengthened. For many Indigenous people, reserves continue to be places of home, recognition, and belonging. (89)

The reserve system began through treaty negotiations first with the French and British and later with the Canadian government. As the settler population increased, demand for access to and control of land increased, and government agents met with Indigenous leaders to negotiate treaties. In exchange for their land, the state promised to provide "land reserved for Indians"; this land became known as reserves. The laws of the Indian Act regulated life on the reserve, and Indian agents were assigned to each reserve. The agents, as representatives of the federal government, were responsible for enforcing the Indian Act.

The implementation of a pass system gave the Indian agent full control over people's lives. People required a pass from the Indian agent to leave the reserve. Sometimes the Indian agent would restrict movement, adding to tensions between Indigenous and settler communities. The governing system of elected chief and council was (and still is) imposed on reserve communities through the Indian Act.

Living conditions on reserves vary greatly from community to community. Some reserve communities close to urban areas allow for band members to commute to school or work, while others are isolated, with few employment opportunities. Isolated reserves often do not have a high school, and children as young as thirteen must travel to urban centres and live with boarding families in order to finish their secondary education. Many reserves face challenges with housing, poverty, clean water, education, and adequate and culturally safe health services. While reserves may or may not be located on a nation's traditional territory, they can be places where Indigenous people connect with family, community, and culture. Indigenous people are advocating for awareness of reserve life and are working within their communities to create positive places. Young people like Shannen Koostachin, who advocated for education, or Autumn Peltier, who advocates for clean water, are pushing back against Canada's assimilationist and colonial policies.

Resources

Indigenous Corporate Training Inc., "8 First Nation reserve FAQs," *Working Effectively with Indigenous Peoples*, March 6, 2015, https://www.ictinc.ca/blog/8-first-nation-reserve-faqs.

Alex Williams, dir., *The Pass System* (Peterborough, ON: Tamarack Productions, 2016), documentary, 50:00, http://thepasssystem.ca/home-2/.[12]

Residential Schools

> In many ways it is impossible to document the impact of residential schools on our family. (78)

The Indian residential school system began in the 1880s. In 1920, under the Indian Act, it became mandatory for all Indigenous children to attend these schools. Parents were forced to send their children to school or risk being arrested or imprisoned. Indian agents had the authority to forcibly remove children if parents tried to hide them.

The Indian residential schools were government-funded and church-run institutions solely for First Nations, Métis, and Inuit children, created with the goal of cultural assimilation. The Canadian government wanted to assimilate all Indigenous people until there was no longer an "Indian problem ... no Indian question and no Indian department."[13] Residential schools were often hundreds of kilometres away from reserves, making it very difficult for families to visit or take their children home during winter or summer breaks. It was difficult for children to run away, and some who did try died of exposure as they attempted to find their way home.

Children who attended the schools not only had to adjust to a new way of life but had to live in poorly maintained buildings and were fed meals that were inadequate in terms of nutrition and quality. Students were separated from their siblings and were only allowed to speak English. There are countless reports of physical, emotional, and sexual abuse by the adults who ran the schools. As many as six thousand children died while attending residential schools.

Even though the last residential school closed in 1996, the effects are long-lasting. The trauma that children experienced has permeated families and communities and will continue to impact Indigenous people for generations. In 2008, then–prime minister Stephen Harper issued a formal apology. In that same year, under the terms of the Indian Residential Schools Settlement Agreement, the Truth and Reconciliation Commission of Canada (TRC) was established. The goal was to expose the truth of the harm done to Indigenous people, families, and communities. In addition to exposing the truth, the TRC was to provide the beginning of a process for healing and reconciliation between Indigenous and non-Indigenous Canadians. The TRC's work took six years and concluded with a six-volume final report and ninety-four calls to action for reconciliation. The history, archival documents, and survivor testimony that the TRC uncovered are permanently housed in the National Centre for Truth and Reconciliation in Winnipeg, Manitoba. The centre continues to maintain educational programming and initiatives to educate about the residential school system and promote reconciliation.

Resources
Kent Monkman, dir., *Sisters and Brothers* (Montreal: National Film Board of Canada, 2015), film, 3:43, https://www.nfb.ca/film/sisters_brothers/.
Tim Wolochatiuk, dir., *We Were Children* (Montreal: National Film Board of Canada, 2012), film, 1:45:00, https://www.nfb.ca/film/we_were_children/.

Salvage Era

While Canadians are starting to learn about the impacts of cultural genocide perpetrated through residential schools, most don't know that in Canada laws were passed that

> made it a crime to speak our languages, practise our culture, and pass on stories and ceremonies to our children and grandchildren. (26)

In 1884, the Indian Act was amended, making Potlatches and other ceremonial gatherings illegal. As mentioned earlier, participants who were caught could be sent to jail and have their ceremonial items confiscated. The items confiscated were often sold or put in museums. One of the more well-known seizures of ceremonial items was during Chief Dan Cranmer's Potlatch in 1921. It was one of the largest Potlatches recorded. Twenty people were arrested and six hundred sacred items, including masks, regalia, and family heirlooms, were confiscated.[14]

It wasn't just sacred items that were confiscated, though; sometimes the bones or remains of Indigenous peoples were taken and sold for personal collections or put in museums. The British Columbia Royal Museum had approximately seven hundred ancestral remains and is in the process of returning them to the territories from which they were taken.[15] The museum has also begun to repatriate stolen or confiscated items from the years during the Potlatch ban, trying to investigate how the items came to the museum and where they belong. Many museums now offer free admission to Indigenous people. The Canadian Museum for Human Rights in Winnipeg notes that its free admission is in the spirit of the United Nations Declaration on the Rights of Indigenous Peoples and that the "declaration recognizes the rights of Indigenous peoples to maintain, control, protect and develop their cultural heritage and traditional cultural expressions."[16]

Another instance of stolen Indigenous property is highlighted in the documentary film *Totem: The Return of the G'psgolox Pole*. In 1929, the Department of Indian Affairs gave permission for Olof Hanson to cut down a totem pole and take it to Sweden, where it was donated by Hanson to the Swedish Museum of Ethnography. Members of the Haisla Nation searched for the pole for years before learning that it was on display in the Swedish museum. In 1994, the Swedish government agreed to return the pole if the Haisla people would create a replica to stand in place of the original pole in the museum. The Haisla Nation agreed, a replica was created and presented to the museum in Sweden, and the original was returned to Kitamaat Village.[17]

Resources

Christopher Auchter, dir., *Now Is the Time* (Montreal: National Film Board of Canada, 2019), video, 16:00, https://www.nfb.ca/film/now-is-the-time/.

Christine Buckley, "The Impact of Anthropology on Native American Culture," *UConn Today*, August 19, 2011, https://today.uconn.edu/2011/08/the-impact-of-anthropology-on-native-american-culture/.

Sixties Scoop and Child Welfare

> My strongest memory from when I finally found a way to talk with our mother about her life was her sense of insult. Her words stay with me: "They judged us incapable, as if we did not know how to take care of ourselves and our children." The disdain she expressed toward those who judged reflected a deep sense of pride in her own and her family's capacities to take care of themselves and each other. (9)

The removal of First Nations, Inuit, and Métis children from their homes during the 1960s is referred to as the Sixties Scoop. As residential schools were being closed across Canada, the rate of Indigenous children being taken and placed in foster homes rose significantly. In 1955, less than 1 percent of children in care in British Columbia were Indigenous; by 1964, that number had risen to 34.2 percent.[18] The statistics were similar in other areas of Canada. Children were taken when parents or their homes were judged unfit. Poverty and lack of access to housing contributed to the high rates of removal. The

Government of Canada was responsible for living conditions on reserves, including the provision of housing, education, health care, and economically sustainable livelihoods; the state was therefore responsible for creating the conditions it used as justification for taking Indigenous children and placing them with non-Indigenous families.

The lack of understanding of Indigenous cultures and ways of knowing and being, along with racism that existed among settler Canadians, negatively impacted Indigenous children who were placed in the care of settler Canadian families. Children experienced the loss of both their biological families and their culture, language, and identity. The Sixties Scoop is widely recognized as an assimilation and colonization tactic by the Canadian government. Class action lawsuits have been filed in several provinces for the harm done to Indigenous people during the Sixties Scoop, and in 2017 Ontario Superior Court Justice Edward Belobaba ruled that the government was liable. A settlement of $800 million was announced as restitution for Sixties Scoop survivors.[19]

The overrepresentation of Indigenous children in child welfare agencies did not end in the 1960s. The apprehension of First Nations, Inuit and Métis children continues as of this writing at an alarmingly disproportionate rate. Often, statistics regarding Indigenous children rely on status Indians, and instances of non-status, Métis, and Inuit children in care are underrepresented. Also, data collection by child welfare agencies varies from region to region; therefore it is difficult to know precise numbers of Indigenous children in care. In 2016, 8 percent of Canadian youth identified as Indigenous, yet more than 50 percent of the children under fourteen in care were Indigenous.[20]

On January 1, 2020, new legislation to reduce the number of Indigenous children taken into care was enacted. An Act Respecting First Nations, Inuit and Métis Children, Youth and Families was co-developed in consultation with Indigenous people and is intended to promote increased sovereignty over child welfare options that take into consideration the best interests of the child and Indigenous jurisdiction over child and family services. This is one step in the direction of reconciliation and the healing and empowerment of Indigenous communities.

Resources

Michael Hutchinson, *The Case of the Missing Auntie* (Toronto, ON: Second Story Press, 2020).

Raven Sinclair, "Identity Lost and Found: Lessons from the Sixties Scoop," *First Peoples Child and Family Review* 3, no. 1 (2020): 65–82.

Stereotypes

> I would take my Grade 1 students to the library and see the villages on display, the longhouses made out of popsicle sticks, tipis made out of toothpicks, and sugar-cube igloos. (80)

A simplified representation of an individual or a group, by basic or obvious characteristics – often exaggerated and/or demeaning – limits people's understanding of those they do not immediately recognize as being like them. This can be dangerous because it can generalize about individuals and groups, erasing diversity both within and between Indigenous nations. Stories have the power to connect people across differences, but they can also create barriers. The Nigerian-born novelist Chimamanda Ngozi Adichie talks about the "single story" that represents people in only one way; if told repeatedly, it becomes how people are identified. She reminds us of the danger of the single story: "The single story creates stereotypes, and the problem with stereotypes is not that they are untrue, but that they are incomplete. They make one story become the only story."[21] Dehumanizing stereotypical representations continue to be relied on as justification for the erasure of sovereignty.

While the making of sugar-cube igloos may seem innocent, it cannot stand in for learning about the Inuit, their history, and their culture. The art and stories shared in this book reflect vibrancy, diversity, and our ongoing presence.

Resources

Thomas King, dir., *I'm Not the Indian You Had in Mind* (National Screen Institute, 2007), film, 5:28, https://vimeo.com/39451956.

Peter A. Leavitt et al., "'Frozen in Time': The Impact of Native American Media Representations on Identity and Self-Understanding," *Journal of Social Issues* 71, no. 1 (2015): 39–53, https://cpb-us-e1.wpmucdn.com/sites.ucsc.edu/dist/0/245/files/2014/08/Leavitt-Covarrubias-Perez-Fryberg-2015_JSI.pdf.

Treaties

> The provision of education is not free – it is a treaty right. (89)

Treaties are binding legal agreements between two or more nations that address rights, responsibilities, and relationships with the land. Since time immemorial, Indigenous people have been making treaties, initially with each other and later with newcomer nations. In Canada, there are pre-Confederation, Numbered and modern treaties. Treaties were made between Indigenous Nations and the British Crown, and after Confederation the Canadian government took on responsibility for the historical treaties and entered into its own treaty negotiations with Indigenous Peoples as need demanded; these are the Numbered Treaties, and there are eleven of them.

The Royal Proclamation of 1763 set a precedent for the British Crown to obtain lands in North America by treaty. Treaty obligations and processes are acknowledged and upheld in section 25 of the Canadian Charter of Rights and Freedoms, stating that the charter should "not be construed so as to abrogate or derogate from any aboriginal, treaty or other rights or freedoms that pertain to the aboriginal peoples of Canada."[22] Indigenous rights to land are acknowledged by the British Crown as well as the Canadian government, and because of this, the only way to obtain land from Indigenous nations legally is through treaty negotiations. Many of the treaties made with Indigenous Peoples provided for continued use of the land, housing, food, education, and health care. Currently, Indigenous people who have status under the Indian Act still access their treaty rights. Sometimes people think that Indigenous people get education, housing, and health care for free. It is not free; it is a result of the agreements our ancestors negotiated.

Resources
"Treaties," Ontario Ministry of Indigenous Affairs, https://www.ontario.ca/page/treaties.
Christina Saunders, "Getting Ready for Treaties Recognition Week," *ETFO Voice*, Fall 2017, http://etfovoice.ca/feature/getting-ready-treaties-recognition-week.

United Nations Declaration on the Rights of Indigenous Peoples

> We have always known, and the United Nations Declaration on the Rights of Indigenous Peoples affirms and protects, our collective and individual rights, including our right to cultural practices, control of our economies, and leadership in social and political institutions. (4)

The United Nations adopted its Declaration on the Rights of Indigenous Peoples (UNDRIP) on September 13, 2007. Article 43 of the declaration states that nations are responsible for establishing "minimum standards for the survival, dignity and well-being of the Indigenous peoples of the world."[23] UNDRIP sets out a basic framework for protecting the rights of Indigenous people, including the right to self-determination. Originally, 144 countries voted to support the declaration; 4 countries (Australia, Canada, New Zealand,

and the United States) voted against; and 11 countries (Azerbaijan, Bangladesh, Bhutan, Burundi, Colombia, Georgia, Kenya, Nigeria, Russian Federation, Samoa, and Ukraine) abstained. In 2010, Canada issued a "Statement of Support" that endorsed the principles of UNDRIP, and in 2015, the declaration was implemented with the support of the prime minister. In 2016, Canada finally expressed full support for the declaration – although the implementation of UNDRIP continues to be a work in progress.

Resources

Global Encounters International Student Video Conference, "UNDRIP: United Nations Declaration on the Rights of Indigenous Peoples – International Video Conference: Teacher's Guide," 2017, http://tcge.tiged.org/images/news/files/UNDRIP TeachersGuide.pdf.

United Nations Human Rights, *10th Anniversary, UN Declaration on the Rights of Indigenous Peoples*, November 28, 2017, video, 9:14, https://youtu.be/yhw5Koo05xE.

Urban Indigenous Identity

> Our understanding of being Indigenous is rooted in our relationship with our mother, our family, and the broader urban Indigenous community. (130)

According to the 2016 census, over half of Indigenous people in Canada live in an urban setting.[24] Winnipeg, Edmonton, Vancouver, Calgary, and Toronto have the highest concentrations of Indigenous people in the country. Urban communities include a diversity of people with mixed ancestry. Urban Indigenous people may or may not have connections with their traditional territories and sometimes have limited access to culture-specific programs. For example, if you are Anishinaabe and you live in Toronto, you can find cultural resources, including ceremony, Elders, and access to language classes, but if you are Inuit or Mi'kmaq, finding ceremony or language from your nation is not necessarily as easily available.

Friendship centres and Indigenous community services often have an "all are welcome" policy that allows all urban Indigenous people access to services. Most urban Canadian cities do not have a single geographic location where urban Indigenous people tend to live, which can make it difficult for Indigenous people living in urban areas to have access to services that reflect their experience and culture. It also means they may experience racism or ignorance when trying to access health care, education, employment, or housing. Governments are recognizing the ever-increasing urban Indigenous population and the need to be responsive to these communities. For example, the Government of Ontario recently began working with the Ontario Federation of Indigenous Friendship Centres, the Métis Nation of Ontario, and the Ontario Native Women's Association to create the *Urban Indigenous Action Plan* to better respond to the needs of urban Indigenous communities.[25]

Resources

Susan D. Dion and Angela Salamanca, "inVISIBILITY: Indigenous in the City – Indigenous Artists, Indigenous Youth and the Project of Survivance," *Decolonization: Indigeneity, Education and Society* 3, no. 1 (2014): 159–188, https://jps.library.utoronto.ca/index.php/des/article/view/20709.

Urban.Indigenous.Proud, short film collection (Ontario Federation of Indigenous Friendship Centres and National Film Board of Canada, 2018), https://www.nfb.ca/channels/urban-indigenous-proud-series/.

Wampum Belts

> Long before the arrival of Europeans, Indigenous Peoples had an established practice of recording treaty agreements in wampum. (86)

A wampum belt is a belt-like object woven together with two kinds of beads, made from quahog and whelk shells, and its materials and iconography create meaning through symbols. As a mnemonic device, leaders "read the talk" embedded in the wampum to establish and renew agreements between nations.[26]

The Dish with One Spoon Wampum Belt documents a treaty between the Haudenosaunee and the Anishinaabe. It represents a shared commitment to equitable and sustainable land use.[27] The earth is the one dish that feeds both nations, who agree to take from the earth only what is required and to use all that is taken. Agreements symbolized by wampum were often revised each year with a feast or ceremony, revisiting the treaty terms through a reading of the wampum. Some of the early treaties between Europeans and Indigenous Peoples were made with wampum. Kaswentha, also known as the Two Row Wampum, documents a 1613 treaty between the Haudenosaunee Confederacy and Dutch settlers. It has two purple rows with a white background. The purple rows represent the Haudenosaunee canoe and the Dutch boat, side by side, not interfering with each other's ways of life. The white rows represent peace, friendship, and respect. The purple rows are parallel, signifying two sovereign nations, each retaining its own governance, traditions, and culture. Other important wampum belts are the Four Nations Alliance Belt, the Peace Treaty Wampum Belt, the Hiawatha Wampum Belt, and the Treaty of Niagara covenant agreement, also known as the Covenant Chain Wampum.

Resources

Alex Shares His Wampum Belt (Anishinabek Nation, June 23, 2021), video, 2:03, https://www.youtube.com/watch?v=iTaaOR3Y8qo.

The Two Row Wampum and the Covenant Chain of Treaties (Two Row, January 4, 2013), video, 2:33, https://youtu.be/amtCICqZk5w.

NOTES

Introduction: Indigenous Presence

Portions of this introduction are adapted from Susan D. Dion, *Braiding Histories: Learning from Aboriginal Peoples' Experiences and Perspectives* (Vancouver: UBC Press, 2009).

1 Susan D. Dion, "Mediating the Space Between: Voices of Indigenous Youth and Voices of Educators in Service of Reconciliation," *Canadian Review of Sociology* 53, no. 4 (2016), 471.
2 For a discussion on the discourse of the Romantic, Mythical Other, see Susan D. Dion, *Braiding Histories*.
3 Truth and Reconciliation Commission of Canada, *Truth and Reconciliation Commission of Canada: Calls to Action*, 2015, https://ehprnh2mwo3.exactdn.com/wp-content/uploads/2021/01/Calls_to_Action_English2.pdf.
4 Susan D. Dion, *The Listening Stone: Learning from the Ontario Ministry of Education's First Nations, Métis and Inuit–Focused Collaborative Inquiry 2013–2014* (Oakville, ON: Council of Ontario Directors of Education, 2014), https://www.ontariodirectors.ca/downloads/Listening_Stone/Dion_LS_Final_Report%20Sept_10-2014-2.pdf; *The Listening Stone Project Year Two: Deliberate Inquiry, Complex Questions, Deep Learning – The First Nations, Métis and Inuit–Focused Collaborative Inquiry 2014–2015* (Oakville, ON: Council of Ontario Directors of Education, 2015), https://www.ontariodirectors.ca/downloads/Listening_Stone/Code_Report%20_%20Listening_Stone-Year_2-2014_15.pdf; *The Listening Stone Project Year Three: Starting Points, Turning Points, Learning Points – Lessons from the First Nations, Métis and Inuit–Focused Collaborative Inquiry 2015–2016* (Oakville, ON: Council of Ontario Directors of Education, 2016), https://www.ontariodirectors.ca/downloads/Listening_Stone/LSY3_Report_Nov_1_2016-Final.

pdf; *The Listening Stone Project Year Four: Investments in Teaching, Learning and Students – Lessons from the Indigenous Education–Focused Collaborative Inquiry 2016–2017* (Oakville, ON: Council of Ontario Directors of Education, 2018), https://www.ontariodirectors.ca/downloads/Listening_Stone/LSPY4_Report_August_3_2018.pdf.

5 Marie Battiste, *Decolonizing Education: Nourishing the Learned Spirit* (Saskatoon, SK: Purich, 2013); Russell Bishop, Mere Berryman, Tom Cavanagh, and Lani Teddi, "Te Kotahitanga: Addressing Educational Disparities Facing Māori Students in New Zealand," *Teaching and Teacher Education* 25, no. 5 (2009): 734–42; Dion, *Braiding Histories*; Susan D. Dion, "Disrupting Molded Images: Identities, Responsibilities and Relationships – Teachers and Indigenous Subject Material," *Teaching Education* 18, no. 4 (2007): 329–42; Dwayne Donald, "Indigenous Métissage: A Decolonizing Research Sensibility," *International Journal of Qualitative Studies in Education* 25, no. 5 (2012): 533–55; Teresa Strong-Wilson and Julia Ellis, "Children and Place: Reggio Emilia's Environment as Third Teacher," *Theory into Practice* 46, no. 1 (2007): 40–47; Jennifer Tupper, "The Possibilities of Reconciliation through Difficult Dialogues: Treaty Education as Peacebuilding," *Curriculum Inquiry* 44, no. 4 (2014): 469–88.

6 Anne Godlewska, Jackie Moore, and C. Drew Bednasek, "Cultivating Ignorance of Aboriginal Realities," *Canadian Geographer* 54, no. 4 (2010), 419.

7 Patrick Wolfe, "Settler Colonialism and the Elimination of the Native," *Journal of Genocide Research* 8, no. 4 (2006): 387–409.

8 Lorenzo Veracini, *The Settler Colonial Present* (Basingstoke, UK: Palgrave Macmillan, 2015), cited in Augustine S.J. Park, "Settler Colonialism and the Politics of Grief: Theorising a Decolonising Transitional Justice for Indian Residential Schools," *Human Rights Review* 16 (2015): 274.

9 "Alberta's K–12 student population includes a self-identified Indigenous population of approximately seven percent. The number of self-identified Indigenous teachers and leaders in the provincial education system workforce is less than one percent, resulting in a less than representative workforce and role models for all students." (College of Alberta School Superintendents, *Indigenous Teacher Survey Report* [January 2019], 29, https://cass.ab.ca/wp-content/uploads/2019/01/Indigenous-Teacher-Survey-Report-Draft-2019-01-23-Final.pdf.) Teaching is not the only profession that lacks Indigenous representation; social work, medicine, law, and policing have a similar problem.

10 Verna St. Denis, *A Study of Aboriginal Teachers' Professional Knowledge and Experience in Canadian Schools* (Saskatoon, SK: Canadian Teachers' Federation, 2010), 11, https://www.oise.utoronto.ca/otso/UserFiles/File/ABORIGINAL_Report2010_EN_Web.pdf.

11 Lisa Korteweg and Alexandra Bissell, "The Complexities of Researching Youth Civic Engagement in Canada with/by Indigenous Youth: Settler-

Colonial Challenges for Tikkun Olam Pedagogies of Repair and Reconciliation," *Citizenship Education Research Journal* 5, no. 1 (2015): 15.

12 Haydn Watters, "Truth and Reconciliation Chair Urges Canada to Adopt UN Declaration on Indigenous Peoples," *CBC News*, June 1, 2015, https://www.cbc.ca/news/politics/truth-and-reconciliation-chair-urges-canada-to-adopt-un-declaration-on-indigenous-peoples-1.3096225.

13 Daniel Heath Justice, *Why Indigenous Literatures Matter* (Waterloo, ON: Wilfrid Laurier University Press, 2018), 75.

14 Thomas King, *The Truth about Stories: A Native Narrative* (Toronto: House of Anansi Press, 2003); N. Scott Momaday, *The Names* (Tucson: University of Arizona Press, 1976); Jo-Ann Archibald, *Indigenous Storywork: Educating the Heart, Mind, Body, and Spirit* (Vancouver: UBC Press, 2008); Gerald Vizenor, *Manifest Manners: Postindian Warriors of Survivance* (Lebanon, NH: University Press of New England, 1994).

15 Armand Ruffo, "Inside Looking Out: Reading 'Tracks' from a Native Perspective," in *Looking at the Words of Our People: First Nations Analysis of Literature*, ed. Jeannette Armstrong, (Penticton, BC: Theytus Books, 1993).

16 Archibald, *Indigenous Storywork*.

17 N. Scott Momaday, in C.L. Woodward, *Ancestral Voice: Conversations with N. Scott Momaday* (Lincoln: University of Nebraska Press, 1989), 100.

18 Vanessa Dion Fletcher, personal communication with the author, 2002.

19 Lenore Keeshig-Tobias, "Stories Are Not Just Entertainment," in *Through Indian Eyes: The Native Experience in Books for Children*, ed. Beverly Slapin and Doris Seale, 98–101 (Gabriola Island, BC: New Society, 1992); Paula Gunn Allen, introduction to *Spider Woman's Granddaughters: Traditional Tales and Contemporary Writing by Native American Women*, ed. Paula Gunn Allen, 1–25 (New York: Fawcett Books, 1989).

20 Royal Commission on Aboriginal Peoples, *Report of the Royal Commission on Aboriginal Peoples* (Ottawa: Supply and Services Canada, 1996).

21 Vine Deloria Jr., *God Is Red: A Native View of Religion*, 2nd ed. (Golden, CO: Fulcrum, 1994), 100.

22 Greg Sarris, *Keeping Slug Woman Alive: A Holistic Approach to American Indian Texts* (Berkeley: University of California Press, 1993).

23 Jocelyn Hazelwood Donlon, "Hearing Is Believing: Southern Racial Communities and Strategies of Story-Listening in Gloria Naylor and Lee Smith," *Twentieth Century Literature* 41, no. 1 (1995): 18.

24 Kimberly M. Blaeser, "Writing Voices Speaking: Native Voices and an Oral Aesthetic," in *Talking on the Page*, ed. Laura J. Murray and Keren Rice, 59–60 (Toronto: University of Toronto Press, 1999).

25 Dion, *Braiding Histories*.

26 Manitoba Métis Federation, "Louis Riel Quotes," http://www.mmf.mb.ca/louis_riel_quotes.php.

27 Dion, *Braiding Histories*.

Chapter 1: Requisites for Reconciliation

1 Susan D. Dion, *Braiding Histories: Learning from Aboriginal Peoples' Experiences and Perspectives* (Vancouver: UBC Press, 2009).
2 Dion, *Braiding Histories*, 178.
3 For a discussion of working through, see Dion, *Braiding Histories*, 62–63.
4 Minnie Bruce Pratt, *Rebellion: Essays 1980–1991* (Ithaca, NY: Firebrand Books, 1991).
5 Roger Simon and Wendy Armitage, "Teaching Risky Stories: Remembering Mass Destruction through Children's Literature," *English Quarterly* 28, no. 1 (1995): 29.
6 Jocelyn Hazelwood Donlon, "Hearing Is Believing: Southern Racial Communities and Strategies of Story-Listening in Gloria Naylor and Lee Smith," *Twentieth Century Literature* 41, no. 1 (1995): 20.
7 I describe four specific contexts; however, different versions of these questions and comments arise in similar situations. They are representative of familiar questions I have been asked in recent years.
8 Section 91(24) of the Constitution Act, 1867 provides that the federal government has the legislative jurisdiction over "Indians and lands reserved for the Indians."
9 Patrick Wolfe, "Settler Colonialism and the Elimination of the Native," *Journal of Genocide Research* 8, no. 4 (2006): 387–409.

Chapter 2: Seeing Yourself in Relationship with Settler Colonialism

1 Quoted in Roger Simon, *The Touch of the Past: Remembrance, Learning, and Ethics* (New York: Palgrave Macmillan, 2005), 24.
2 Reni Eddo-Lodge, *Why I'm No Longer Talking to White People about Race* (London: Bloomsbury, 2017); Cleveland Hayes and Brenda Juárez, "You Showed Your Whiteness: You Don't Get a 'Good' White People's Medal," *International Journal of Qualitative Studies in Education* 22, 6 (2009): 729–44.
3 Each of the totem poles has its own plaque providing more detailed information. But it was the more general plaque, for all of the poles, that Libby responded to. Her realization at that moment signified her noticing her own learning.
4 Robin DiAngelo, *White Fragility: Why It's So Hard for White People to Talk about Racism* (Boston: Beacon Press, 2018).
5 Richard Wagamese, *Embers: One Ojibway's Meditations* (Madeira Park, BC: Douglas & McIntyre, 2016), 12.
6 To give a sense of the placement of the position within the hierarchy, a senior assistant deputy minister is the most senior executive position reporting to the deputy minister, a Governor-in-Council appointee, and

supporting the minister. In my case, the minister is the Minister for Crown-Indigenous Relations, who is responsible for exercising leadership within the Government of Canada in relation to the affirmation and implementation of the rights of Indigenous Peoples recognized and affirmed by section 35 of the Constitution Act, 1982 and the implementation of treaties and other agreements with Indigenous Peoples; negotiating treaties and other agreements to advance the self-determination of Indigenous Peoples; and advancing reconciliation with Indigenous Peoples, in collaboration with Indigenous Peoples and through renewed nation-to-nation, government-to-government, and Inuit-Crown relationships.

Chapter 3: The Historical Timeline: Refusing Absence, Knowing Presence, and Being Indigenous

1 Deborah Britzman, *Lost Subjects, Contested Objects* (Albany: State University of New York Press, 1998), 118.
2 Susan D. Dion, *Braiding Histories: Learning from Aboriginal Peoples' Experiences and Perspectives* (Vancouver: UBC Press, 2009), 58.
3 Quoted in Kimberly M. Blaeser, "Writing Voices Speaking: Native Authors and an Oral Aesthetic," in *Talking on the Page: Editing Aboriginal Oral Texts*, ed. Laura Jane Murray and Keren Dichter Rice (Toronto: University of Toronto Press, 1999), 53.
4 Laura Jane Murray and Keren Dichter Rice, introduction to *Talking on the Page: Editing Aboriginal Oral Texts*, ed. Laura Jane Murray and Keren Dichter Rice (Toronto: University of Toronto Press, 1999), xii.
5 Murray and Rice, introduction to *Talking on the Page*, xi.
6 Murray and Rice, introduction to *Talking on the Page*, xiii.
7 Kimberly M. Blaeser, "Writing Voices Speaking," 56.
8 *Dr. Susan Dion Shares Her Historical Timeline Lecture*, Professional Learning Supports (Ontario Ministry of Education, 2018), video, 47:34, http://hdl.handle.net/2429/80924.
9 See Ontario Ministry of Education, *People of Native Ancestry: A Resource Guide for the Primary and Junior Divisions* (Toronto: Ontario Ministry of Education, 1977). See also Ontario Ministry of Education, *People of Native Ancestry: A Resource Guide for the Intermediate Division* (Toronto: Ontario Ministry of Education, 1975).
10 Minnesota Historical Society, "The Doctrine of Discovery," *The US-Dakota War of 1862*, https://www.usdakotawar.org/history/newcomers-missionaries/doctrine-discovery.
11 Quoted in J.R. Miller, *Skyscrapers Hide the Heavens: A History of Indian-White Relations in Canada*, rev. ed. (Toronto: University of Toronto Press, 1991), 189.

12 Duncan Campbell Scott, National Archives of Canada, Record Group 10, vol. 6810, file 470-2-3, vol. 7, 55 (L-3) and 63 (N-3).
13 P.H. Bryce, quoted in "Bryce Report" *Canadian Museum of History*, June 18, 2017, https://www.historymuseum.ca/blog/bryce-report/.

Chapter 4: Learning from Contemporary Indigenous Artists

1 Greg Hill, "Afterward: Looking Back to Sakahàn," in *Sakahàn: International Indigenous Art*, ed. Greg Gill, Candice Hopkins, and Christine Lalonde, 136–40 (Ottawa: National Gallery of Canada, 2013), 16.
2 Vanessa Dion Fletcher, "Curatorial Statement," in *Aanikoobijigani Gikinoohamaagewinan: Noonkom Ishinamowinan Ancestral Teachings: Contemporary Perspectives*, exhibit catalogue (Toronto: Thunderbird Aboriginal Arts Culture and Entrepreneur Centre, 2011), 8.
3 Leanne Simpson, *Dancing on Our Turtle's Back: Stories of Nishnaabeg Re-Creation, Resurgence, and a New Emergence* (Winnipeg: ARP Books, 2011), 51.
4 Heather Igloliorte, "No History of Colonialism," in *Decolonize Me*, eds. Heather Igloliorte, Steve Loft, Brenda L. Croft (Ottawa: Ottawa Art Gallery and the Robert McLaughlin Gallery, 2012), 25.
5 France Trépanier and Chris Creighton-Kelly, *Understanding Aboriginal Arts in Canada Today: A Knowledge and Literature Review* (Ottawa: Canada Council for the Arts, 2011), 15.
6 Charlotte Townsend-Gault, "Kinds of Knowing," in *Land, Spirit, Power: First Nations at the National Gallery of Canada* (Ottawa: National Gallery of Canada, 1992), 99.
7 Vanessa Dion Fletcher, personal communication with the author, 2021.
8 Vanessa Dion Fletcher is my daughter. We have collaborated on a number of projects. Originally Vanessa was going to author this chapter entirely, but her schedule did not allow for that degree of collaboration. We did have many conversations about the work, and she put me in touch with Sara Roque, who was able to assist with the organization and art selection, and contributed to discussions about the annotations.
9 Vanessa Dion Fletcher, personal communication with the author, July 2018.
10 Vanessa Dion Fletcher, "Art and Indigenous Identity" (guest lecture for Artists in Toronto District School Board Schools Speaker Series, Toronto, Urban Indigenous Education Centre, 2014).
11 Thomas King, *The Truth about Stories: A Native Narrative* (Toronto: House of Anansi Press, 2003), 36.
12 King, *The Truth about Stories*, 10.

13 Mary Anne Barkhouse, "Mary Anne Barkhouse," *Resilience: 50 Indigenous Art Cards and Teaching Guide*, 2017, https://resilienceproject.ca/en/artists/mary-anne-barkhouse.
14 In published material Joseph Jacobs is identified as Tuscarora. In my correspondence with his family, I was told that Joseph was Cayuga.
15 Bruce Fisher, "Joseph Jacobs: Narratives in Stone," *The Public*, May 13, 2015, http://www.dailypublic.com/articles/05132015/joseph-jacobs-narratives-stone.
16 Fisher, "Joseph Jacobs."
17 King, *The Truth about Stories*.
18 Fisher, "Joseph Jacobs."
19 Ruth Cuthand, *I'm Not the Indian You're Looking For*, https://www.ruthcuthand.ca/.
20 Adrian Stimson, "Used and Abused," *Humanities Research* 15, no. 3 (2009): 75.
21 Vanessa Dion Fletcher, personal communication with the author, 2018.
22 George Littlechild, quoted in Portia Priegert, "Winnipeg Project Looks at the Sixties Scoop," *Galleries West*, April 9, 2017, https://www.gallerieswest.ca/magazine/stories/george-littlechild-and-the-sixties-scoop/.
23 Nicole Meawasige, "Reflections on Urban Indigenous Art" (unpublished manuscript, 2019).
24 Erica Commanda, "Bonnie Devine's *Battle for the Woodlands* Battles the Status Quo," *Muskrat Magazine*, January 13, 2016, http://muskratmagazine.com/bonnie-devines-battle-for-the-woodlands-battles-the-status-quo/.

Chapter 5: The Braiding Histories Stories

1 Julie Cruikshank, *Life Lived Like a Story* (Vancouver: UBC Press, 1990), ix.
2 Susan D. Dion, *Braiding Histories: Learning from Aboriginal Peoples' Experiences and Perspectives* (Vancouver: UBC Press, 2009).
3 Walter Benjamin, *Illuminations*, ed. Hannah Arendt, trans. Harry Zohn (New York: Schocken Books, 1968), 87.
4 I use the word *alterity* as opposed to *otherness* to signal incommensurability. By contrast, *other* is based on comparisons involving deviation from a certain normative standard.
5 The primary source for this (re)telling is a series of interviews completed in the preparation of Susan D. Dion, "Braiding Histories: Responding to the Problematics of Canadians Hearing a First Nations Perspective of Post-contact History" (PhD diss., Ontario Institute for Studies in Education, University of Toronto, 2002).

6 We worked closely on these stories and consider them to be co-written. When a story includes a first-person narrative, we identify which of us occupies the position of "I."
7 The primary source for this (re)telling is Ingeborg Marshall, *A History and Ethnography of the Beothuk* (Montreal/Kingston: McGill-Queen's University Press, 1996).
8 The primary sources for this (re)telling are W.B. Cameron, *The War Trail of Big Bear* (Toronto: Ryerson, 1926); Hugh A. Dempsey, *Big Bear: The End of Freedom* (Lincoln: University of Nebraska Press, 1984); and William B. Fraser, "Big Bear, Indian Patriot," *Alberta Historical Review* 14, no. 2 (1966): 1–13.
9 Rudy Wiebe, *The Temptations of Big Bear* (Toronto: Knopf Canada, 1995).
10 Dempsey, *Big Bear*, 157.
11 Dempsey, *Big Bear*, 44.
12 Dempsey, *Big Bear*, 63.
13 Dempsey, *Big Bear*, 69.
14 Dempsey, *Big Bear*, 106.
15 The primary source for this (re)telling is [As told to] Janet Silman, *Enough Is Enough: Aboriginal Women Speak Out* (Toronto: The Women's Press, 1987).
16 Now Sandra Lovelace Nicholas.
17 This (re)telling is based on a series of interviews completed in the mid 1990s. The story was reviewed and updated by Bernard Kerrigan in 2021.
18 This (re)telling is based on interviews completed in Fall 2020.
19 This (re)telling is based on interviews conducted in 2019. It was edited and approved by Oonig Paul Ward, with guidance and assistance from his father, Jeff Ward, at Membertou, Heritage Centre, March 5, 2021.
20 This (re)telling is based on a series of interviews conducted in 2019.

Conclusion: Wuleelham – Make Good Tracks

1 Simon Ortiz, quoted in Kimberly M. Blaeser, "Writing Voices Speaking: Native Authors and an Oral Aesthetic," in *Talking on the Page: Editing Aboriginal Oral Texts*, ed. Laura Jane Murray and Keren Dichter Rice (Toronto: University of Toronto Press, 1999), 56.

Glossary and Additional Resources

1 Statistics Canada, *Linguistic Characteristics of Canadians* (Language, 2011 Census of Population), October 2012, catalogue no. 98-314-X2011001,

https://www12.statcan.gc.ca/census-recensement/2011/as-sa/98-314-x/98-314-x2011001-eng.cfm.
2 Statistics Canada, "The Aboriginal Languages of First Nations People, Métis and Inuit," *Census in Brief* (Census of Population, 2016), October 25, 2017, catalogue no. 98-200-X2016022, https://www12.statcan.gc.ca/census-recensement/2016/as-sa/98-200-x/2016022/98-200-x2016022-eng.cfm.
3 Vine Deloria Jr., *God Is Red: A Native View of Religion*, 2nd ed. (Golden, CO: Fulcrum Publishing, 1994), 62.
4 Heather Conn, "Powley Case," *Canadian Encyclopedia*, Historica Canada, December 3, 2018, https://www.thecanadianencyclopedia.ca/en/article/powley-case.
5 National Indian Brotherhood/Assembly of First Nations, *Indian Control of Indian Education: Policy Paper* (Ottawa: Assembly of First Nations, 1972).
6 Tabitha Marshall, Michael Posluns, and Anthony J. Hall, "Assembly of First Nations," *Canadian Encyclopedia*, Historica Canada, February 7, 2006, https://www.thecanadianencyclopedia.ca/en/article/assembly-of-first-nations.
7 Naithan Lagace and Niigaanwewidam James Sinclair, "The White Paper, 1969," *Canadian Encyclopedia*, Historica Canada, September 24, 2015. https://www.thecanadianencyclopedia.ca/en/article/the-white-paper-1969.
8 Thomas King, *The Truth about Stories: A Native Narrative* (Toronto: House of Anansi Press, 2003), 98.
9 King, *The Truth about Stories*, 98.
10 "Potlatch," *Living Tradition: The Kwakwaka'wakw Potlatch on the Northwest Coast*, U'mista Cultural Society, 2021, https://umistapotlatch.ca/potlatch-eng.php.
11 Bob Joseph, *21 Things You May Not Know about the Indian Act: Helping Canadians Make Reconciliation with Indigenous Peoples a Reality* (Port Coquitlam, BC: Indigenous Relations Press, 2018).
12 The documentary can be viewed on demand at CBC Gem, and on Vimeo for a small donation (http://thepasssystem.ca/screenings/).
13 Duncan Campbell Scott, National Archives of Canada, Record Group 10, vol. 6810, file 470-2-3, vol. 7, 55 (L-3) and 63 (N-3).
14 "The Potlatch Ban," Bill Reid Centre, Simon Fraser University, 2016, https://www.sfu.ca/brc/online_exhibits/masks-2-0/the-potlatch-ban.html.
15 Terri Theodore, "New Royal B.C. Museum Policy Highlights Return of Stolen, Confiscated Indigenous Remains, Artifacts," *Globe and Mail*, May 19, 2019, https://www.theglobeandmail.com/canada/british-columbia/article-new-royal-bc-museum-policy-highlights-return-of-stolen-confiscated/.
16 "Understanding Our Admission Policy in Relation to Indigenous Peoples," Canadian Museum of Human Rights, 2021, https://humanrights.ca/visit/

plan-your-visit/understanding-our-admission-policy-in-relation-to-Indigenous-peoples.
17 "The Haisla Prepare to Welcome Their Totem Pole Back Home," Turtle Island Native Network, June 27, 2006, http://www.turtleisland.org/culture/culture-haisla.htm.
18 Patrick Johnston and Canadian Council on Social Development, *Native Children and the Child Welfare System* (Toronto: Canadian Council on Social Development, in association with James Lorimer & Co., 1983).
19 Ontario Sixties Scoop Steering Committee, "Sixties Scoop Survivors' Decade-Long Journey for Justice Culminates in Historic Pan-Canadian Agreement," *Cision*, October 6, 2017, https://www.newswire.ca/news-releases/sixties-scoop-survivors-decade-long-journey-for-justice-culminates-in-historic-pan-canadian-agreement-649748633.html.
20 CBC Radio, "The Millennium Scoop: Indigenous Youth Say Care System Repeats Horrors of the Past," *The Current*, January 25, 2018, https://www.cbc.ca/radio/thecurrent/a-special-edition-of-the-current-for-january-25-2018-1.4503172/the-millennium-scoop-Indigenous-youth-say-care-system-repeats-horrors-of-the-past-1.4503179.
21 Chimamanda Ngozi Adichie, "The Danger of a Single Story," filmed in July 2009, TEDGlobal 2009 video, 18:49, https://www.ted.com/talks/chimamanda_ngozi_adichie_the_danger_of_a_single_story.
22 *Canadian Charter of Rights and Freedoms*, s. 25, Part I of the Constitution Act, 1982, RSC 1985, app. II, no. 44.
23 United Nations General Assembly, *United Nations Declaration on the Rights of Indigenous Peoples: Resolution Adopted by the General Assembly on 13 September 2007*, https://www.un.org/development/desa/indigenouspeoples/wp-content/uploads/sites/19/2018/11/UNDRIP_E_web.pdf.
24 Statistics Canada, "Aboriginal Peoples in Canada: Key Results from the 2016 Census," *The Daily*, October 25, 2017, https://www150.statcan.gc.ca/n1/daily-quotidien/171025/dq171025a-eng.htm.
25 Ontario Ministry of Indigenous Relations and Reconciliation, Ontario Federation of Indigenous Friendship Centres, Métis Nation of Ontario, and Ontario Native Women's Association, *The Urban Indigenous Action Plan*, n.d., https://files.ontario.ca/uiap_full_report_en.pdf.
26 Lisa Myers and Rachelle Dickenson, *Reading the Talk: Michael Belmore, Hannah Claus, Patricia Deadman, Keesic Douglas, Vanessa Dion Fletcher, Melissa General* (Oshawa, ON: Robert McLaughlin Gallery, 2014), 15.
27 Fred Glover, "A Dish with One Spoon," *Canadian Encyclopedia*, Historica Canada, March 31, 2020, https://www.thecanadianencyclopedia.ca/en/article/a-dish-with-one-spoon.

BIBLIOGRAPHY

Adichie, Chimamanda Ngozi. "The Danger of a Single Story." Filmed July 2009. TEDGlobal video, 18:49. https://www.ted.com/talks/chimamanda_ngozi_adichie_the_danger_of_a_single_story.
Archibald, Jo-Ann. *Indigenous Storywork: Educating the Heart, Mind, Body, and Spirit*. Vancouver: UBC Press, 2008.
Barkhouse, Mary Anne. *Resilience: 50 Indigenous Art Cards and Teaching Guide*. 2017. https://resilienceproject.ca/en/artists/mary-anne-barkhouse.
Battiste, Marie. *Decolonizing Education: Nourishing the Learned Spirit*. Saskatoon, SK: Purich, 2013.
Benjamin, Walter. *Illuminations*. Edited by Hannah Arendt. Translated by Harry Zohn. New York: Schocken Books, 1968.
Bishop, Russell, Mere Berryman, Tom Cavanagh, and Lani Teddy. "Te Kotahitanga: Addressing Educational Disparities Facing Māori Students in New Zealand." *Teaching and Teacher Education* 25, no. 5 (July 2009): 734–42.
Blaeser, Kimberly M. "Writing Voices Speaking: Native Authors and an Oral Aesthetic." In *Talking on the Page: Editing Aboriginal Oral Texts*, edited by Laura Jane Murray and Keren Dichter Rice, 53–68. Toronto: University of Toronto Press, 1999.
Britzman, Deborah. *Lost Subjects, Contested Objects*. Albany: State University of New York Press, 1998.
Cameron, W.B. *The War Trail of Big Bear*. Toronto: Ryerson, 1926.
Canadian Charter of Rights and Freedoms, s 25, Part I of the *Constitution Act, 1982*, RSC 1985, app. II, no. 44.
Cardinal, Gil, dir. *Totem: The Return of the G'psgolox Pole*. 2003; Montreal: National Film Board of Canada. DVD.
CBC Radio. "The Millennium Scoop: Indigenous Youth Say Care System Repeats Horrors of the Past." *The Current*, January 25, 2018. https://www.

cbc.ca/radio/thecurrent/a-special-edition-of-the-current-for-january-25-2018-1.4503172/the-millennium-scoop-Indigenous-youth-say-care-system-repeats-horrors-of-the-past-1.4503179.

College of Alberta School Superintendents. *Indigenous Teacher Survey Report.* January 2019. https://cass.ab.ca/wp-content/uploads/2019/01/Indigenous-Teacher-Survey-Report-Draft-2019-01-23-Final.pdf.

Commanda, Erica. "Bonnie Devine's *Battle for the Woodlands* Battles the Status Quo." *Muskrat Magazine,* January 13, 2016. http://muskratmagazine.com/bonnie-devines-battle-for-the-woodlands-battles-the-status-quo/.

Constitution Act, 1867 (UK), 30 & 31 Victoria, c 3. https://canlii.ca/t/ldsw.

Constitution Act, 1982, being Schedule B to the *Canada Act 1982* (UK), 1982, c 11. https://canlii.ca/t/ldsx.

Cruikshank, Julie. *Life Lived Like a Story.* Vancouver: UBC Press, 1990.

Deloria, Vine, Jr. *God Is Red: A Native View of Religion.* 2nd ed. Golden, CO: Fulcrum, 1994.

Dempsey, Hugh A. *Big Bear: The End of Freedom.* Lincoln: University of Nebraska Press, 1984.

DiAngelo, Robin. *White Fragility: Why It's So Hard for White People to Talk about Racism.* Boston: Beacon Press, 2018.

Dion, Susan D. *Braiding Histories: Learning from Aboriginal Peoples' Experiences and Perspectives.* Vancouver: UBC Press, 2009.

–. "Braiding Histories: Responding to the Problematics of Canadians Hearing a First Nations Perspective of Post-contact History." PhD diss., Ontario Institute for Studies in Education, University of Toronto, 2002.

–. "Disrupting Molded Images: Identities, Responsibilities and Relationships – Teachers and Indigenous Subject Material." *Teaching Education* 18, no. 4 (2007): 329–42.

–. *The Listening Stone: Learning from the Ontario Ministry of Education's First Nations, Métis and Inuit–Focused Collaborative Inquiry 2013–2014.* Oakville, ON: Council of Ontario Directors of Education, 2014. https://www.ontariodirectors.ca/downloads/Listening_Stone/Dion_LS_Final_Report%20Sept_10-2014-2.pdf.

–. *The Listening Stone Project Year Four: Investments in Teaching, Learning and Students – Lessons from the Indigenous Education–Focused Collaborative Inquiry 2016–2017.* Oakville, ON: Council of Ontario Directors of Education, 2018. https://www.ontariodirectors.ca/downloads/Listening_Stone/LSPY4_Report_August_3_2018.pdf.

–. *The Listening Stone Project Year Three: Starting Points, Turning Points, Learning Points – Lessons from the First Nations, Métis and Inuit–Focused Collaborative Inquiry 2015–2016.* Oakville, ON: Council of Ontario Directors of Education, 2016. https://www.ontariodirectors.ca/downloads/Listening_Stone/LSY3_Report_Nov_1_2016-Final.pdf.

–. *The Listening Stone Project Year Two: Deliberate Inquiry, Complex Questions, Deep Learning – The First Nations, Métis and Inuit–Focused Collaborative Inquiry 2014–2015*. Oakville, ON: Council of Ontario Directors of Education, 2015. https://www.ontariodirectors.ca/downloads/Listening_Stone/Code_Report%20_%20Listening_Stone-Year_2-2014_15.pdf.

–. "Mediating the Space Between: Voices of Indigenous Youth and Voices of Educators in Service of Reconciliation." *Canadian Review of Sociology* 53, no. 4 (2016): 468–73.

Dion Fletcher, Vanessa. "Curatorial Statement." In *Aanikoobijigani Gikinoohamaagewinan: Noonkom ishinamowinan Ancestral Teachings: Contemporary Perspectives*. Exhibit Catalogue. Toronto: Thunderbird Aboriginal Arts Culture and Entrepreneur Centre, 2011.

Donald, Dwayne. "Indigenous Métissage: A Decolonizing Research Sensibility." *International Journal of Qualitative Studies in Education* 25, no. 5 (2012): 533–55.

Donlon, Jocelyn Hazelwood. "Hearing Is Believing: Southern Racial Communities and Strategies of Story-Listening in Gloria Naylor and Lee Smith." *Twentieth Century Literature* 41, no. 1 (1995): 16–35.

Eddo-Lodge, Reni. *Why I'm No Longer Talking to White People about Race*. London: Bloomsbury, 2017.

Fisher, Bruce. "Joseph Jacobs: Narratives in Stone." *The Public*, May 13, 2015. http://www.dailypublic.com/articles/05132015/joseph-jacobs-narratives-stone.

Fraser, William B. "Big Bear, Indian Patriot." *Alberta Historical Review* 14, no. 2 (1966): 1–13.

Global Encounters International Student Video Conference. "UNDRIP: United Nations Declaration on the Rights of Indigenous Peoples – International Video Conference: Teacher's Guide." 2017. http://tcge.tiged.org/images/news/files/UNDRIPTeachersGuide.pdf.

Godlewska, Anne, Jackie Moore, and C. Drew Bednasek. "Cultivating Ignorance of Aboriginal Realities." *Canadian Geographer* 54, no. 4 (2010): 417–40.

Government of Ontario. *The Urban Indigenous Action Plan*. Updated January 12, 2021, https://www.ontario.ca/page/urban-indigenous-action-plan.

Gunn Allen, Paula. Introduction to *Spider Woman's Granddaughters: Traditional Tales and Contemporary Writing by Native American Women*, edited by Paula Gunn Allen, 1–25. New York: Fawcett Books, 1989.

Hayes, Cleveland, and Brenda Juárez. "You Showed Your Whiteness: You Don't Get a 'Good' White People's Medal." *International Journal of Qualitative Studies in Education* 22, no. 6 (November 2009): 729–44.

Hill, Greg. "Afterward: Looking back to Sakahàn." In *Sakahàn: International Indigenous Art*, edited by Greg Gill, Candice Hopkins, and Christine Lalonde, 136–40. Ottawa: National Gallery of Canada, 2013.

Igloliorte, Heather. "No History of Colonialism." In *Decolonize Me*, edited by Heather Igloliorte, Steve Loft, and Brenda L. Croft, 18–27. Ottawa: Ottawa Art Gallery and the Robert McLaughlin Gallery, 2012.

Johnston, Patrick, and Canadian Council on Social Development. *Native Children and the Child Welfare System*. Toronto: Canadian Council on Social Development in association with James Lorimer & Co., 1983.

Joseph, Bob. *21 Things You May Not Know about the Indian Act: Helping Canadians Make Reconciliation with Indigenous Peoples a Reality*. Port Coquitlam, BC: Indigenous Relations Press, 2018.

Justice, Daniel Heath. *Why Indigenous Literatures Matter*. Waterloo, ON: Wilfrid Laurier University Press, 2018.

Keeshig-Tobias, Lenore. "Stories Are Not Just Entertainment." In *Through Indian Eyes: The Native Experience in Books for Children*, edited by Beverly Slapin and Doris Seale, 98–101. Gabriola Island, BC: New Society, 1992.

King, Thomas. *The Truth about Stories: A Native Narrative*. Toronto: House of Anansi Press, 2003.

Korteweg, Lisa, and Alexandra Bissell. "The Complexities of Researching Youth Civic Engagement in Canada with/by Indigenous Youth: Settler-Colonial Challenges for Tikkun Olam Pedagogies of Repair and Reconciliation." *Citizenship Education Research Journal* 5, no. 1 (2015): 14–26.

Marshall, Ingeborg. *A History and Ethnography of the Beothuk*. Montreal/Kingston: McGill-Queen's University Press, 1996.

McLaren, Nadia, dir. *Muffins for Granny*. 2007; Toronto, ON: Mongrel Media, 2019. DVD.

Meawasige, Nicole. "Reflections on Urban Indigenous Art." Unpublished manuscript, 2019. Typescript.

Miller, J.R. *Skyscrapers Hide the Heavens: A History of Indian-White Relations in Canada*. Rev. ed. Toronto: University of Toronto Press, 1991.

Momaday, N. Scott. *The Names*. Tucson: University of Arizona Press, 1976.

Murray, Laura Jane, and Keren Dichter Rice. Introduction to *Talking on the Page: Editing Aboriginal Oral Texts*, edited by Laura Jane Murray and Keren Dichter Rice, xi–xxi. Toronto: University of Toronto Press, 1999.

Myers, Lisa, and Rachelle Dickenson. *Reading the Talk: Michael Belmore, Hannah Claus, Patricia Deadman, Keesic Douglas, Vanessa Dion Fletcher, Melissa General*. Oshawa, ON: Robert McLaughlin Gallery, 2014. https://michaelbelmore.com/wp-content/uploads/2018/01/catalogue_2015_reading-the-talk_michael-belmore.pdf.

National Indian Brotherhood/Assembly of First Nations. *Indian Control of Indian Education: Policy Paper*. Ottawa, ON: Assembly of First Nations, 1972.

Ontario Ministry of Education. *People of Native Ancestry: A Resource Guide for the Intermediate Division*. Toronto: Ontario Ministry of Education, 1975.

–. *People of Native Ancestry: A Resource Guide for the Primary and Junior Divisions*, Toronto: Ontario Ministry of Education, 1977.

Ontario Ministry of Indigenous Relations and Reconciliation, Ontario Federation of Indigenous Friendship Centres, Métis Nation of Ontario, and Ontario Native Women's Association. *The Urban Indigenous Action Plan*. n.d. https://www.ontario.ca/page/urban-Indigenous-action-plan.

Ontario Sixties Scoop Steering Committee. "Sixties Scoop Survivors' Decade-Long Journey for Justice Culminates in Historic Pan-Canadian Agreement." *Cision*, October 6, 2017. https://www.newswire.ca/news-releases/sixties-scoop-survivors-decade-long-journey-for-justice-culminates-in-historic-pan-canadian-agreement-649748633.html.

Park, Augustine S.J. "Settler Colonialism and the Politics of Grief: Theorising a Decolonising Transitional Justice for Indian Residential Schools." *Human Rights Review* 16 (2015): 273–93.

Pratt, Minnie Bruce. *Rebellion: Essays 1980–1991*. Ithaca, NY: Firebrand Books, 1991.

Priegert, Portia. "Winnipeg Project Looks at the Sixties Scoop." *Galleries West*, April 9, 2017. https://www.gallerieswest.ca/magazine/stories/george-littlechild-and-the-sixties-scoop/.

Royal Commission on Aboriginal Peoples. *Report of the Royal Commission on Aboriginal Peoples*. Ottawa: Supply and Services Canada, 1996.

Ruffo, Armand. "Inside Looking Out: Reading 'Tracks' from a Native Perspective." In *Looking at the Words of Our People: First Nations Analysis of Literature*, edited by Jeannette Armstrong, 161–76. Penticton, BC: Theytus Books, 1993.

Sarris, Greg. *Keeping Slug Woman Alive: A Holistic Approach to American Indian Texts*. Berkeley: University of California Press, 1993.

Simon, Roger. *The Touch of the Past: Remembrance, Learning, and Ethics*. New York: Palgrave Macmillan, 2005.

Simon, Roger, and Wendy Armitage. "Teaching Risky Stories: Remembering Mass Destruction through Children's Literature." *English Quarterly* 28, no. 1 (1995): 27–31.

Simpson, Leanne. *Dancing on Our Turtle's Back: Stories of Nishnaabeg Re-Creation, Resurgence, and a New Emergence*. Winnipeg: ARP Books, 2011.

Smith, Linda Tuhiwai. *Decolonizing Methodologies: Research and Indigenous Peoples*. New York: St. Martin's Press, 1999.

St. Denis, Verna. *A Study of Aboriginal Teachers' Professional Knowledge and Experience in Canadian Schools*. Saskatoon, SK: Canadian Teachers' Federation, 2010. https://www.oise.utoronto.ca/otso/UserFiles/File/ABORIGINAL_Report2010_EN_Web.pdf.

Statistics Canada. "The Aboriginal Languages of First Nations People, Métis and Inuit." *Census in Brief* (Census of Population, 2016), October 25, 2017. Catalogue no. 98-200-X2016022. https://www12.statcan.gc.ca/census recensement/2016/as-sa/98-200-x/2016022/98-200-x2016022-eng.cfm.

–. "Aboriginal People in Canada: Key Results from the 2016 Census." *The Daily*,

October 25, 2017. https://www150.statcan.gc.ca/n1/daily-quotidien/171025/dq171025a-eng.htm.

—. *Linguistic Characteristics of Canadians* (Language, 2011 Census of Population). October 2012. Catalogue no. 98-314-X2011001. https://www12.statcan.gc.ca/census-recensement/2011/as-sa/98-314-x/98-314-x2011001-eng.cfm.

Stimson, Adrian. "Used and Abused." *Humanities Research* 15, no 3. (2009): 71–80.

Strong-Wilson, Teresa, and Julia Ellis. "Children and Place: Reggio Emilia's Environment as Third Teacher." *Theory into Practice* 46, no. 1 (2007): 40–47.

Talaga, Tanya. *Seven Fallen Feathers: Racism, Death, and Hard Truths in a Northern City.* Toronto: House of Anansi Press, 2017.

Theodore, Terri. "New Royal B.C. Museum Policy Highlights Return of Stolen, Confiscated Indigenous Remains, Artifacts." *Globe and Mail,* May 19, 2019. https://www.theglobeandmail.com/canada/british-columbia/article-new-royal-bc-museum-policy-highlights-return-of-stolen-confiscated/.

Tobique Women's Group as told to Jane Silman. *Enough Is Enough: Aboriginal Women Speak Out.* Toronto: The Women's Press, 1975.

Townsend-Gault, Charlotte. "Kinds of Knowing." In *Land, Spirit, Power: First Nations at the National Gallery of Canada.* Ottawa: National Gallery of Canada, 1992.

Trépanier, France, and Chris Creighton-Kelly. *Understanding Aboriginal Arts in Canada Today: A Knowledge and Literature Review.* Ottawa: Canada Council for the Arts, 2011.

Truth and Reconciliation Commission of Canada. *Canada's Residential Schools: The Legacy.* Vol. 5 of *Final Report of the Truth and Reconciliation Commission of Canada.* Winnipeg: Truth and Reconciliation Commission of Canada, 2015. https://publications.gc.ca/collections/collection_2015/trc/IR4-9-5-2015-eng.pdf.

—. *Honouring the Truth, Reconciling for the Future: Summary of the Final Report of the Truth and Reconciliation Commission of Canada.* 2015. https://publications.gc.ca/site/eng/9.800288/publication.html.

—. *Truth and Reconciliation Commission of Canada: Calls to Action.* 2015. https://ehprnh2mwo3.exactdn.com/wp-content/uploads/2021/01/Calls_to_Action_English2.pdf.

Tupper, Jennifer. "The Possibilities of Reconciliation through Difficult Dialogues: Treaty Education as Peacebuilding." *Curriculum Inquiry* 44, no. 4, (2014): 469–88.

United Nations General Assembly. *United Nations Declaration on the Rights of Indigenous Peoples: Resolution Adopted by the General Assembly on 13 September 2007.* https://www.un.org/development/desa/indigenouspeoples/wp-content/uploads/sites/19/2018/11/UNDRIP_E_web.pdf.

Veracini, Lorenzo. *The Settler Colonial Present.* Basingstoke, UK: Palgrave Macmillan, 2015.

Vizenor, Gerald. *Manifest Manners: Postindian Warriors of Survivance*. Lebanon, NH: University Press of New England, 1994.
Wagamese, Richard. *Embers: One Ojibway's Meditations*. Madeira Park, BC: Douglas & McIntyre, 2016.
Watters, Haydn. "Truth and Reconciliation Chair Urges Canada to Adopt UN Declaration on Indigenous Peoples." *CBC News*, June 1, 2015. https://www.cbc.ca/news/politics/truth-and-reconciliation-chair-urges-canada-to-adopt-un-declaration-on-indigenous-peoples-1.3096225.
Wiebe, Rudy. *The Temptations of Big Bear*. Toronto: Knopf Canada, 1995.
Wolfe, Patrick. "Settler Colonialism and the Elimination of the Native." *Journal of Genocide Research* 8, no. 4 (2006): 387–409.
Woodward, C.L. *Ancestral Voice: Conversations with N. Scott Momaday*. Lincoln: University of Nebraska Press, 1989.

CONTRIBUTORS

Susan D. Dion is a Lenape-Potawatomi scholar with Irish-Quebecois ancestry who has been working in the field of Indigenous education for more than thirty years. A professor in the Faculty of Education at York University, her research focuses on the complexities of teaching and learning from Indigenous people's experiences and perspectives. Susan is a mother and a Gokamis, with three adult children, Matthew, Claire, and Vanessa, and three grandchildren, Samuel, Owen, and Lillian. She learns from them and from her students about how our past continues to impact our present. She draws on the power of art and story to teach us how to live and work in ways that contribute to a more just future.

Michael Dion, co-author of the Braiding Histories Stories, is of Potawatomi-Lenape mixed with Quebecois-Irish ancestry. He is a son, brother, uncle, and great-uncle. He takes these roles very seriously and has found great joy living up to the responsibilities that each requires. Love, friendship, humour, cooking, and caring are his ways of making his world a joyful place. Michael has been living with HIV/AIDS for over thirty years.

Sheyfali Saujani is a freelance writer and producer living in Toronto. She was a producer with CBC Radio and worked with a variety of network and local shows until her retirement. She is partially blind and, as a disability activist, advocates for greater access to print content. Sheyfali continues to pursue post-graduate studies and has worked on a number of creative projects related to disability representation.

Libby Stephenson is a settler. She was born in Ontario and grew up in a loving family with two parents and two siblings. It was stable and secure. She always wanted to be an educator, and has been for the past thirty years. She has loved her career, but more important to her is her family. She is a wife, mother, daughter, sister, and aunt. All of these connections make her proud and feel loved. Libby is on a journey – learning to unlearn a history she was taught.

Joe Wild is a career public servant with the Government of Canada. He is currently a senior assistant deputy minister with Crown-Indigenous Relations and Northern Affairs and has held various other executive and legal counsel positions with the Government of Canada. He continues to work on renewing Canada's relationship with Indigenous Peoples. Joe lives with his family in Ottawa.

Artists

Joi T. Arcand is a photo-based artist from Saskatchewan. Her work includes digital collage, graphic design, and photography, exploring themes of representation, language, reclaiming and (re)indigenizing spaces.

Mary Anne Barkhouse is a sculptor and artist. Born in Vancouver, BC, and currently living in the Haliburton Highlands in Ontario, she comes from a long line of Northwest Coast artists who are internationally recognized, including Ellen Neel, Mungo Martin, and Charlie James. Her work often includes the use of animal imagery to explore culture and ecological concerns.

Ruth Cuthand is a mixed-media artist from Saskatchewan. Using mediums such as beadwork, painting, drawing, photography, and printmaking, her work examines colonialism and its impact on Indigenous people.

Bonnie Devine is an installation artist, painter, curator, writer, and educator who lives and works in Toronto, Ontario. Her work is influenced by storytelling and narratives of treaty, land, environment, and history of the Anishinaabeg.

Vanessa Dion Fletcher is a mid-career artist who lives and works in Toronto. Reflecting on an Indigenous and gendered body with a neurodiverse mind, she creates art using composite media, primarily working in performance, textiles, and video.

Rosalie Favell is a Métis artist from Winnipeg, Manitoba. Using photography and sometimes digital collage, she creates portraits and self-portraits that explore contemporary Indigenous identity and sense of self.

Joseph Jacobs is a sculptor from the Tuscarora Nation Reservation in New York. His work is made out of stone and portrays stories, teachings, and traditions from Haudenosaunee culture.

George Littlechild is from Alberta. His mixed-media works showcase the beauty of First Nations people and culture while also highlighting the injustices of colonialism.

Nadia Myre is a multidisciplinary artist from Quebec. Her work incorporates traditional mediums to explore issues of identity, language, belonging, resilience, and resistance.

Adrian Stimson is a multidisciplinary artist who lives and works in his home Siksika community. He attended a residential day school, and his father attended residential school.

IMAGE CREDITS

33 Courtesy of Nadine Pedersen.
46 Courtesy of Libby Stephenson.
104 Reproduced by permission of Rosalie Favell (four images).
106 *The Baptism of Pocahontas* courtesy of Architect of the Capitol.
106 *Lucille* courtesy of Library of Congress, Prints and Photographs Division, Edward S. Curtis Collection, LC-USZ62-112239.
109 Reproduced by permission of Mary Anne Barkhouse.
111 Courtesy of House of Commons Collection, Ottawa.
113 Collection of the MacKenzie Art Gallery, reproduced by permission of Ruth Cuthand.
115 Reproduced by permission of Adrian Stimson.
117 © Nadia Myre. Copyright Visual Arts-CARCC, licensed 2021. Reproduced by permission of Nadia Myre.
119 Reproduced by permission of George Littlechild.
121 Collection of Saskatchewan Arts Board, reproduced by permission of Joi T. Arcand.
123 Collection of the Art Gallery of Ontario, reproduced by permission of Bonnie Devine.
125 Collection of Seneca College, reproduced by permission of Vanessa Dion Fletcher (two imges).
131 Courtesy of the Dion family.
134 Courtesy of the Dion family.
138 Courtesy of the Dion family.
140 Courtesy of the Dion family.
141 Reproduced by permission of The Rooms Corporation of Newfoundland and Labrador, Canada.
143 Courtesy of Dennis Minty, Minty Nature Photography.

145 The Rooms Provincial Archives Division, Newfoundland and Labrador, Canada, MG 100.1.
146 The Rooms Provincial Archives Division, Newfoundland and Labrador, Canada, MG 100.1.
148 Library and Archives Canada, C-001873.
150 Library and Archives Canada, Sandford Fleming fonds, c-005181.
153 Library and Archives Canada, Peter Winkworth Collection of Canadiana at the National Archives of Canada, e002140161.
156 Courtesy of Archives of Manitoba, cropped from *Big Bear 3 & Poundmaker, Personalities*, circa 1886, N16092.
172 Courtesy of Toni Goree.
178 Courtesy of Toni Goree.
180 Courtesy of Toni Goree.
182 Courtesy of Susan D. Dion.
185 "See you again" and welcome mat courtesy of Susan D. Dion.
185 Traffic sign courtesy of Oonig Paul Ward.
186 Courtesy of Oonig Paul Ward.
189 Courtesy of Oonig Paul Ward.
193 Courtesy of Liz Hall.
194 Courtesy of Liz Hall (two images).
196 Courtesy of Liz Hall.
200 Courtesy of Liz Hall.
201 Courtesy of Liz Hall.

INDEX

Note: Page numbers with (f) refer to illustrations.

activism, as term, 209–10. *See also* resistance
Adichie, Chimamanda Ngozi, 231
adoptions. *See* child welfare; Sixties Scoop
AFN (Assembly of First Nations), 94, 220–21
Afro-Indigenous people, 7–8. *See also* Black people; Goree, Toni; mixed ancestry
agents, Indian. *See* reserve system
Algonquin: Myre's artworks, 117–19, 117(f), 256; resistance to logging, 210; unceded territory, 58
allies, Indigenous, 31. *See also* reconciliation; reconciliation, requisites; reconciliation, settler storytellers
alterity, as term, 243n4
ancestral teachings: about, 11–12, 102, 213–14; all my relations, 78, 125; artworks, 16, 101–3, 114–15, 124–25, 208; ceremonies, 102, 213–14; community strengths, 98–99; dances, 182(f), 187–88; listening, 43; oral and written literacy, 222–23; resurgence, 98–99; take only what is needed, 150–51, 219. *See also* ceremonies; interconnectedness; languages; oral and written literacy; stories and storytelling
Anishinaabe: Devine's artworks, 123–25, 123(f), 255; place names, 45; wampum belts, 236
anthropologists, 92–93, 227–29. *See also* salvage era
anti-colonialism, 5–6. *See also* resistance
anti-Indigenous racism. *See* racism and discrimination
appropriation of Indigenous culture, 212–13. *See also* images of Indigenous Peoples; stereotypes of Indigenous Peoples
Arcand, Joi T., 121–23, 121(f), 255
Archibald, Jo-ann, 10, 11
Armitage, Wendy, 22
art, Indigenous: about, 12, 16, 100–3, 207–8; ancestral teachings, 16, 98, 101–2, 124–25, 208, 214; beauty, 114–15; carving and carvers, 164, 168–69, 171; creation stories, 108–12; cultural appropriation, 212–13;

259

everyday life, 102–3; in galleries and museums, 101; reclamation, 169; as resistance, 13, 100–3, 108–10, 109(f), 112–19, 207–8; resurgence, 101; salvage era, 92–93, 227–29; settlers' investment in learning, 112; vs stereotypes, 231–32; teaching strategies, 12, 44, 100; terminology, 102. *See also* beadwork; installations; photography; totem poles

artists, Indigenous: artistic processes, 12, 114, 214; knowledge protection, 103. *See also* Arcand, Joi T.; Barkhouse, Mary Anne; Cuthand, Ruth; Devine, Bonnie; Dion Fletcher, Vanessa (Susan's daughter); Favell, Rosalie; Goree, Toni; Jacobs, Joseph; Kerrigan, Bernard; Littlechild, George; Myre, Nadia; Stimson, Adrian

Assembly of First Nations (AFN), 94, 220–21

assimilation: about, 4, 6, 88–93; band councils, 89–90, 93; child welfare system, 229–31; Christian ideals, 91, 169; Indian Act goals, 26, 88–93, 118, 216–17; "Indian problem," 15, 86–87, 91, 118, 226; "passing" as white, 196–97, 199; reserve system, 26, 88–91, 118; residential schools, 226–27; White Paper on (1969), 95–96, 210, 221–22. *See also* child welfare; Indian Act; reserve system; residential schools; Sixties Scoop

Audrey. *See* Dion, Audrey Angela (née Tobias) (Susan's mother)

Aupilardjuk, Pierre, 104(f)

Aztec libraries, 222–23

Baptism of Pocahontas (painting, Chapman), 106(f), 107–8

Barkhouse, Mary Anne, 108–10, 109(f), 255

Battle for the Woodlands (installation, Devine), 123–25, 123(f)

beadwork: about, 114; *Battle for the Woodlands*, 123–25, 123(f); communal elements, 114, 118–19; *Indian Act*, 117–19, 117(f); Mi'kmaq, 189(f); quahog beads, 86, 126, 236; as records, 86, 222, 235–36; *Relationship or Transaction*, 125–27, 125(f), 255; *Smallpox*, 112–15, 113(f), 255; wampum belts, 86, 125–27, 125(f), 222, 235–36, 255. *See also* art, Indigenous

Beam, Carl, 101

Bednasek, C. Drew, 5

Before and After the Horizon (installation, Devine), 123–25, 123(f)

belts, wampum. *See* wampum belts

Benjamin, Walter, 129

Beothuk Nation: canoes, 145(f), 147–48; diseases, 82, 114; genocide, 82, 144, 147; hair combs, 143, 143(f); mamateeks (houses), 146–48, 146(f); Shawnadithit, 81, 141–48, 141(f), 244n7; territory, 82

Bernard. *See* Kerrigan, Bernard

Big Bear. *See* Mistahimaskwa

Black people: Afro-Indigenous people, 7–8; Black Lives Matter, 8, 211, 213; terminology, 175; Toni's ancestry, 173–75. *See also* Goree, Toni; racism and discrimination

Blaeser, Kimberly, 14

blockades. *See* resistance

Braiding Histories: about, 12–13, 16–17, 128–30, 243n5; co-written stories, 12–13, 128–30, 244n6; diversity of stories, 173, 179; interviews, 172–73, 183, 243n5; key questions, 129; Not-So-Perfect Stranger position, 15, 19–20, 29–30, 99. *See also* oral

and written literacy; stories and storytelling
Braiding Histories, (re)tellings. *See* Dion, Audrey Angela (née Tobias) (Susan's mother); Goree, Toni; Hall, Liz; Kerrigan, Bernard; Lovelace Nicholas, Sandra M.; Mistahimaskwa; Shawnadithit; Ward, Oonig Paul
Braiding Histories (Dion), 15, 129
British Columbia: child welfare, 229; fishing rights, 95; Haida Nation, 167–71; Institute for Indigenous Government, 165–68; organizations, 95, 165–66, 220–21; Potlatch ceremonies, 169, 223–24, 228; resistance to resource extraction, 170–71, 210–11; salvage era, 92, 228–29; unlearn the Indian Act, 68–69. *See also* totem poles
Bryce, Peter, 92
buffalo: ancestral teachings, 150–51; disappearance, 87–88, 149–55; Iron Stone protection, 149–51, 157; *Sick and Tired* (installation), 115–17, 115(f)
Burnt Church First Nation (NB), 211

Cabot, John, 82
Canada: dominant narratives, 25, 97. *See also* historical timeline
Canada, government: apology (2008), 62–63, 227; implementation of rights (s. 35), 60–62, 240n6 (Ch. 2); Indigenous affairs departments (recent), 60–61; Indigenous Senators, 163; land claims, 66; listening to Indigenous voices, 66–67, 72; Meech Lake Accord, 96, 210; partnerships and collaboration, 68, 70, 73, 111; UNDRIP rights, 233–34. *See also* Constitution Act, 1982; Constitution Act,

1982, treaty rights (s. 35); Indian Act
Canada, Indigenous relations. *See* historical timeline; Indian Act; Indigenous Peoples
Canada, settler colonialism. *See* reconciliation, settler storytellers; settler colonialism
Cartwright, John, map, 145(f), 146(f)
carving and carvers, 164, 168–69, 171. *See also* art, Indigenous
Catlin, George, 103–5
ceremonies: about, 213–14, 223–24, 228–29; ancestral teachings, 102, 214; ban on, 92–93, 224, 228–29; belonging, 213–14; blanketing, 67; gift-giving, 224; Mi'kmaq Sacred Fire, 188–89; Potlatch, 169, 223–24, 228; reclamation, 169; resources on, 214; ritual, as term, 214; salvage era, 92–93; smudging, 40, 164, 180, 214–15; totem poles, 92, 169–70; wampum belts, 86, 235–36. *See also* spirituality
Chapman, John Gadsby, 106(f), 107–8
Charter of Rights and Freedoms, 232. *See also* Constitution Act, 1982; Constitution Act, 1982, treaty rights (s. 35)
child welfare: about, 229–31; adoptions by Indigenous families, 192–95, 198; *Indian Foster Boy* (mixed media), 119–21, 119(f), 256; legislation (2020), 230–31; *A Place Between* (exhibition), 120–21; racism, 229–30; resources on, 231; statistics, 229–30. *See also* Sixties Scoop
Chrétien, Jean, 95
Christianity: assimilation, 91, 169; *The Baptism of Pocahontas* (painting), 106(f), 107–8; Book of

Genesis, 108–10, 109(f); *Dominion* (photo), 108–10, 109(f), 255; historical timeline, 84, 91; missionaries, 84, 150, 154, 169; on-reserve schools, 91, 136; residential schools, 91–92

circles: about, 215; all my relations, 125; Elders, 40, 74, 215; resources on, 215; in schools, 40; smudging, 40, 164, 180, 214–15

CIRNA (Crown-Indigenous Relations and Northern Affairs), 66

colonialism, as term, 6–7. *See also* settler colonialism

Constitution Act, 1982: Charter rights (s. 25), 232; Meech Lake, 96, 210

Constitution Act, 1982, treaty rights (s. 35): government implementation, 60–62, 240*n*6 (Ch. 2); of Indian, Inuit and Métis Peoples, 219; strength in diversity, 70

Cranmer, Dan, 228

Creation (sculpture, Jacobs), 110–12, 111(f)

creation stories, 108–12, 109(f), 111(f). *See also* stories and storytelling

Cree people: about, 148–57, 150(f), 153(f); ancestral teachings, 114–15, 150–51; Arcand's artworks, 121–23, 121(f), 255; buffalo, 87–88, 149–55; Cuthand's artworks, 112–15, 113(f), 255; diseases, 113–14, 151; Iron Stone protection, 149–51, 157; land dispossession, 151–56; Littlechild's artworks, 119–21, 119(f), 256; Lubicon Cree, 210; plains life, 150–52, 150(f), 153(f); Poundmaker, 153, 156; prophecies, 150–52, 155; residential schools, 192–93; starvation, 151–55; syllabics, 121–23, 121(f); treaties, 87–88, 151–57, 153(f); wars, 154–56; Wihaskokiseyin, 153–54. *See also* Hall, Liz; Mistahimaskwa

cultural genocide, 4, 115(f), 116–17, 120. *See also* assimilation

Curtis, Edward S., 105, 106(f), 107–8

Cuthand, Ruth, 112–15, 113(f), 255

Dallaire, Joanne, 74, 215

dance: circles in, 215; Grass Dancers, 183, 186(f), 187–88, 190; Métis jigging, 219–20; Sky Woman story, 111

Davidson, Robert, 169

de Vitoria, Francisco, 31

Deadman, Patricia, 104(f)

Delaware Nation, 82–83, 136

Deloria, Vine, Jr., 13, 218

Demasduit, 140(f)

Devine, Bonnie, 123–25, 123(f), 255

DiAngelo, Robin, 39

Dion family: about, 9–10, 78–79; Delaware Nation, 82–83, 136; discrimination, 94–95; drumming, 78; family life, 9; history of, 82–83; languages, 78, 136; racism, 9; residential schools, 78, 136; schools, 78–79, 136–37; status under Indian Act, 94–96, 133, 136–37; storytelling, 10–11, 82–83, 132, 140–41; territory, 82; veterans, 137; war veterans, 94–95. *See also* Lenape people

Dion, Audrey Angela (née Tobias) (Susan's mother): about, 78–79, 130–41, 131(f), 138(f), 140(f); assimilation, 79; basketweaver, 136; early life, 132–37; employment, 137–39; in Hamilton, 138–39; identity, 132, 137–39; languages, 78–79, 136, 139; marriage to Lindy, 138–39, 138(f); Moraviantown Reserve, 9, 78–79, 133–37, 140(f); racism, 9, 132–33, 136–39; in Sarnia, 139–41; schools, 78, 136–37; siblings, 78, 134–35; status, 94–96, 133, 136–37; storyteller, 10–11, 132–33, 140–41. *See also* Dion,

Lindy (Audrey's husband, Susan's father)
Dion, Jim (Susan's brother), 164–65
Dion, Lindy (Audrey's husband, Susan's father): about, 138–39, 138(f); early life, 132; in Hamilton, 138–39; Irish-Catholic ancestry, 9, 132, 138–39; marriage to Audrey, 138–39, 138(f); storyteller, 10–11, 132. *See also* Dion, Audrey Angela (née Tobias) (Susan's mother)
Dion, Michael (Susan's brother): about, 254; co-author with Susan, 9–14, 128–30, 172–73; family life, 9, 164–65, 254
Dion, Susan D.: about, 7–9, 254; *Braiding Histories*, 15, 129; childhood, 74–75; co-author with Michael, 9–14, 128–30, 172–73; educator, 7–9, 13, 19–20, 29–30, 79–81, 100, 203–6, 254; family life, 9, 131–32; historical timeline, 36, 75–77; historical timeline video, 241n8; languages, 78; Listening Stone Project, 5, 173, 205, 237n4; oral and written storytelling, 75–77. *See also* Braiding Histories; historical timeline
Dion Fletcher, Vanessa (Susan's daughter): about, 12, 242n8, 255; on Favell's works, 105; on Littlechild's works, 120; on Pocahontas, 107; *Relationship or Transaction* (mixed media), 125–27, 125(f)
discrimination. *See* racism and discrimination
diseases: historical timeline, 84, 113–14; *Sick and Tired* (installation), 115–17, 115(f); smallpox, 151; *Smallpox* (beadwork), 112–15, 113(f), 255; tuberculosis, 82
Dish with One Spoon Wampum Belt, 236

Disney Productions, 105, 107
Displaced Indians (exhibition, Littlechild), 120–21
Doctrine of Discovery, 81, 96, 204. *See also* land; land dispossession
Dominion (photograph, Barkhouse), 108–10, 109(f), 255
Donlon, Jocelyn, 14
drums and drumming: ban on ceremonies, 93, 224, 228; circles, 215; contemporary practices, 42; Grass Dancers, 182(f), 183, 186(f), 187–88, 190; Mi'kmaq symbols, 182(f), 187; spirituality, 192
Duck Lake battle (1885), 156

Edenshaw, Charles, 169
education: about, 205–8; colonialism in, 6–7; community collaboration, 43–44, 46–47, 74, 205–8; curricula, 79–81; lack of Indigenous knowledge, 3, 6–7, 21, 25–26, 79–81, 89; Listening Stone research, 5, 205, 237n4; reconciliation actions in, 43–44, 46–47, 206–8; settlers' investment in learning, 23, 25–27, 57–58, 62–69; teaching strategies, 44, 100. *See also* educators and teachers; post-secondary education; residential schools
education of Indigenous students: about, 205–9; Circle sharing, 40–41; community collaboration, 43–44, 46–47, 74, 225; Elders as educators, 41–43, 48, 74, 205; federal funding, 40, 89; Indigenous control of, 95, 98, 165, 167–68, 220; Indigenous literature on, 39, 41–42; lack of Indigenous knowledge, 6–7, 21, 25–26, 79–81, 89, 170, 205; language and cultural learning, 184–90, 185(f), 189(f); Listening Stone research, 5,

237n4; on-reserve schools, 39–40, 91, 225; pedagogy, 10–13, 17, 100; post-secondary education, 98, 165–68; racism, 40–41; stories and storytelling, 10–13; students' new awareness of culture, 205–6; travel to schools, 39–40, 225; as treaty right, 89. *See also* educators and teachers, Indigenous; residential schools

educators and teachers: community relations, 43–44; lack of Indigenous knowledge, 5–7, 9, 25–26, 35–36, 62, 79–81, 87, 99; Not-So-Perfect Stranger position, 15, 19–20, 29–30, 99. *See also* education; Stephenson, Libby

educators and teachers, Indigenous: lack of Indigenous knowledge, 5–7, 9, 25–26, 79–81, 99; training, 98; under-representation, 6, 238n9. *See also* ancestral teachings; education of Indigenous students; Elders and Knowledge Keepers; Kerrigan, Bernard

Elders and Knowledge Keepers: Afro-Indigenous alliances, 8; ancestral teachings, 78, 99, 102, 169, 213–14; ceremonies, 188–89, 213–14; circles, 40–41, 74, 215; as educators, 41–43, 48, 74, 205; languages, 52, 122, 185. *See also* ceremonies

Embers (Wagamese), 41–42

enfranchisement, 90, 94–95, 137. *See also* Indian Act, status

Ennis, Caroline and Dan, 157–58, 161

Esgenoopetitj (Burnt Church) First Nation (NB), 211

Facing the Camera (photography, Favell), 103–5, 104(f)

family services. *See* child welfare

Favell, Rosalie, 103–5, 104(f), 255

Feit, Harvey, 56–57

fiduciary responsibility, 88, 216–17, 232–33

First Nations: organizations, 95, 165, 220–21; terminology, 83–84. *See also* Indigenous Peoples; Indigenous Peoples, governance

Fisher, Bruce, 110–11

Fletcher, Susan Dion. *See* Dion Fletcher, Vanessa (Susan's daughter)

foster children. *See* child welfare

friendship centres, 235

Frog Lake (1885), 149, 156

fur trade, 84

gender and status. *See* Indian Act, status

George, Dudley, 211

gift-giving ceremonies, 224

Gladstone, Charles, 169

Glancy, Diane, 75

glossary and resources, 17, 77, 209–36

Godlewska, Anne, 5

Gordon, Jessica, 97

Goree, Toni: about, 130, 171–81, 172(f), 178(f), 180(f); career, 178–81; early life, 173–77; education, 177–81, 178(f), 180(f); educator, 173, 179–81; her mother, 175–79, 178(f); identity, 174–76, 179–80; mixed ancestry, 173, 174, 179, 181; motherhood, 176–79, 181; partners, 177–78, 179; spirituality, 175, 177, 179

Gustafsen Lake (BC), 211

Haida Gwaii, 169–71

Haida Nation, 167–71. *See also* Kerrigan, Bernard

Haisla Nation, 228–29

Hall, Liz: about, 130, 190–202, 201(f); brothers, 192, 196–97, 198–99; Cree identity, 191–95, 193(f), 194(f),

197–98; education and awards, 201–2; family history, 192–202, 193(f), 194(f), 196(f), 200(f); marriage and motherhood, 190–91, 200–1, 200(f), 201(f); mixed ancestry and identity, 191–92, 198–99; spirituality, 191–92, 199, 201; status, 198
Hall, Ryan, Caelan, and Isla, 190–91, 200, 200(f), 201(f)
Harper, Elijah, 96, 210
Harper, Stephen, 62–63, 227
Haudenosaunee: Confederacy, 52, 54, 110–12; *Creation* (sculpture), 110–12, 111(f); wampum belts, 86, 236
Heath Justice, Daniel, 10
Here On Future Earth (photography, Arcand), 121–23, 121(f)
Hill, Richard, 107
history: about, 15–16, 75–77; erasure of Indigenous people, 85; linear vs non-linear, 12–13; progress narrative, 85; terminology, 83–84, 85
historical timeline: about, 15–16, 76–77; dominant narrative, 85; editing of text, 77; introduction by S. Dion, 78–81; link to online video, 241*n*8; public interest in, 203–4; resistance timeline (1979–2020), 210–12; resources, 17, 77, 241*n*8; specific topics, 17, 209–36; terminology, 83–84
hunting and fishing, 66–67, 186, 219

identity: after enfranchisement, 137–38; multiple identities, 179, 191, 198–99; "passing" as white, 196–97, 199; portrait photography, 103–5, 104(f); urban Indigenous communities, 234–35; woman married to non-status man, 159, 170
Idle No More, 8, 96–97, 211
images of Indigenous Peoples: about, 100–1; cultural appropriation, 212–13; educational strategies, 100; as Romantic, Mythical Other, 3, 13, 49, 79, 105–8, 106(f), 130; school curricula, 79–81; single vs diverse images, 213, 231; stereotypes, 231–32; totem poles, 33–35, 33(f), 240*n*3 (Ch. 2); urban identities, 234–35. *See also* art, Indigenous; artists, Indigenous; identity; photography; stereotypes of Indigenous Peoples
immigrants: Afro-Indigenous alliances, 7–8; differences with Indigenous Peoples, 52–53, 72; diversity in settler population, 7–8, 32, 53, 72; South Asians, 48–49, 51, 54–55. *See also* Saujani, Sheyfali
implication in colonial relationship, 15, 23–25, 57–58, 62–65, 75, 99. *See also* reconciliation, requisites
Indian, terminology, 49, 83–84. *See also* Indigenous Peoples
Indian Act: about, 90–93, 118, 216–17; assimilation goals, 88, 90–93, 118, 216, 226–27; fiduciary responsibility, 88, 92, 216–17, 230, 232–33; historical timeline, 88, 90–93, 216; *Indian Act* (beadwork), 117–19, 117(f); need for replacement, 68–69, 96, 118, 216; reserve system, 224–26; resources on, 216–17; treaty rights, 52, 89, 95–96, 216, 232–33; White Paper on (1969), 95–96, 210, 221–22. *See also* child welfare; Indigenous Peoples; Indigenous Peoples, governance; reserve system; residential schools; Sixties Scoop
Indian Act, status: about, 90, 95–96, 216; access to rights, 96, 159; Dion family, 94–96, 133, 136–37; enfranchisement, 90, 94–95, 137; housing control, 94, 159–61; Lovelace's

resistance, 93–94, 157–63; marriage to status vs non-status man, 57, 159–61, 170; war veterans, 94–95
Indian Act (installation, Myre), 117–19, 117(f), 256
Indian agents. *See* reserve system
Indian Control of Indian Education: Policy Paper (1972), 95, 220
Indian Foster Boy (mixed media, Littlechild), 119–21, 119(f), 256
Indian Horse (Wagamese), 41
Indian Residential Schools Settlement Agreement, 220–21, 227
Indigenous Education–Focused Collaborative Inquiry Initiative (Listening Stone Project), 5, 43, 205, 237n4
Indigenous Peoples: about, 4–5; community strengths, 98–99; before contact, 81–82; cultural pride, 55; demographics, 230, 234; government apology (2008), 62–63, 227; inherent rights, 60; organizations, 95, 220–21; resurgence, 26, 98–99; terminology, 49, 83–84, 85; treaty rights, 60; urban communities, 98, 234–35; victimhood narratives, 27–30, 39; in world wars, 94–95. *See also* assimilation; Elders and Knowledge Keepers; historical timeline; Indigenous Peoples, governance; Indigenous Peoples, women; Inuit; Métis Nation; racism and discrimination; resistance
Indigenous Peoples, culture. *See* ancestral teachings; art, Indigenous; ceremonies; languages; spirituality; stories and storytelling
Indigenous Peoples, education. *See* education of Indigenous students; educators and teachers, Indigenous; stories and storytelling
Indigenous Peoples, governance: about, 93; administration of treaty rights, 89–90; elected chiefs and councils, 54, 89–90, 93, 160; historical timeline, 89–90, 93; media coverage, 52, 54; settlers' investment in learning, 54, 112; Six Nations Confederacy, 52, 54, 112; UNDRIP rights, 233–34. *See also* Indian Act; self-determination and sovereignty; treaties
Indigenous Peoples, images and stereotypes. *See* images of Indigenous Peoples; stereotypes of Indigenous Peoples
Indigenous Peoples, reconciliation. *See* reconciliation; reconciliation, settler storytellers
Indigenous Peoples, women: Indian Act control of status, 93–94, 95–96; marriage to status vs non-status man, 57, 159–61, 170; Métis women, 84–85; MMIWG, 97, 205–7, 211; on-reserve housing, 94, 159–60; Pocahontas, 38, 106(f), 107–8; resistance, 93–94, 96–97, 157–63; Sky Woman creation story, 111–12. *See also* Indian Act, status
Innu of Labrador, 82, 210
installations: *Battle for the Woodlands* (Devine), 123–25, 123(f); *Indian Act* (Myre), 117–19, 117(f); *Sick and Tired* (Stimson), 115–17, 115(f)
Institute for Indigenous Government, 165–68
interconnectedness: all my relations, 78, 125; ancestral teachings, 124–25; *Battle for the Woodlands* (installation), 123–25, 123(f); *Dominion* (photo), 108–10, 109(f). *See also* ancestral teachings; circles
International Year of Indigenous Languages, 217

Inuit: child welfare system, 229–31; diseases, 113–14; exclusion from Indian Act, 216; Inuit Tapiriit Kanatami, 94; stereotypes, 231–32; terminology, 83. *See also* Indigenous Peoples

Ipperwash Provincial Park (ON), 211

Jacobs, Joseph, 110–12, 111(f), 243*n*14, 255
Jehovah's Witnesses, 199, 201
Jigonsaseh, 112
Joe's story. *See* Wild, Joe
Johnson, Ursula, 104(f)
Johnston, Basil, 121
journalism. *See* media

Kanehsatà:ke Mohawks, 57, 96, 211
Kaswhentha treaty, 86
Kawagama Lake (ON), 45–46
Kelowna Accord, 220–21
Kerrigan, Bernard: about, 130, 164–71, 244*n*17; carver, 168–69, 171; educator, 164–71; Haida identity, 167–71; lawyer, 164, 167; spirituality, 168–69, 171; status, 170
King, Thomas, 10, 108, 111–12, 222–23, 232
Kinsella, Noel, 162
knowledge sharing. *See* ancestral teachings; circles; Elders and Knowledge Keepers; stories and storytelling
Koostachin, Shannen, 225
Kwakiutl: M.A. Barkhouse's artworks, 108–10, 109(f), 255

land: about, 24–25, 218–19; all my relations, 78, 125; ancestral teachings, 124–25, 219; *Battle for the Woodlands* (installation), 123–25, 123(f); historical timeline, 96; Indigenous control, 171; key questions, 170; reconciliation requisites, 28–30, 44, 45; resources on, 170, 219; responsible relationship, 96, 170–71, 218–19; settlers' lack of knowledge, 6–7, 24–25, 50–51, 99; and spirituality, 218–19; territorial boundaries, 218–19; treaty rights, 24, 232–33. *See also* reserve system; treaties; water
land dispossession: about, 6, 24–25; Doctrine of Discovery, 81, 96, 204; historical overview, 25, 96; historical timeline, 85–90; LANDBACK, 8, 212; reconciliation requisites, 24–25, 28–30, 44; Romantic Other as justification, 3; *terra nullius*, 81, 96, 204; territorial acknowledgments, 28, 44, 58, 62; timeline of resistance, 210–12; treaties, 24–25, 232–33. *See also* reserve system; treaties
languages: about, 217–18; ban on, 52, 217; *Indian Act* (installation), 117–19, 117(f); Indigenous terminology, 83; Lenape, 78, 83, 122, 136, 139, 203; Michif, 220; Mi'kmaq, 184–86, 185(f); *Northern Pawn, South Vietnam* (photography), 121–23, 121(f); on-reserve schools, 91, 217; in residential schools, 52, 122, 217; resources on, 218; revitalization, 26, 122–23, 217–18; statistics on, 122, 217–18
learning. *See* ancestral teachings; education; education of Indigenous students; Elders and Knowledge Keepers; stories and storytelling
learning, settlers' investment in. *See* reconciliation, requisites
Learning from the Indigenous Education–Focused Collaborative Inquiry Initiative (Listening Stone Project), 5, 43, 205, 237*n*4

Legault, John, 196, 198
Lenape people: about, 82–83, 136; Delaware Nation, 82–83, 136; Dion Fletcher's artworks, 125–27, 125(f), 255; languages, 78, 83, 122–23, 136, 139, 203; Moraviantown Reserve, 9, 78–79, 83, 133–36, 140(f). *See also* Dion family
Libby's story. *See* Stephenson, Libby
listening: about, 11–12, 13–14, 72, 207–8; action by, 207–8; ancestral teachings, 43; positionality, 13–14, 22; questioning by, 22–23; reading as, 11; responsibilities in, 11–12, 13–14, 22–23, 73, 207–8; settlers as listeners, 29–30, 59–60, 66–67, 72. *See also* oral and written literacy; stories and storytelling
Listening Stone Project (Indigenous Education–Focused Collaborative Inquiry Initiative), 5, 43, 205, 237*n*4
literacy, oral and written. *See* listening; oral and written literacy; stories and storytelling
literature, Indigenous, 10, 14, 39, 41–42
Littlechild, George, 119–21, 119(f), 256
Liz. *See* Hall, Liz
Longfish, George, 120
Lovelace Nicholas, Sandra M.: about, 93–94, 157–63, 244*n*16; Maliseet identity, 159–61, 163; resistance by, 157–63; as Senator, 163; status, 94, 157–61; Tobique Women's Group, 94, 158, 160, 210; UN complaint, 94, 158, 161–63
Lubicon Cree, 210

Macdonald, John A., 90, 91
Maliseet people: Lovelace's identity, 159, 161, 163; Tobique Women's Group, 94, 158, 160, 210; Toni's ancestry, 174. *See also* Goree, Toni; Lovelace Nicholas, Sandra M.
Martin, Paul, 207
McAdam, Sylvia, 97
McDougall, John and George, 151–52
McKenzie, Arlene, 180
McLaren, Nadia, 92
McLean, Sheelah, 97
McLeod, Betsy, and family, 192–94, 193(f), 194(f), 198
McMaster, Gerald, 120
Meawasige, Nichole, 124
media: Indigenous voices, 54; lack of Indigenous coverage, 52, 54; non-Indigenous reporters on Indigenous news, 53, 55–56, 72; racialized reporters, 51, 53; *Turtle Island News*, 55–56
Meech Lake Accord, 96, 210
Membertou First Nation (NS), 182(f), 183, 185, 185(f). *See also* Ward, Oonig Paul
Metepenagiag Mi'kmaq Nation (NB), 183, 184. *See also* Ward, Oonig Paul
Métis Nation: about, 84–85, 219–20; child welfare system, 229–31; culture, 219–20; Duck Lake battle, 156; exclusion from Indian Act, 216; Favell's photography, 103–8, 104(f); historical timeline, 84–85; Powley test on identity, 219; resources on, 220; L. Riel, 16, 61, 101, 156, 219; terminology, 83, 85; treaty rights, 219. *See also* Indigenous Peoples
Michael. *See* Dion, Michael (Susan's brother)
migration. *See* immigrants
Mi'kmaq people: Beothuk ancestors, 82; drums and symbols, 182(f), 187; Grass Dancers, 183, 186(f), 187–88, 190; land claims, 66; language and culture, 182(f), 184–87, 185(f), 189(f);

Membertou, 182(f), 185, 185(f); resistance by, 211–12; spirituality, 182(f), 184, 187, 188–89; treaty rights, 66–67, 186, 211–12. *See also* Goree, Toni; Ward, Oonig Paul

Missing and Murdered Indigenous Women and Girls (MMIWG), National Inquiry, 97, 205–7, 211

Mistahimaskwa: about, 87–88, 148–57, 148(f), 156(f), 244n8; Iron Stone protection, 149–51, 157; resistance to treaties, 87–88, 149, 151–57, 156(f). *See also* Cree people

mixed ancestry: mixed-race, as term, 85; self-identification, 181; urban communities, 234–35. *See also* Goree, Toni; Hall, Liz

MMIWG (Missing and Murdered Indigenous Women and Girls), 97, 205–7, 211

Momaday, N. Scott, vi, 10

Moore, Jackie, 5

Moraviantown Reserve (ON), 9, 78–79, 83, 133–36, 140(f)

Morrisseau, Norval, 44

Muffins for Granny (film), 92

museums: Potlatch items, 169, 223–24, 228; repatriation of items, 228; salvage era, 92–93, 227–29. *See also* salvage era

Muskaday, Chief, 193–95

Muskeg Lake Cree Nation, 121–22

Myre, Nadia, 117–19, 117(f), 256

Mythical Other stereotype, 3, 13, 49, 79, 105–8, 106(f), 130. *See also* images of Indigenous Peoples; stereotypes of Indigenous Peoples

National Indian Brotherhood (NIB), 94–95, 220–21. *See also* resistance

National Inquiry into Missing and Murdered Indigenous Women and Girls, 97, 211

native, as term, 49, 83. *See also* Indigenous Peoples

Native Women's Association, 94, 235

New Brunswick, 61, 184, 211. *See also* Lovelace Nicholas, Sandra M.; Ward, Oonig Paul; Wild, Joe

newcomers. *See* immigrants

Newfoundland and Labrador, 82, 145(f), 146(f), 210. *See also* Beothuk Nation

newspapers. *See* media

NIB (National Indian Brotherhood), 94–95, 220–21. *See also* resistance

Nicholas, Sandra Lovelace. *See* Lovelace Nicholas, Sandra M.

non-Indigenous people. *See* immigrants; settler colonialism

non-status Indigenous people. *See* Indian Act, status

North American Iceberg (photo collage, Beam), 101

Northern Pawn, South Vietnam (photography, Arcand), 121–23, 121(f), 255

Not-So-Perfect Stranger position, 15, 19–20, 29–30, 99

Nova Scotia, 211. *See also* Goree, Toni; Mi'kmaq people; Wild, Joe

occupations. *See* resistance

Ontario: community collaboration, 43–44, 46–47, 74, 205–6; curriculum, 79–81; reconciliation actions, 205–8; urban Indigenous communities, 234–35

Oonig. *See* Ward, Oonig Paul

oral and written literacy: about, 10–14, 21–23, 75–77, 130, 222–23; editing written texts, 77; hierarchies of, 222; im/permanence of, 222; *Indian Act* (beadwork), 117–19, 117(f); mnemonic devices, 86, 126, 236; oral texts, 76–77; positionality,

13–14, 22; questioning by, 22–23; resources on, 222–23; responsibilities, 11–12, 13–14, 22–23, 73, 207–8; "single story," 231; tellers/writers and listeners/readers, 11, 22–23, 130, 209; wampum belts, 86, 235–36; written texts, 14, 76–77. *See also* listening; stories and storytelling
Ortiz, Simon, 207–8
other, as term, 243*n*4

pass system, 225. *See also* reserve system
peace and friendship treaties, 232, 236
Peace Maker, 111–12
pedagogy, Indigenous, 10–13, 17. *See also* education of Indigenous students; educators and teachers, Indigenous; stories and storytelling
Peltier, Autumn, 225
Perfect Stranger position, 15, 19–20, 29–30, 99
Perley, Glenna, 157–58, 160–63
photography: E.S. Curtis's works, 103–4, 106(f), 107–8; *Dominion*, 108–10, 109(f); *Facing the Camera*, 103–8, 104(f); *Northern Pawn, South Vietnam*, 121–23, 121(f), 255
A Place Between (exhibition), 120–21
Pocahontas, 38, 106(f), 107–8
Poitras, Jane Ash, 120
positionality, 13–14, 22. *See also* stories and storytelling
post-secondary education, 98, 165–68. *See also* education of Indigenous students
Potawatomi: Dion family, 7, 136, 254; Dion Fletcher's artworks, 125–27, 125(f). *See also* Dion family
Potlatch ceremonies, 169, 223–24, 228
Poundmaker, 153, 156

power relations: cultural appropriation, 212–13; hierarchical worldview, 110; partnerships and collaboration, 68, 70, 73, 111; power in stories, 12–13; white supremacy, 6, 29–30
Powless, Lynda, 51–56, 58, 72
Powley case, Métis rights, 219
press. *See* media

quahog beads, 86, 126, 236. *See also* wampum belts
Queen Charlotte Islands (now Haida Gwaii), 169–71

racism and discrimination: Afro-Indigenous alliances, 7–8; Black Lives Matter, 8, 211, 213; child welfare system, 229–30; Indigenous students, 40–41, 92; institutional racism, 63; school children, 92, 136–37, 163; settlers' lack of knowledge of, 5–7; sexual discrimination under Indian Act, 93–94; South Asian immigrants, 52–53, 72; urban communities, 95, 234–35; white privilege and supremacy, 6, 8, 29–30, 37–39
radio. *See* media
reading. *See* oral and written literacy
reconciliation: about, 7, 15, 19–20, 31–33, 99, 203–4; disruptive questions, 19–23; fairness, 207; guilt and shame, 36, 39, 65; key questions, 28–29, 36; listening to Indigenous voices, 59–60, 72; motivations, 28; Not-So-Perfect Stranger position, 15, 19–20, 29–30, 99; oppressor narratives, 27–28, 39; partnerships and collaboration, 43–44, 46–47, 68, 70, 73, 74–75, 111; public interest in, 99, 203–4; settlers' lack of knowledge, 5–7, 9,

24–26, 35–36, 62, 79–81, 87, 99; TRC (Truth and Reconciliation Commission), 4–5, 17, 37–38, 97, 211, 227; victimhood narratives, 27–30, 39

reconciliation, requisites: about, 7, 15, 23–30, 203–4; impact, 23–24, 28–29, 63–64, 66–70; implication in relationship, 15, 23–25, 57–58, 62–65, 75, 99; investment in learning, 7, 15, 23, 25–27, 39–47, 57–58, 62–64, 99, 112, 203–4; key questions, 28–29, 36; shared interest, 23, 27–28

reconciliation, settler storytellers, 15, 31–33, 71–73. *See also* Saujani, Sheyfali; Stephenson, Libby; Wild, Joe

Relationship or Transaction (mixed media, Dion Fletcher), 125–27, 125(f), 255

repatriation. *See* salvage era

representations. *See* images of Indigenous Peoples; stereotypes of Indigenous Peoples

requisites for reconciliation. *See* reconciliation, requisites

research project, Listening Stone, 5, 205, 237n4

reserve system: about, 24–25, 88–90, 98, 224–26; assimilation goals, 26, 89–91, 118; community strengths, 98, 224–25; education, 225; historical timeline, 88–91; housing control, 159–60; Indian Act, 90–91, 216–17, 225–26; Indian agents, 88, 91, 225–26; isolation on, 26, 89, 98, 224–25; pass system, 225; reconciliation requisites, 24–25; resources on, 226; status and rights, 137, 159–60; treaties, 88, 225–26, 232–33. *See also* Indian Act; land; land dispossession

residential schools: about, 91–92, 226–27; abuse, 92, 226–27; ban on languages, 52, 217, 226; curriculum, 91–92; Dion family, 78, 136; generational trauma, 63, 92, 227; government apology (2008), 62–63, 227; historical timeline, 91–92; Indian Act, 92, 226; Indian Residential Schools Settlement Agreement settlement, 220–21, 227; living conditions, 92, 226–27; Liz's mother, 192–93, 197; resources on, 227; *Sick and Tired* (installation), 115–17, 115(f); Sixties Scoop after, 229–30; unmarked graves, 65, 226

resistance: about, 93–98, 209–12; activism, as term, 209–10; alliances, 7–8, 97; art as, 13, 100–3, 108–10, 109(f), 112–19, 207–8; ban on, 93; to cultural appropriation, 212–13; historical events, 93–98, 210–12; historical timeline (1979–2020), 210–12; Idle No More, 8, 96–97, 211; land and treaties, 96; organizations, 95, 220–21; power of stories, 207–8; to resource extraction, 170–71, 210–11; resources on, 212; to treaties, 87–88; urgent matters, 65–66; to White Paper (1969), 95–96, 210, 221–22; women's rights, 93–94, 96–97, 157–63. *See also* Indigenous Peoples; Lovelace Nicholas, Sandra M.; Mistahimaskwa; Truth and Reconciliation Commission (TRC)

Riel, Louis, 16, 61, 101, 156, 219

ritual, as term, 214. *See also* ceremonies

Romantic, Mythical Other stereotype, 3, 13, 49, 79, 105–8, 106(f), 130. *See also* images of Indigenous Peoples; stereotypes of Indigenous Peoples

Roque, Sara, 12, 242n8
Royal Proclamation (1763), 232

sacred relations. *See* spirituality
salvage era: about, 92–93, 227–29; ancestral remains, 228; ban on ceremonies, 78, 93, 224, 228; Potlatch items, 169, 223–24, 228; totem poles, 169
Sappier, Sandra. *See* Lovelace Nicholas, Sandra M.
Saujani, Sheyfali: about, 15, 32, 47–58, 72–73, 254; career as journalist, 50–56; early life, 47–50; friendship with L. Powless, 51–56, 58, 72; implication in colonial relationship, 55–58; investment in learning, 56–58, 72; lack of Indigenous knowledge, 49–51, 55–56; as South Asian immigrant from Uganda, 47–49, 53–54, 57–58; stereotypes, 49–50, 57. *See also* reconciliation, settler storytellers
Saul, John Ralston, 39
Saulis, Eva, 157–58
schools. *See* education; education of Indigenous students
Scott, Duncan Campbell, 91
self-determination and sovereignty: about, 57; artworks, 108–10, 109(f); government minister's duties, 240n6 (Ch. 2); need for new laws, 68–69, 96, 118, 216; settlers' lack of knowledge, 6–7, 57, 99; sovereignty, 166–67; status of women, 57; stereotypes, 57; UNDRIP rights, 233–34. *See also* Indigenous Peoples, governance
Senators, Indigenous, 163
settler colonialism: about, 5–7, 29–30; beadwork as resistance, 114–15, 118–19; Christian justifications, 81; guilt and shame, 36, 39, 65; historical timeline, 85–90; Listening Stone research, 5, 205, 237n4; oppressor narratives, 27–28; racist justifications, 81; white privilege and supremacy, 6, 8, 29–30, 37–39. *See also* assimilation; Canada; historical timeline; images of Indigenous Peoples; Indian Act; Indigenous Peoples; resistance; stereotypes of Indigenous Peoples
settler colonialism, reconciliation. *See* reconciliation; reconciliation, requisites; reconciliation, settler storytellers
settler colonialism, resistance to. *See* art, Indigenous; resistance
Seven Fallen Feathers (Talaga), 39
Shawnadithit, 81, 130, 141–48, 141(f), 244n7. *See also* Beothuk Nation
Sheyfali's story. *See* Saujani, Sheyfali
Sick and Tired (installation, Stimson), 115–17, 115(f), 256
Siksika: Stimson's artworks, 115–17, 115(f), 256
Simon, Roger, 22
Sinclair, Murray, 7
Six Nations: Confederacy, 51–52, 54, 112; *Creation* (sculpture), 110–12, 111(f)
Sixties Scoop: about, 229–31; assimilation goals, 120, 230; financial restitution, 230; *Indian Foster Boy* (mixed media), 119–21, 119(f); resources on, 231; restitution, 230; statistics, 120, 229. *See also* child welfare
Sky Woman creation story, 111–12
Smallpox (beadwork, Cuthand), 112–15, 113(f), 255
Smith, Linda Tuhiwai, 128, 129
smudging, 40, 164, 180, 214–15. *See also* ceremonies

South Asians, 48–49, 51–55. *See also* Saujani, Sheyfali
sovereignty. *See* self-determination and sovereignty
spirituality: ancestral teachings, 213–14; ban on ceremonies, 223–24, 228; connections with nature, 191; historical timeline, 84; Iron Stone protection, 149–51, 157; lakes as spirit beings, 124; and land, 218–19; Potlatch ceremonies, 169, 223–24, 228; records of events, 222; reincarnation, 168–69; sacred items, 92–93. *See also* ancestral teachings; ceremonies
Stanley Mission (SK), 192, 194(f), 195
status. *See* Indian Act, status
Stephenson, Libby: about, 15, 32–47, 71–73, 254–55; educator, 35, 37–38, 40, 42–47, 71; implication in colonial relationship, 35, 37–38, 45–46, 71–72; investment in learning, 39–47, 71–72; lack of knowledge, 33–36, 33(f), 35–37, 240n3 (Ch. 2); social position, 35; totem poles reflections, 33–35, 33(f), 240n3 (Ch. 2). *See also* reconciliation, settler storytellers
stereotypes of Indigenous Peoples: about, 79, 231–32; children's books, 38, 49–50; competency, 57, 229; cultural appropriation, 212–13; defined, 231; Disney images, 38, 105, 107; disruptive questions, 19–23; vs diversity of images, 213, 231–32; films, 38; how to counter, 19–21, 213; marker of knowledge gaps, 75; Pocahontas as Indian Princess, 38, 106(f), 107–8; resources on, 232; as Romantic, Mythical Other, 3, 13, 49, 79, 105–8, 106(f), 130; "single story," 231; ways of knowing, 18–20. *See also* images of Indigenous Peoples
stereotypes of South Asians, 51, 54–55, 231–32
Stimson, Adrian, 104(f), 115–17, 115(f), 256
stories and storytelling: about, 10–14, 73, 129, 207–9; ancestral teachings, 10–11, 111–12, 114–15; creation stories, 108–12, 109(f), 111(f); diversity vs stereotypes, 231–32; education for action, 207–8; knowledge frames, 21–22; meaning-making, 10–12, 209; as pedagogy, 10–13, 17; positionality, 13–14, 22; prophecies, 150–52, 155; as resistance, 129; responsibilities in, 11–12, 13–14, 22–23, 73, 207–8; "single story," 231; Sky Woman, 111–12; as (re)tellings, 128–30, 243n5. *See also* images of Indigenous Peoples; listening; oral and written literacy; stereotypes of Indigenous Peoples
stories of Indigenous peoples. *See* Braiding Histories; Dion, Audrey Angela (née Tobias) (Susan's mother); Goree, Toni; Hall, Liz; Kerrigan, Bernard; Lovelace Nicholas, Sandra M.; Mistahimaskwa; Shawnadithit; Ward, Oonig Paul
stories of settlers and reconciliation. *See* Saujani, Sheyfali; Stephenson, Libby; Wild, Joe
students. *See* education; education of Indigenous students
Susan. *See* Dion, Susan D.
Sweden, repatriation, 228–29

Tadodaho, 112
Talaga, Tanya, 39
talking circles. *See* circles

teachers. *See* educators and teachers; educators and teachers, Indigenous
teachings, ancestral. *See* ancestral teachings; circles; Elders and Knowledge Keepers; stories and storytelling
Temagami First Nation (ON), 210
terminology, Indigenous, 49, 83–84, 85
terra nullius, 81, 96, 204. *See also* land dispossession
territory, 218–19. *See also* land; land dispossession
territorial acknowledgments, 28, 44, 58, 62
Thunder Bay (ON), 39–41
timeline. *See* historical timeline
Tobias, Effie (née Dodge) and Victor, and family (Audrey's parents, Susan's grandparents), 133–37, 134(f)
Tobias, George (Audrey's brother), 140(f)
Tobique First Nation (NB), 158, 163. *See also* Lovelace Nicholas, Sandra M.
Tobique Women's Group, 94, 158, 160, 210
Toni. *See* Goree, Toni
Toronto: Indigenous communities, 234–35. *See also* Ontario
totem poles: colonial representations, 33–35, 33(f), 240*n*3 (Ch. 2); contemporary carvers, 169; Potlatch ceremonies, 169, 223–24, 228; as records, 222; salvage era, 92, 228–29; student knowledge, 80; *Totem* (film), 228–29
Trading Series (beadwork, Cuthand), 112–15, 113(f), 255
TRC (Truth and Reconciliation Commission), 4–5, 17, 37–38, 97, 211, 227

treaties: about, 86, 232–33; historical timeline, 86–90; Numbered treaties, 151–56, 153(f), 232; peace and friendship treaties, 236; pre-Confederation treaties, 86, 232; promises, 88, 93, 155, 232–33; reconciliation requisites, 24–25; records, 86, 222, 235–36; reserve system, 225–26; resistance to, 87–88; resources on, 233, 236; rights under Indian Act, 96, 216, 218–19; settlers' lack of knowledge, 6–7, 24–25, 51, 61, 99; status for access to rights, 95–96; wampum belts, 86, 125(f), 126–27, 235–36. *See also* Constitution Act, 1982, treaty rights (s. 35); Indian Act; reserve system; wampum belts
Trudeau, Pierre Elliott, 95–96, 221–22
Truth and Reconciliation Commission (TRC), 4–5, 17, 37–38, 97, 211, 227
tuberculosis, 82, 84, 113–14
Turtle Island News, 55–56
Tuscarora: J. Jacobs's artworks, 110, 111(f), 112, 243*n*14, 255
Two Row Wampum, 86, 236. *See also* wampum belts
2SLGBTQ+ people, 207, 211

Uganda, 47–49, 52–53. *See also* Saujani, Sheyfali
UN International Covenant on Civil and Political Rights: Lovelace's complaint, 94, 158, 161–63
UNDRIP (United Nations Declaration on the Rights of Indigenous Peoples), 4, 60, 228, 233–34
UNESCO International Year of Indigenous Languages, 217
United States: *The Baptism of Pocahontas* (painting, Chapman), 106(f), 107–8; Delaware Nation,

82–83, 136; Indigenous terminology, 83–84
urban Indigenous communities, 98, 234–35. *See also* identity

Vancouver: Stanley Park totem poles, 33–35, 33(f), 240*n*3 (Ch. 2)
Veracini, Lorenzo, 6
Vizenor, Gerald, 10
voting rights, 137

Waboose, Felicia, 42–43
Wagamese, Richard, 41–42
Walking with Our Sisters (exhibition), 206–7
Walpole Island, 136
wampum belts: about, 86, 126–27, 235–36; historical timeline, 86, 235–36; as records, 86, 222, 235–36; *Relationship or Transaction* (mixed media), 125–27, 125(f), 255; resources on, 236; treaties, 86, 125(f), 126–27, 235–36. *See also* beadwork
Wandering Spirit, 154–55
war: *Battle for the Woodlands* (installation), 123–25, 123(f); veterans' enfranchisement, 90, 94–95, 137; veterans' status, 94–96, 133
Ward, Jeff and Tyler, 183, 188, 190, 244*n*19
Ward, Oonig Paul: about, 130, 181–90, 182(f), 244*n*19; career, 183, 187; childhood, 184–89; Grass Dancer, 183, 186(f), 187–88, 190; Mi'kmaq language and culture, 181–90, 182(f), 185(f), 189(f); spirituality, 182(f), 184, 187, 188–89
water: ancestral teachings, 124–25; *Battle for the Woodlands* (installation), 123–25, 123(f); spirit beings, 124; waterways in colonialism, 85–86. *See also* land; land dispossession
Western Great Lakes Covenant Chain Confederacy: wampum belt reproduction, 125–27, 125(f)
Wet'suwet'en Nation (BC), 8, 211
White Paper (1969), 95–96, 210, 221–22
white privilege and supremacy, 6, 8, 29–30, 37–39, 163. *See also* racism and discrimination; settler colonialism
Wihaskokiseyin, 153–54
Wild, Joe: about, 15, 32–33, 58–73, 255; career in Crown-Indigenous relations, 32–33, 60–61, 63–67, 72–73, 255; early life, 58–59, 61–62; implication in colonial relationship, 58–60, 62–65, 67–68, 70–71; importance of listening, 59–60, 66–67, 72–73; investment in learning, 62–69, 72–73; lack of knowledge, 32–33, 61–63; land acknowledgment, 58, 62, 71; positive impact, 63–64, 66–70. *See also* reconciliation, settler storytellers
Wilson, Nina, 97
Wolastoqiyik. *See* Maliseet people
wolves, 108–10, 109(f)
worldviews, Indigenous: artworks, 108–10, 109(f), 126–27; vs hierarchies, 108–10, 109(f); in languages, 217; relations *with* land, 218–19; time relationships, 114. *See also* ancestral teachings; art, Indigenous; ceremonies; interconnectedness; land; languages; spirituality
written literacy. *See* oral and written literacy

Printed and bound in Canada by Friesens
Set in Calibri and Sabon by Artegraphica Design Co. Ltd.
Copy editor: Merrie-Ellen Wilcox
Proofreader: Helen Godolphin
Indexer: Judy Dunlop
Cover designer: Lara Minja
Cover image: Vanessa Dion Fletcher, *Relationship or Transaction*, 2014